PHILOSOPHY IN INDIAN POLITICS

About the Author

Rabindranath Mukherji is a leading scholar on contemporary socio-economic developments. He did his Ph.D. on modern finance in 1979. He has to his credit many books, including *Economics of Soviets Foreign Trade and Aid : A Critique, Comprador Bourgeoisie in India, Finance Capital and Crisis*, and *Peasant Question in India*. He has a number of papers published in the economic journals and books edited by eminent teachers in economics.

PHILOSOPHY IN INDIAN POLITICS

Rabindranath Mukherji

CONCEPT PUBLISHING COMPANY, NEW DELHI-110059

Cataloging in Publication Data—DK
Courtesy: D.K. Agencies (P) Ltd. <docinfo@dkagencies.com>

Mukherji, R. (Rabindranath), 1943-
Philosophy in Indian politics / Rabindranath Mukherji.
p. cm.
Includes bibliographical references (p.)
Includes index.
ISBN 8180691594

1. Philosophy in politics. 2. India—Politics and government. Title.

DDC 320.01 21

ISBN-81-8069-159-4

First Published, 2005

Published and Printed by

Ashok Kumar Mittal
Concept Publishing Company
A/15-16, Commercial Block, Mohan Garden
NEW DELHI-110059 (INDIA)

Phones : 25351460, 25351794
Fax : 091-11-25357103
E-mail : publishing@conceptpub.com

In

Memory

of

Ishwar Chandra Vidyasagar

(6 September 1820–28 July 1891)

PREFACE

The relation between politics and philosophy is very close, automatic and intimate though the latter remains intricately wrapped within the canvas of the former. Philosophy is the inner-kernel of politics, which grows upon the economic base of the society in a particular period of historical development.

Subjective idealism originating from religious philosophy, runs to counter the rationalist thought, necessary for social reforms, and their growth and development for a real social democracy. It confronts the rationalist thought for objective idealism and also objective reality centering round the practical life of social man. It has taken the colour and vulgar abstraction of religion to complicate the transition of a very stratified and hierarchical feudal society like India, oppressed under the yoke of colonialism and imperialism. Since the first decade of the twentieth century, it has grown unprecedented and been transmitted into the present state, throwing man in the marsh of sectarianism and communalism. It only helps maintain the age-old *status quo* and serves reaction in the society.

The book, in its six chapters, analyses the inter-relation and conflict between the two trends of philosophy in the operation of the Indian politics in the nineteenth and the twentieth centuries. The subjective idealism with communal and religious stance greatly overwhelmed the nascent rationalism in politics resulting in decay and degeneration in the Constitution of national unity and self-feeling, and continual anarchy in the Indian society. Nevertheless, the dul between the two continues and that is shaping the course of development of the Indian politics in the present time.

I am indebted to many persons who helped me with their

opinions and observations in the formation of idea and in the writing of this volume. I thank the staff of the Concept Publishing Company, who sincerely arranged to publish the work within a short period of time.

Calcutta
17 July, 2003

R. Mukherji

CONTENTS

INTRODUCTION

The trend of rational thought of India had its own indigenous origin. The evolution of language communities, spread of Indian knowledge systems and humanist values in opposition to the dominant Brahminical Hinduism of the past can be attributed to claim that some strains and features of modernity were existent which were, broadly speaking, somewhat common to the humanist appeal of the West. It grew, in India, during the sixteenth and eithteenth centuries. Subsequent western domination over India should not blind one to the part played by Eurasia in the origin of modernity itself.

Colonialism, far from seeking simply to impose modernity on Indian society, was more concerned with its denial. British rule in India arose very early in the history of European global expansion directly by colonialism and that was founded in some extremely archaic instruments of imperial domination.

These continue to pattern India's colonial development until well into the twentieth century, precluding it form achieving many of the social attributes of modernity. When, in spite of colonialism's resistance, the attributes began to emerge especially through the rationalist humanist approach and work of the secular and foresighted founder leaders of the Indian National Congress, the contradiction between the British Colonialism and people of India came to gradually focused and unravelled. The British rule became increasingly conservative and set itself against India's transition from feudalism to bourgeois full participation in the global modernity.

As the liberal education and ideas on human rights, social condition and economic approach relatively disseminated, the bourgeois landlord and capitalist classes of India, who made their fortunes during the British rule, became alarmed. To counter the emerging rational thought based on social reality, they took recourse to religion and idealise the ethos and institutions of the ancient and medieval societies. The religion and scripture became their medium, and the philosophy of the religious scriptures became the weapon for propagating the idea of obedience and devotion for the existing social order, which served their interest best. Religious books, cults and rites, and secret activity for their growth were encouraged for active practice and it was financed for thwarting the spread of rational and secular approach in education and social thought.

The Indian National Congress became a victim of this conspiracy by the comprador landlord and capitalist classes, in the aftermath of the First World War (1914-1918). This period marked the ascendancy of M.K. Gandhi in the Congress leadership. To Gandhi, there was no dichotomy between the religion and politics. He sang Ramdhun before addressing political meetings of national movement. To him Rama was the soul and Ravana, the non-soul. He outright brought in ideas of *Swaraj,* Non-violence, Holy war, *Satyagraha,* Ramrajya – the old religious and spiritual concepts from the ancient Hindu religious scriptures and their ethos – in the politics of the Indian National Congress to look back and transform its character into spiritualism. Answering to a question whether he would favour retention of foreign missionaries when India became Independent, he said that if he had the power he would ban conversion. (*cf.* Sitaram Goel, History of Hindu-Christian Encounters). On Ambedkar's intention to renounce Hinduism, Gandhi said, that if he became a Christian, he would cease to be an Indian and that the fraternity in Islam was confined to "believers". He said in an interview in March 1931, "Every nation considers its own faith be as good as that of any other. Certainly the great faiths held by the people of India are adequate for her people. India stands in no need for conversion from one faith to another" and that the "venerations of the *Bible*, the *Quran*, the *Gita* and the like is like idol worship". He also declared that "the idea of conversion was assuredly the deadliest poison which ever shook the foundation of truth". He preferred withdrawal of missionaries on the charge of proselytising and observed that Christianity in India was synonymous with materialistic civilisation and imperialistic exploitation by the strong white races of the weaker traces of the world. ("Citations" from T.H. Chowdhury conversions fraudulent or fair, *South-Asia*

Politics, December 2002, New Delhi, pp. 8-14.)

Little did he feel that such a philosophical stand would not practically pave the path of national liberation movement nor was it seriously criticised for its negative impact to the organisation, development and transition of India's complex feudal society to a civil society, worthy of a bourgeois democracy. In fact, such ideas spread the germs of dissent, misunderstanding, suspicion and division among different communities and castes of the Indian people. Non-violence was of no avail in the practical life of the society actually based on private property, class rule and labour exploitation. Class struggle however grew apace and it was countered with religious and communal stand and continuous verbosity on *Swaraj*.

Tej Bahadur Sapru severely criticised the Congress party's dominating attitude for imposing its own flag, song and Vidyamandir school teachings etc., in the Congress ruled states during 1937-39. He observed, "whether British imperialism survives or dies is not the question but if it should die it will be succeeded by the rule of dictatorship, the more intolerable, because politics will be mixed up with religious sanctions, unbelievers like me who have never believed in surrendering their conscience or independence of judgement to leaders whose claim to obedience is based more upon the sanctity attaching to them rather than upon their wisdom or judgement, will have seriously to ask themselves whether they can live in this country under the new system. Frankly I am in a state of revolt..."(*cf.* Rima Hooja, ed, *Crusader for Self-Rule : Tej Bahadur Sapru and the Indian National Movement).* The reasonable attitude, exposing the political reality, is quite clear in these words.

The contradiction of the emerging Indian bourgeoisie naturally manifested in the religious and communal forms over time. Contending sections of the bourgeoisie very much required support of the old social forces and institutions and the latter found their solace by aligning with the former. Jawaharlal Nehru said in *An Autobiography* that "many a Congressman was a communalist under his nationalist cloak but the Congress leadership stood firm and on the whole, refused to side with either a communal party or rather with any communal group". His profession of the idea of socialism cut notice and his speech of December 1948 acceded that "no government can be absolutely uncompromising where its own citizens are concerned. It tries or should try to win over as many people as possible to its own side. Nevertheless, it is always a dangerous thing to compromise with something that is definitely evil".

Advocacy for compromise with communal ideology became an inherent phenomenon in the Indian society and its political parties. Even an earlier report on the Kanpur Riots Enquiry Committee 1931, said that "....the power of the Congress collectively and wholeheartedly to fight communalism was altogether undermined. The complicated nature of the problem, the preoccupations of the political leaders and the exigencies of electoral campaigns, all made it almost impossible for the Congress openly and directly to come to grips of communalism". Nehru's profession of the idea of democratic socialism did not touch the ground reality, far from making an impact on the Indian society. He confessed in his *The Discovery of India* (1946) that "almost unwares, a vague idealist approach would creep into my mind, something rather akin to the *Vedanta* approach". Idealist Vedanta philosophy and socialism cannot unite for general human welfare and emanicipation of labour from feudal and capitalist exploitation.

India bereft of the philosophy of human dignity, right, equality and freedom and groaning under its age-old social and economic structure, internal inequalities, different religious and caste divisions, was relegated to a veritable ground of growing communalism—a category of religio-economic interest group—under the British rule. The British colonial power strived to gain its objective by petty parliamentary reforms which further aggravated the problem while the vested interest groups of Indian landlords and capitalists fought among themselves with the shields of religion. As a result, the people's mood and psychology was severely beaten and suppressed. Religion obviously played a key role under the canopy of Indian politics. The Congress supremo, Gandhi asserted: "My religion is Hinduism which for me, is the religion of humanity and includes the best of all religions known to me". He held, "I am led to my religion through truth and non-violence. I often describe my religion as religion of truth. Of late, instead of saying God...Denial of truth we have not known... We are all sparks of truth. The sum total of these sparks is indescribeable, as yet unknown truth, which is God. I am daily led nearer to it by constant prayer," and that "to be true to such religion, one has to lose oneself in continuous and continuing service in life." He elaborated, "The deeper I study Hinduism, the stronger becomes the belief in me that Hinduism is broad as the universe. Something within me tells that, for all the deep veneration I show to several religions, I am all the more a Hindu nonetheless for it." He also made it clear, "My devotion to truth (God) has drawn me to politics...Those who say that religion has nothing to do with politics do not know what religion means." (Citation from Jagmohan, "Vivekananda and Gandhi," *The Statesman*, Kolkata, 16 January 2003, p. 6.) Gandhi, while speaking of religion in this language, remained at the helm of the Indian National Congress leadership. He thus combined religion and politics into the one and inseparable whole with the old ethos and epos of Hinduism, in the name of practical Vedanta and specially through social service. Spiritualism and social service are two constituents of any social religion in which charity of the rich being the core is condensed and it actually works as the dispenser in the social order.

It obviously works for maintaining the *status quo*, idealization of the existing economic system and rule of the propertied class in a society with the religious-feudal culture. Historical developments spearheaded the growth of spiritualism in different forms *viz*., Hindu-feudal, Christian-feudal and Islamic-feudal cultures. Gandhism contributed largely to the substance and growth of Hindu-feudal culture through the so-called social service in political arena. With a peculiar fantasy, the Vedantists sought to introduce "equal privilege" for the lower strata by retaining caste system—the age old hereditary division of labour in the Indian society. The Vedantist's thought is *atman* (soul) and its liberation. It is an old religious philosophy based on individual asceticism and spiritualism. It has no practical value to the social man whose universal concern is the emanicipation of labour in real world, not liberation in the religious world. Practical Vedanta, through the tradition of the *Puranas*, was reduced to *dana, vrata, tirtha, Avatara, bhakti*, priest-craft and petty reformism with the charity of the rich in the name of Hinduism.

This does not help to make social man and contribute to the solution of problems in social life.

No sensible person can say that any religion would pass on without spreading confusion and suspicion among other communities and castes in the society. It no doubt attracted many with its Hindu theistic appeal and politically it pushed back the minorities (ethnic, religious and language) into deep introspection on their economic rights, privileges and culture. Added to this factor, the British Government's decision to introduce a show of parliamentary democracy in a country constituently divided on communal and caste lines, much more complicated the problem. The political unity of the communities in India for struggle against their common adversary—colonialism and imperialism—faded in the oblivion. A radical outlook embracing freedom of the country and condition of the actual life of the common people could not develop owing to the manoeuvre of the grave reserve of reaction in the Indian society entrenched with its religious and idealist philosophy and instigation of the British colonial power, rising communalism and general weakness of the Leftist organisation in the country.

The reality was that the theology of the majority community in idealist philosophy was concentrated in Gandhism and equated as nationalism while the dissent of the minority against this stance was sweepingly labelled as the religious sectarianism (communalism) by the institutions of the majority community in the sphere of politics. The developments of the two are inter-related and the result of their interactions has been quite deleterious in the country over the years.

The Indian politics fell to such an abyss of philosophy in the 1920s through 1940s, although, generally, there was no lack of people's interest, enthusiasm, and of progress in materialist philosophy which grew relatively during the nineteenth and beginning of the twentieth centuries. Curiously enough, Indian movement had split and degenerated into communalism that sought to get inspiration from the theism and religion.

All this no doubt marked a philosophical retrogression on the political plane, although a considerable portion of the works of Bankim Chandra Chattopadhyay and those of Jagadish Chandra Bose ad Ramendra Sundar Trivedi in earlier period contained excellent writings on science and natural philosophy. In political thought, India's philosophical backwardness increased more in comparison with the rationalist developments in the west. India continued to lag far behind.

A very brief outline of the progress of the materialist philosophy in the 19th Century would seem necessary and pertinent in this connection to show its rich content and the difference between the theological idealist and materialist schools of thought.

"Matter bears all reality and mechanical energy originates from it. Energy is a state of matter. In the primordial state, when nothing happened, matter and its state, mechanical energy, were one. Afterwards, when something began to happen, this state must apparently have become different from its earlier one. Matter and motion or as it is now called energy can neither be created nor destroyed. "It would imply a contradiction if, on the one hand, we maintained that all ideas had their origin in the world of sensation, and, on the other, that a word was more than a word; that besides the beings known to us by our senses, beings which are one and all individuals, there existed also beings of a general, not individual, nature. An unbodily substance is the same absurdity as an unbodily body. Body, being substance, are but different terms for the same reality. *It is impossible to separate thought from matter that thinks.* This matter is the substratrum of all changes going on in the world. The word infinite is meaningless, unless it states that our mind is capable of performing an endless process of addition. Only material things being perceptible to us, we cannot know anything about the existence of God. My existence alone is certin. Every human passion is a mechanical movement which has a beginning and an end. The objects of impulse are what we call good. Man is subject to the same law as nature. Power and freedom are identical".

"*Motion is the mode of existence of matter.* Never anywhere has there been matter without motion, nor can there be. Motion in cosmic space, mechanical motion of smaller masses on the various celestial bodies, the vibration of molecules as heat or as electrical or magnetic currents, chemical decomposition and combination, organic life —at each given moment each individual atom of matter in the world is one or another of these forms of motion, or in several forms at once. All rest, all equilibrium, is only relative, only has meaning in relation to one or another definite form of motion. On the earth, for example, a body may be in mechanical equilibrium, may be mechanically at rest; but this in no way prevents it from participating in the motion of the earth and in that of the whole solar system, just as little as it prevents its most minute physical particles from carrying out the vibrations determined by its temperature, or its atoms of matter from passing through a chemical process. Matter without motion is just inconceivable as motion without matter. Motion is, therefore, as uncreatable and indestructible as matter itself; as the older philosophy (Descartes) expressed it, the quantity of motion existing in the world is always the same. Motion, therefore, cannot be created; it can only be transmitted. When motion is transmitted from one body to another, it may be regarded as active and as the cause of motion in so far as it transmits itself, as passive in so far as it is transmitted. We call this active motion *energy,* and the passive, the *manifestation of energy.* Hence it is as clear as daylight that the energy is as great as its manifestation, because in fact *the same* motion takes place in both." "A motionless state of matter therefore proves to be one of the most empty and non-sensical of ideas—a 'delirious fantasy' of the purest water". Life is a product of matter organised in a definite manner, the *mode of existence of proteins*, and so, never a spark of sensation.

Along with presence of certain other chemical combinations, "wherever we find life, we find it associated with proteins, and wherever we find a protein not in the process of dissolution, there also without exception we find phenomena of life".

In the early history of all civilised peoples, tribal and village communities lived with common ownership of the land. There was no "large landed proprietors". "From India to Ireland the cultivation of landed property in extensive tracts were originally carried on by such tribal and village communities; sometimes the arable land was tilled jointly for account of the community, and sometimes in separate plots temporarily allotted to families by the community, while woodland and pasture-land continued to be used in common." With the emergence and growth of unequal property status with the development and expansion of exchange of product, the original natural division of labour and the ancient common ownership of the land was more deeply undermined, and more rapidly did the commune move towards its "dissolution and transformation into a village of small-holding peasants."

For thousands of years oriental despotism and the changing rule of conquering nomad people were unable to injure these old communities; the gradual destruction of their primitive home industry by the competition of the products of large-scale industry brought them nearer and nearer to dissolution. The formation of a primitive aristocracy, in the case of the Celts, the Germans and the Punjab (of undivided India) took place even "on the basis of common ownership of the land, and was not at first based in any way on force, but on voluntariness and custom". Despite this, the old primitive communities could remain in existence for thousands of years—as in India and among the Slavs throughout the nineteenth century—before intercourse with the external world gave rise to the "internal inequalities" of property as a result of which they began to breakup.

One can reasonably make up a philosophical trend from the developments of the ancient society. "The philosophy of antiquity was primitive, natural materialism. As such, it was incapable of clearing up the relation between thought and matter. But the need to get clarity on this question led to the doctrine of a soul separable from the body, then to the assertion of the immortality of this soul and finally to monotheism. The old must materialism was, therefore, negated by idealism. But in the course of further development of philosophy, idealism, too, became untenable and was negated by modern materialism. This modern materialism, the negation of the negation, is not the mere re-establishment of the old, but adds to the lasting foundations of this old materialism the whole intellectual content of two thousand years of progress in philosophy and natural science, as well as in these two thousand years of history itself. Generally speaking, it is no longer philosophy at all, but a simple world outlook which has to be verified and implemented not in a science of sciences standing apart, but in the positive sciences". "The unity of the world does not consist in its being, although its being is a precondition of its unity, since it must surely first *be* before it can be *one*. Indeed, being is always an open question beyond the point where our sphere of observation ends. The real unity of the world consists in its materiality, and this is proved not by a few juggling phrases, but by a long and laborious development of philosophy and natural science". (*cf.* Frederick Engels, *Anti Duhring*, Foreign Language Press, Peking, 1976, p. 73 and p. 434, 429, 102, 74, 224, 206, 189, 176-177 and 54 ff.)

With this perspective, it becomes imperative and consistent to show the philosophical trends and developments of the Indian politics in the nineteenth and twentieth centuries. The rationalist thought spread in the country mainly with the establishment of the educational and political institutions in the dense mist of theological atmosphere and subjectivism predominant in the Indian society. It can be viewed as the precursor of subsequent developments. It certainly made a considerable impact on the social psychology steeped with ignorance. But this trend dominated for a relatively short period, as it was opposed and hounded by the vestiges of the old—its powerful adversary. Religion and idealist philosophy was largely rigged up in the same period by the indigenous vested interest and that gathered more strength and momentum in collaboration with the colonial power to challenge the nascent rationalist thought in Indian politics.

The unprecedent growth and advance of subjective idealism mainly through Gandhism has remained to be dominant in the Indian politics with its manifold nature. On the contrary, reforms, objective idealism and consequently, class struggle grew in a characteristic manner against the religious and idealist philosophy over the years. The ideas of reformism in the arena of social democracy have made a dent and they have conditioned the necessity and emergence of materialist view of life and society. It has followed a circuitous but uninterrupted course in the process of historical development. Within the ambit of India's British transplanted parliamentary democracy, vulgar materialism clothed with the tapestry of religion rules and is setting forth a definite coercive trend that undermines the composite social-fabric of a vast country like India.

For a long time it has been in a state of decay and negation, and its product, in the positive sense, will be the re-emergence and growth of a radical opposition, a force, under the banner of militant materialism with the unique world view, to counter and transform India's existing anarchic social order enmeshed with the domination of international capital.

1

SUBJECTIVISM AND RATIONALIST THOUGHT

The first hundred years of the British colonialism in India was characterised with the establishment of rule of the East India Company after a series of wars with the native forces of India, which reached its natural limits after the end of Anglo-Sikh war in 1849. With the suppression of the native forces, East India Company, a trading organisation, extended its political design for territorial annexation causing destruction, misery, and destitution to the static and hierarchical Indian society. The structure of the Indian society based on the common ownership of land, village communities and their hereditary and natural division of labour, an economy operating with the unity of agriculture and handicrafts, traditional values originating from the natural economy and concentrated in religion, myths and folk cultures were all severely undermined by two different types of land systems *viz.*, zamindari and ryotwari resting on the newly introduced private property on land under the company rule, sweep of trade, commercial agriculture and new international division of labour required for this purpose.

This change in the property ownership and a little change in the mode of production brought only an apparent stability, and there accumulated many grievances arising out of the alienation and destitution of the different sections of the Indian people.

The social grievances concentrated and actually began to shape the general discontent which took the form of large-scale armed resistance in unison by the Indian people through the 1820s. It developed into the great rebellion or the first war of Indian independence in 1857. This indicated the growing trend of India's protest and active resistance against the notorious common enemy and most oppressive British colonialism on the Indian soil. It raised the banner of rebellion against the alien reactionary British colonial force suppressing the Indian people. It can be hardly stressed that this war of Independence overthrew the despotism of the East India Company and forced the British Parliament to take over the administration of India on behalf of the Crown, from the East India Company.

It signalled a change in the method of the country's administration without resolving the social contradictions, but resulting in the establishment of the organs of the modern state machinery under the aegis and domination of the British bourgeoisie firmly committed to the ideals and philosophy of colonisation. Material ingredients of this state *viz.*, private property in land, new international division of labour, trade had already grown and developed through the past one hundred years to support and prepare some ground for the bourgeois mode of production in the Indian subcontinent. The new elements of material production were under the control and domination of the British capital, its trade and commerce. Native Indian capital mainly grew through the internal trade and its relation with the British capital and external trade, and that was largely owned by the comprador traders, suppliers and agency operators, of the majority community in India. The big landlords and their feudators sustaining on a chain of tenancy system had their field day and exploited the small and poor peasants and day labourers in the field. There also grew a rising middle class of salary earners in the colonial government establishment over the years. English education spread among the middle class to support and run the direct foreign rule and colonial order in the country. According to one estimate, till the first half of nineteenth century, in India, some 860 titles of books were published, out of which as many as 176 comprised *Puranas*, *Vedas*, *Vedantas* and *Upanishads*. Establishment of three universities in 1857 helped to spread education further in course of time.

The weak but emerging Indian bourgeoise, as a result of this process naturally required intellectual support and moral and spiritual inspiration for its own interest and progress. Western logic and philosophy was then being introduced and it had made only a very late start and tardy progress. Western ideas, especially in metaphysics, naturally could make no substantial progress with institutional support and constant efforts of some notable Indian and British scholars and administrators in the nineteenth century.

This philosophical approach for pursuit of knowledge with the logic and metaphysics however made some positive development in the method and process of enquiry into the social condition of the Indian society. A slow and weak trend of rational approach towards analysis of the existing reality of the social life grew in the intellectual realm of India, and later on, it made a considerable political impact to unravel the contradiction between the colonial power and Indian society. It was the result of the work of some Indian progressive thinkers who were themselves products of the western philosophy and more especially of metaphysics.

The western metaphysics as the theory dealing with reality and knowledge, was introduced to India in the early period of the nineteenth century and it made a little advance in two different spheres and directions and led to two different trends. Consequently, it flowed in two different branches *viz.*, social science and religion. In one branch it rightly made some very good attempt and progress in analysing the social phenomenon and understanding the objective reality in a secular manner. It followed a radical course to critically analyse and understand the existing social order of things in India. In the political arena it made its imprint and expression through liberalism. In the other branch, metaphysics was grossly corrupted in use and it got entangled and enmeshed with the religion and spiritualism which held Indian society captive for a long time. This branch was fused within the religion of India and with the help of metaphysics, a systematic attempt was carried on to collate, review and reinterpret the *Upanishad*, *Vedanta*, *Brahma Sutra* and other religious thoughts and myths. It can be hardly be stressed that this course of metaphysics greatly helped to refurbish the scriptures and led to the great revival of Hinduism with its reforms and startling manifold developments, under the influence of Christianity in the late nineteenth century. This trend developed with the reform movement and its activities in India from Rammohan to Dayananda, Ramakrishna, Narendranath, Aurobindo and it had continued through the twentieth century. The result was the re-emergence and resurgence of religion and spritualism in the colonial and feudal India, and not for a social India with the radical monist view of the world. It was due to the fact that the stronger force in the corrupt trend had slowly and gradually coaxed and dominated over the nascent rationalist force in the works of the liberals exposing the antagonistic contradiction between the colonial power of Great Britain and colonial India.

The modern rationalist idea in India however began to spread slowly and gradually, it made some impact despite stiff opposition from powerful conservative forces in the society.

This idea can be said to have started with the literary works of Raja Rammohan Roy (1772-1833) and Young Bengal Movement of the 1820s. Although himself an exponent of *Vedanta*, Rammohan mainly followed the *Upanishad* and felt existence of spirit in every thing. (Brajendranath Seal, *Rammohan Roy : The Universal Man*, pp. 11-12). He believed in monotheism and was partially influenced by *Adwaitaism*. As a reformer with political insight he thought that "the present system of religion adhered to by the Hindus is not well calculated to promote their political interest. The distinction of castes introducing innumerable divisions and sub-divisions among them has entirely deprived them of patriotic feeling... It is, I think necessary that some change should take place in their religion at least for in sake of their political advantage and social comfort." (Citation from *Tatwabodhini Patrika*, Baishakh, Saka 1777, A.D. 1855) He understood that learning of *Vedanta* would be meaningless in the practical life of the society. With this idea he wrote in a letter addressed to the Governor-General Amherst stating that the teaching of *Vedanta* would not be congenial, "nor will youths be fitted to be better members of society by the *Vedanta* doctrines, which teach them to believe that all visible things have no real existence". This exposed the falacy of the *Vedanta* philosophy. Highlighting the ideas of old western materialist philosopher, Bacon, he wrote in the same letter on public education rightly stressing the social necessity that:

"If it had been intended to keep the British Nation in ignorance of real knowledge, the Baconian philosophy would not have been allowed to displace the system of the schoolmen which was the best calculated to perpetuate ignorance. In the same manner the Sanskrit system of education would be the best calculated to keep this country in darkness if such had been the policy of the British legislature. But as the improvement of the native population is the object of the Government, it will consequently promote a more liberal and enlightened system of instruction, embracing Mathematics, Natural Philosophy, Chemistry, Anatomy with other useful sciences." (S.D. Collet, *The Life and Letters of Raja Rammohan Roy*, Appendix II.)

Rammohan Roy made a strong argument for a new system of education in his letter to the Governor General, Lord Amherst in 1823 wherein he wrote, "The Sanskrit language...is well known to have been for ages a lamentable check to the diffusion of knowledge" in the society. "Neither can much improvement arise," and he added that "from such speculation as the following which are the themes suggested by the *Vedanta*–in what manner is the soul absorbed in the Deity". Here Rammohan showed his uprightness and rationality to question the "speculation" in the *Vedanta*. It is true that he translated several *Upanishads* and the *Brahmasutra* in English and Bengali but he himself was not swayed by the very speculative ideas of *Adwaitavad* of Shankaracharya and others. He wrote *Vedantasar* and founded a school in 1825 accepting only the *Upanishad* and its supreme spirit and he rejected the Vedanta Philosophy propounded by other teachers in the later period of history. This aspect had been clarified by his disciple Debendranath Tagore who was also an eminent Sanskrit scholar in his times.

In appreciation of his efforts, Jeremy Bentham, the utilitarian thinker, commented, "Rammohan has cast off thirty-five millions of gods and learnt from us to embrace reason in all important field of religion." (Citation in A.F. Salahuddin Ahmed, *Social Ideas and Social Change in Bengal : 1818-1835*, Leiden, 1965, p. 39)

Rammohan was opposed to social discrimination. He organised a protest movement against the Jury Act that infringed the rights of the Indians in the judiciary. He sent through J. Crawford, a complaint to the British parliament on the discrimination against the Hindu and Muslim for appointment to the jury. This complaint in 1828 was signed by more than 200 Indians among whom as many as 95 were Muslim.

In 1839, Tatwabodhini Sabha was established under the aegis of Debendranath Tagore (1817-1905) who was an erudite scholar of the *Upanishad* and *Vedanta* philosophy. He was a student of Ram Chandra Vidyabagish who became the mentor of the Sabha. Debendranath became the leader of the Brahmo Samaj established by Rammohan Roy in 1828. Ramchandra became the first Acharya of the Samaj which he led with great ability and devotion.

The positive aspect of the Brahmo religion is in "Loving Him and doing the works He loveth". It prohibits the worship of any created being or thing as the Creator distinguishes the believers from all who are addicted to the worship of *avatars* or incarnations who believe in the necessity of mediators, symbols or idols of any description. The faith is based on "fundamental truths" of religion, attested by reason and conscience and it refuses to permit man, book, image to stand in the way of the direct communication of man's soul with the Supreme Spirit. Brahmoism belongs to the Hindu community and seeks to purify the community's heritage of customs, usages, rites and ceremonies and adopt them to the needs of person's conscience and community. Brahmo Samaj and its leaders accept the *Upanishad* as *Vedanta*, preach theology with sanctification of this scripture. Debendranath wrote, they had no faith on the premises and resolutions of the *Vedanta* philosophy. "We accepted the Brahmo concept of the *Upanishad* and *Vedanta*. We did not regard *Vedanta* philosophy as Shankaracharya had projected life and Brahma as the one. We want to worship God. If the worshipped and worshipper become the same, then who would worship whom? Therefore, we could not put on our views in favour of the *Vedanta* philosophy: As we were against idolatry, so we also opposed *Adwaitavad* (*Vedanta* philosophy). We could not fully accept Shankaracharya's version of the *Upanishad*. For he interpreted its entire thought on taking it in favour of *Adwaitavad*". Debendranath and his associates accepted only the *Upanishad* as *Vedanta*—and they had "no faith on the propositions of the *Vedanta* philosophy." It can be noted that the thought on reform was set in progress.

Debendranath wrote a new commentary in place of the extant interpretation of the *Upanishad*, which was serialised in the journal of the Tatwabodhini Sabha. It showed the relationship of devotees and worshippers with the God and had preached monotheism anew. (*Autobiography of Maharshi Debendranath Tagore*, Calcutta, 1909, pp. 10-20, pp. 610-611). This was certainly a change. By worshipping the Supreme Spirit, Brahmoism no doubt followed subjective idealism but it challenged the *Adwaitavad* that was entrenched with the age-old reaction. *Vedanta* philosophy was criticised by a powerful section of the intellectuals in the nineteenth century. In fact, it was negated and discarded as the source of truth and knowledge by the Brahmo Samaj which was at one with the pristine Hinduism of the age of *Upanishad*.

The name of Akshay Kumar Datta can be mentioned in regard to the concept of social organisation and development. Among his important writings are *Charupath*, *Padarthavidya* and many other essays on the socio-economic condition of the country, which showed his rational bend of mind. He held that produce is equivalent to labour; labour and prayer amounts to the product; and hence power of prayer would be zero. Debendranath Tagore himself acknowledged in his autobiography that, while his mind was set in quest for self-realisation and Brahmo, Akshay Kumar Datta searched for "the relationship between the external matter and human mind—Difference between the earth and the sky." Debendranath called him an atheist. Akshay Kumar Datta was a close friend of Vidyasagar and functioned as the editor of *Tatwabodhini Patrika*. He declared in 1850 that the *Vedas* were not oracles of God and literature on world history was the real *Vedanta*. This is known from the autobiography of Rajnarayan Bose. As he wrote, "The Babu (Akshay Kumar Datta) long ago abjured his belief in Brahmoism and turned to be an agonostic". This was a common approach towards a practical life of the society, rationality and atheism.

To Akshay Kumar, the real meaning of religion (*Dharma*) is the adherence to the laws of nature. His two-volume work (1851-53) on the inquiry of relationship between human nature and external matter carries rich thought on this subject. He followed George

Coomb's "Constitution of Man" in preparing this book. Only natural law in his opinion may be viewed as the rule of God. One can be happy if he observes that law, instead of prayer. To work for the good of mankind, according to Akshay Kumar, is the proper worship of God. He opposed prejudice and dependence. Dependence is despicable to the concept of hell preached by the Hindu, Muslim and Christian. He made a scathing criticism against the atrocities of the indigo planters on the Indian peasants in the *Tatwabodhini Patrika*. He felt that the root cause of ruin to the peasants was the indigo planters. Akshay Kumar Datta had differences with Rammohan on many subjects but he regarded him as the pioneer of modernity who played the sombre martial instrumental music in favour of science.

Pandit Iswarchandra Vidyasagar, a noble personage, in his notes[1] on the Sanskrit College, Calcutta, dated 12 April, 1852 wrote, "True it is that the most part of the Hindu system of philosophy do not tally with the advanced ideas of modern times, yet it is undeniable that to a good sanskrit scholar their knowledge is absolutely required. By the time that the students come to the *Darshana* or philosophy class their requirements in English will enable them to study the modern philosophy of Europe. Thus they shall have an ampler opportunity of comparing the system of philosophy of their own, with the new philosophy of the western world. Young men thus educated will be better able to expose the *errors* of ancient Hindu philosophy than if they were to derive their knowledge of philosophy simply from European sources. One of the principal reasons why I have ventured to suggest the study of all the prevalent systems of philosophy in India is that the student will clearly see that the propounders of different systems have attacked each other and have pointed out each other's errors and fallacies. Thus he will be able to judge himself. His knowledge of European philosophy shall be to him an invaluable guide to the understanding of the merits of the different systems.

"Another advantage is, that students so prepared, wishing to transfer the philosophy of the west into a native dress will possess a stock of technical words, already in some degree familiar to intelligent natives."

As Principal of the Sanskrit College, he observed in his letter dated 7 September, 1853 addressd[2] to the Secretary of the Council of Education to the Government, "we have better treatises in our curriculum. With regard to Bishop Berkeley's Inquiry, I beg leave to remark that the introduction of it as a class book would beget more mischief than advantage. For certain reasons, which it is needless to state here, we are obliged to continue the teaching of the *Vedanta* and *Sankhya* in the Sanskrit College. That the *Vedanta* (sic!) and *Sankhya* are fast systems of philosophy is no more a matter of dispute. *These systems false as they are, command unbounded reverence from the Hindus*. Whilst teaching these in Sanskrit course, we should oppose them by sound philosophy in the English course to counteract their influence. Bishop Berkeley's Inquiry, which has arrived at similar or identical conclusions with the *Vedanta* or *Sankhya* and which is no more considered in Europe as a sound system of philosophy, will not serve that purpose. On the contrary, when, by the perusal of that book, the Hindu students of Sanskrit will find that the theories advanced by the *Sankhya* and *Vedanta* systems are corroborated by a philosopher of Europe, their reverence for the two systems may increase instead of being diminished. Under the circumstances I regret I cannot agree with Dr. Ballantyne in recommending the adoption of Bishop Berkeley's work as a class book."

"...Even if we take it for granted that we shall be able to point out agreement between the two, it appears to me to be a hopeless task to conciliate the learned of India to the acceptance of the advancing sciences of Europe. They are a body of men whose *long standing prejudices are unshakable*. Any idea when brought to their notice either in the form of a new truth or in the form of expansion of truths the germs of which their *shastras* contain, they will not accept. It is but natural they would obstinately adhere to their old prejudices.... *The bigotry of learned of India, I am ashamed to state is not in the least inferior to that of the Arab*. They believe that their *shastras* have all emanated from omniscient *rishis* and, therefore, they cannot but be infallible. When in the way of discussion or in course of conversation any new truth advanced by European science is presented before them, they laugh and ridicule. Lately, a feeling is manifesting among the learned of this part of India, especially in Calcutta and its neighbourhood, that when they hear of a scientific truth, the germs of which may be traced out in their *shastras*, instead of showing any regard for that truth, they triumph and the superstitious regard for their own *shastras* is redoubled. From these considerations, I regret to say that *I cannot persuade* myself to believe that there is *any hope* of reconciling the learned of India to the reception of new scientific truth. Dr. Ballantyne's views (on the recommendation of class books) may be successfully carried out in the North West provinces where his experience has made him arrive at his conclusions with regard to the learned of India." (Italics added)

Vidyasagar set the trend of modern philosophical movement in India against fast systems of *Sankhya* and *Vedanta* of the classical Indian philosophy. He presented a very brief outline of the objective reality on modern philosophy in popular Bengali language sifting facts from various English books. He wrote in the preface to *Bodhodoya* (Book IV 1851) that, "on the study of the few subjects dealt with, there is possibility of accruing greater benefit than reading unrealistic imagined stories". In this text, he outlined the concepts of matter, conscious matter, mankind, sense-organs, speech and language, time, numeration, size and weight of things, metals, purchase-sale-money, water-river-sea, plant, labour-right, animal, agriculture, industry-commerce and society. It is interesting that in this 37-page booklet, the words on God and the Crown are restricted in a very few words. The first edition of *Bodhodoya* did not contain[3] even a word on God but at the request of others, he later on added that the God may be like a formless (*nirakara*) sensation (*chaitanya*) but nobody can see him. During a conversation with Vidyasagar at his residence, meditator Ramakrishna, expressed his contentment and said that he had just witnessed the sea. Vidyasagar said that he might then carry some saline water, meaning the reality of the world. Listening to Ramkrishna's (Gadadhar) statement on the attainment of God Vidyasagar questioned, "when did I ever worship God"? This at once completely silenced Gadadhar.

Bodhodoya begins with the thing and matter. "Matter is of three kinds; conscious, unconscious and plant. Things which have life, can wilfully move, they are conscious matters; for example, man, animal, bird, worm, insect etc.; those things which have no life, remain, where you put them, cannot move from one place to another, they are called unconscious matter; for example, metal, stone, soil etc. And those things which grow on earth, they are plant matter; for example, tree, creeper and grass etc.

"Sense-organ is the gateway or medium of knowledge, and all kinds of knowledge are perceived with the sense-organs of the body. Without sense organs, we cannot know even a little of any subject. Cornea of the eye is transparent as glass. Beyond the eye-ball there lies a soft thin screen. Light passes inside the eye-ball through the cornea, from the matter we observe. Then, the same matter is *reflected* on the soft thin screen in the miniature form, and only from that our sense perception grows."

Bodhodoya, speaks of the existence of commodities in the form of individual or private property "as those objects belong to some person or others." "One acquires the goods through labour and without labour nothing is obtained. People earn money by labour. There are some common goods on which people have equal right; all persons can get these things without labour. Air, sunlight, rain and river water—-on all these and such other things, all people have equal right. Except these things, if some one wishes to obtain any other thing, he must have to *toil*, as there is *no possibility* of getting that *without labour* in the society."

"Activity concerned with the ploughing and sowing is agriculture. Persons directly engaged in this pursuit for production are peasants. Actually, it is an occupation of dignity. Like the living beings, plants cannot thrive without air, light, heat, water and suitable food; therefore, attention has to be paid so that there is no dearth in proportion of any of these things for agriculture. As all animals breathe, plants do the same act. As man catches disease without inhaling clean air, so also, unclean air is incongenial to the plant."

"There is no doubt that the assistance of the *three classes* of people, viz., peasant, artisan and merchant is extremely necessary. But all of our wants are never met by them. For learning, knowledge and treatment of disease, assistance of other kinds of people is necessary. Thus different classes of people are engaged in assistance with each other. Society is organised with all these classes of population.

"Brain, a substance of soft matter, lies within the skull of head. Now-a-days, the European scientists say that the brain is the place of mind and intellect. Nerves are thread-like matters set inside and spread throughout the body. They have relations and connections with the brain. So, when any thing comes into contact with the sense perception, the *idea* is formed about it."[4] (italics added)

It would be of much interest to view and relate the similarity of the above content on *idea* in Iswarchandra's *Bodhodoya* in the light of Marx's observation in "Afterword to the Second German Edition" of *Capital* (Vol. I) in 1873. There, Marx wrote, "My dialectic method is not only different from the Hegelian, but is its direct opposite. To Hegel, the life-process of the human brain i.e., the process of thinking, which, under the name of 'the idea', he even transforms into an independent subject, is the demiurgos of the real world, and the real world is only the external, phenomenal form of 'the idea'. With me, on the contrary, the ideal is nothing else than the material world reflected by the human mind, and translated into forms of thought."[5]

Further, with great insight Vidyasagar[6] critically observed the religious character of the Indian society. As he wrote :

> "Oh religion! It is difficult to comprehend your inner significance. How you are protected and how you are destroyed is known to you only.
>
> "Thanks to the customs of the country! What unspeakable grace you have! You are dominating on your faithful devotees under bondage by putting them in the harsh chains.
>
> "Oh India! How wretched you are. You were known to be holy land everywhere by virtue of the practices of your earlier sons; but your sons at present have made you such a holy land with their wilful acts and practices that, on hearing it, blood of all body is dried up. On seeing your present condition, it is difficult to decide on introspection, at what time your wretchedness would be removed.
>
> "Ah mute women! For what sin you are born in India, I do not know. "Ah people of India! How long would you lie on the

pleasure bed, remaining in deep sleep of superstition. Once open your eye of intellect, and you see the stream of sins in anti-social and unlawful practices in the holy land of India.

"Unfortunately, you are so much hypnotised with the age-old ever accumulated superstition, so much enslaved with the old customs and practices and so firmly determined to preserve them, that it cannot be expected that you would be followers of the very right path by suddenly sacrificing the superstitions, prevailing customs and practices and banishing the determined commitment of service to protect the evil order."

"In the earlier times, our country was very much developed in industries and artisan works. Muslin of Dhaka, a fine quality of cotton and silk fabric was sold at high prices in Europe. Ornaments of gold and silver produced at Cuttack and other places were adored in all countries. Without knowledge and enterprise, these industries have been ruined. All efforts should be made so that they may revive and develop again."

Vidyasagar exposed these social phenomena in his writings. It actually carries the nascent philosophical materialism and national feeling, and its conflict with the colonial interest of Great Britain.

In 1827, Lord Amherst, Governor General of the East India Company met Emperor Shah Alam II, and openly told him that the English were no longer under the descendants of Taimur. The royal family fell in great despair on hearing this news. Maharastrians humiliated the Emperor but did never disregard the royal authority. Now the Emperor's right to the kingdom was to go out of his hand for ever. Vidyasagar, outlining this political development of the time, observed that "the vast majority of the Indians became very much aggrieved on this behaviour of the English".[7] In these few words, the contradiction between the British colonialism and the Indian people was highlighted for public knowledge.

Rammohan Roy was conversant in nine languages, and in the words of Vidyasagar, he took much care to preach worshipping of Parabrahmo as depicted in the *Vedanta* system of Indian philosophy but distinct from the idolatry, among his countrymen. He was appointed as lawyer of the Emperor to defend his case in the court of appeal in England but the latter rejected the appeal. Rammohan's six Persian letters[8] disclose his intention and secret plan for revolutionary struggle of the Indians against the East India Company, by rallying around and under the authority of Mughal Emperor Shah Alam II. Vidyasagar wrote that even the persons opposed to the views of Rammohan praised his intellect and viewed that "There is no doubt that Rammohan Roy was an extraordinary personage of this country."

The social condition in India under the domination of the British rule in the 1880s became so pernicious, exploiting and oppressive that Vidyasagar used to say to his friends in close circles that they had "no other way out, but to build up native army in the forests"[9] and fight for driving out the colonial English in order to alleviate and improve the condition of the country.

The academic works on social condition confirmed the growing conflict between India and Great Britain. The broad sweep of history brought some change in administration of education and social thought, and consequently, some consciousness and radicalism particularly among one section of the newly educated class. Communal harmony till then remained intact. The appeal of this section was common, rational and secular to the people of India reflecting the antagonistic contradiction between the British colonial power and a colonial India.

One can at case relate and compare these facts revealing the contradiction between India and the colonial power of Great Britain with the observations of Karl Marx on the Indian situation in the early 1850s through 1880s. His sympathy to the cause of India and its people had no bounds. Marx with his profound materialist insight of philosophy could see a long way of the social development.

There is indeed a striking similarity in their views on the antagonistic contradiction between the Indian people and British colonialism. This was quite obvious in the process of historial development.

Some important incidents exposing rationality and the attitude independent of religion and spiritualism in this period can be mentioned. On hearing that Shibnath Shastri had embraced Brahmoism and for this reason his father Haran Shastri, leaving his native place, made his abode in Benaras (Kashi), Vidyasagar said with regret that Shibnath had not committed such a wrong that his father in sorrow would have to settle at Benaras. When Haran Shastri came to Calcutta for meeting, Vidyasagar asked him "Have you been adept in consuming *ganja*? If some one dies at Kashi, he becomes an incarnate of Shiva. Shiva is a confirmed consumer of *ganja*. If you could make a little practice of it, it would have been an advantage for you to become Shiva." In Vidyasagar's biography written by his younger brother Shambhuchandra, another incident had been recorded on his views about religion. It states that one day two missionaries came to Vidyasagar's house to ask him for a discussion on religion. He said to them, "what is religion, is beyond knowledge of man at the present time, and there is no necessity of knowing it." On being pestered by the two missionaries, Vidyasagar retorted that he would not like to be caned for others. In one of his letters to his brother, Vidyasagar affirmed, "I am not a slave of the native custom (*achar*)" His biographer Chandicharan Bandyopadhyay records that :

> Vidyasagar with deep regret uttered that "the salvation of India would be long delayed. By stopping cultivation of man with primitive nature and old ideas, removing seven layers of soil and making new man it would be better for the country like India." Such was his critical view and resplendant rationality with deep insight to the social problem of the country. Ballentyne, Haliday, Moyet, Carr and Gordon Young—all high officials of the East India Company—were aware of Vidyasagar's very firm and consistent view on the affairs of the Sanskrit college. He did not agree to change even a word of his important report on the academics of the college, inspite of the directions from Gordon Young. As he was opposed to the policy of the government's education department he unhesitatingly resigned from the office of the college in 1858 stating "self-respect is many times precious than service."

From these passages one can fairly have an idea of the rationalist philosophy which Vidyasagar and his associates held fast. Poet Rabindranath Tagore wrote that Vidyasagar was born in that great period which grasped the present and did not refuse the future. The flowing Ganga, said Rabindranath, had changed its old course and is connected with the sea. It is the flowing Ganga of the time with which Vidyasagar's course of life was in unison. For this reason, Vidyasagar, in the words of the poet, was modern. Kshudiram Bose who was very much known to Vidyasagar, called him an agnostic. In recent articles, authors like Badruddin Umar, Golam Murshid and Ahmad Shariff write that realisation in the life of Vidyasagar was that of an atheist philosopher and of a scientist caring for human life. Rammohan was agnostic, Vidyasagar was really an atheist and nationalist. They boldly declared that the Vedanta philosophy was a false system and native Naya Darshana was useless in practical life, and thus paved the path of philosophy and social progress in the country. (Golam Murshid, ed., *Vidyasagar Sardha Satabarsha Purti Smarak Grantha,* 1970, pp. 3-4, p. 13 and p. 217)

The trend of the movement can be followed from Shibnath Sashtri's comments : "The principles and practices of Hindu religion were openly rediculed and condemned, and angry disputes were held on moral subjects; the sentiments of Hume had been widely diffused and warmly patronised. Reason was now promoted to be a god, and custom voted to be the idol of fools.....it was then resolved that nothing but a liberal education could enfranchise the minds of the people." (*Ramtanu Lahiri O Tatkalin Bangasamaj*, Calcutta, 1957, p. 102).

A reference must be made in this context, on the formation of Arya Samaj in 1875, which spread its activity on a large scale in the North and Western India over the years. It was founded by Swami Dayananda who was born in a Nagar Brahman family of Gujarat. His original name was Mulshankar. He studied sanskrit literature. He was deeply versed in Vedic knowledge and came to the conclusion of his own thought.

Swami Dayananda gave a new interpretation of Hinduism. He opposed and overthrew idolatry. He discarded *Adwatic* interpretation of the *Vedanta-Sutras*. He negated Sayana's interpretation of the *Veda*, and Sankara's interpretation of the *Vedanta*. He upheld, that, matter is *co-eternal* with *Brahman*. Hence the world is no illusion. His *parabrahma* is a *fighting* god. Like the reform movements of the medieval period, Dayananda's religious concepts were moulded by the local environment of the North and Western India. He acknowledged that the *Veda* is eternal and a revealed one. It preaches monotheism, the *parabrahman* of which is not a philosophic abstraction but a fighting god, the lord of hosts. As such all other religions are "false".

He argued that all other interpretations of the Hindu scriptures are erroneous, and the epigonous developments are to be rejected. All must *go back* to the *Vedas* and *Vedic* rites, and these are such as interpreted by Swami Dayananda. One god, one scripture and one law was his ideal. Arya Samaj sanctions conversion of persons of other faiths into Hinduism. (Bhupendranath Datta, *Swami Vivekananda-Patriot-Prophet*, 1954, pp. 63-64)

Swami Dayananda rejected all earlier interpretations of the *Veda* and *Vedanta sutras*. He rightly criticised idolatry and recognised matter and reality of the world. But he mistakenly found matter as "co-eternal", confused it with the *Brahmana* and finally prescribed a return to the period of the Veda under the cult of a fighting god! He failed to look further in the path of philosophical materialism. Viewed from this angle, the postulate and principle of Swami Dayananda is quite opposite to the nascent rational philosophical school of Rammohan, Vidyasagar and his followers in Bengal.

Calcutta Journal The in 1819 reported the discussion of social problems by the Atmiya Sabha established by Rammohan, in the following words :

> "At the meeting in question the necessity of an infant widow passing her life in a state of celibacy, the practice of polygamy and of suffering about widows to turn with the corpse of their husbands were condemned." Rammohan's letter to Lord Amherst in 1823 clearly evinced his attitude against study of religious philosophy and its classical literature. He said "This seminary (Sanskrit school), similar in character to those which existed in Europe before the time of Lord Bacon, can only be expected to load the minds of youth with grammatical and metaphysical distinctions *of little or no practical use* to the possessors or to society." (Quoted from N. N. Chattopadhyay, *The Life of Rammohan Roy*, pp. 389-90)

Criticism of religion and its inhuman rites is the first transit point in the movement towards philosophical materialism. Opposition to, and negation of the *Vedanta* philosophy or *Adwaitavad* by the enlightened India represented by Vidyasagar, Rammohan, Debendranath and Akshay Kumar Datta had, in fact, broken new ground and heralded a new era of thought and materialism in the country. Vidyasagar rejected Bishop Barkeley's book, Inquiry, in 1852, which was later criticised and negated by the great social revolutionary leader, V.I. Lenin in his *Materialism and Empirio Criticism* in 1909, as idealist philosophy. How many scholars could dare find the defects and challenge the *Adwaita Vedanta* and *Inquiry* in the same vein at that time? It was possible for Vidyasagar to oppose the old system with his great intellect, vast knowledge and sterling integrity. He also edited a book on Indian philosophy exposing the nature of different schools of thought in the 1850s. His name will ever shine in the history of philosophical thought in India.

The keynote to the philosophy of rationalism, speaking in the words of Rammohan, is still modern to the democratic masses of the society. As he declared, "If mankind are brought into existence, and by nature formed to enjoy the comforts of society and the pleasure of an improved mind, they may be *justified in opposing* any system, religious, domestic and political which is inimical to the happiness of society or calculated to debase the human intellect" (Quoted in Bimanbihari Majumdar, *History of Political Thought*, p. 18). Following the same ideal and contention, he observed that "The enemies to liberty and friends of despotism have never been and never will be ultimately successful." (Quoted in A.F. Salahuddin Ahmed, *Social Ideas and Social Change in Bengal :* 1818-1835; Leiden, 1965, p. 32).

Briefly speaking, it becomes self-evident that the rationalist idea and materialist thought was slowly and gradually making inroads in the Indian society in the nineteenth century. It can be certainly said as the beginning of the enlightenment and modernisation in our country. This movement helped to usher in national feeling, national self-respect and patriotism. Analysis of this subject can be extended with the works of other important Indian personalities and development of social institutions at that time. However, for the time being, an attempt can be made to show the relation and consistency of the ideas of enlightenment with the salient features of philosophical materialism for the sake of analysis and elucidation.

On the Indian situation, Karl Marx wrote in the early 1850s, that "the more the industrial interest became dependent on the Indian market, the more it felt the necessity of creating fresh productive powers in India, after having ruined her native industry." (*On Colonialism*, Moscow, 1956, p. 48).

"Just as Italy has, from time to time, been compressed by the conqueror's sword into different national masses, so as we find Hindusthan, when not under the pressure of the Mohammedan, or the Mogul, or the Briton, dissolved into as many independent and conflicting states as it numbered towns or even villages...this strange combination of Italy and of Ireland, of a world of voluptuousness and of world of woes, is anticipated in the ancient traditions of the religion of Hindusthan. That religion is at once a religion of sensualist exuberance, and a religion of self-torturing asceticism, religion of the Lingam and of the Juggernaut; the religion of the Monk, and of the Bayadere". (*Ibid.*, pp. 3l-32)

The great materialist philosopher further commented, "I share not the opinion of those who believe in a golden age of Hindusthan....if you will go still more back to antiquity, take the mythological chronology of the Brahmin itself, who places the commencement of Indian misery in an epoch even more remote than the Christian creation of the world." "There cannot, however, remain any doubt but that the misery inflicted by the British on Hindusthan is of an essentially different and infinitely more intensive kind than all Hindusthan had to suffer before.... This is no distinctive feature of British colonial rule, but only an imitation of the Dutch.... All the civil wars, invasions, revolutions, conquests, famines, strangely complex, rapid and destructive as the successive action in Hindusthan may appear, did not go deeper than its surface. England has broken down the entire framework of Indian society, without any symptoms of reconstitution yet appearing. This loss of the world, with no gain of a new one, imparts a particular kind of melancholy to the present misery of the Hindu, and separates Hindusthan, ruled by Britain, from all its ancient traditions and from the whole of its past history." (*Ibid*, pp. 32-33)

"Indian society has no history at all, at least no known history. What we call its history, is but the history of the successive intruders who founded their empires on the passive basis of that unresisting and unchanging society.

"Arabs, Turks, Tartars, Moguls, who had successively overrun India, soon became Hinduized, the barbarian conquerors being by an eternal law of history, conquered themselves by the superior civilisation of their subjects. The British were the first conquerors superior, and, therefore, inaccessible to Hindu civilisation. They destroyed it by breaking up the native communities, by uprooting the native industry, and by levelling all that was great and elevated in the native society. The historic pages of their rule in India report hardly anything beyond that destruction. The regeneration hardly transpires through a heap of ruins. Nevertheless, it has began." (*Ibid.*, pp. 76-77)

On 19 February, 1881 Marx, wrote to N. F. Danielson "......In *India* serious complication, if not a general outbreak, is in store for the British Government..... There is an actual conspiracy going on wherein Hindus and Mussalmans cooperate; the British Government is aware that something is 'brewing', but this shallow people (I mean the Governmental men), stultified, by their own parliamentary ways of talking and thinking, do not even desire to see clear, to realise the whole extent of the imminent danger. To delude others and by deluding them to delude yourself this is : *parliamentary wisdom* in a nutshell. *Tant mieux* (so much the better)"[10]. Thus Marx exposed the growing antagonistic contradiction between the British colonialism and the people of India. A brief outline on the result of the scientific study and research on natural phenomenon, human organisation and thought can be given in this regard for the sake of objective reality and clarity of standpoint on the actual developments in the nature and human society.

"Everything that the human race has done and thought is concerned with the satisfaction of deeply felt needs and the assuagement of pain. One has to keep this constantly in mind if one wishes to understand spiritual movements and their development. A little consideration will suffice to show us that the most varying emotions preside over the birth of religious thought and experience. With primitive man it is above all fear that evokes religious notions—fear of hunger, wild beasts, sickness, death. Since at this stage of existence understanding of causal connections is usually poorly developed, the human mind creates illusory beings more or less analogous to itself on whose wills and actions these fearful happenings depend. Thus one tries to secure the favour of these beings by carrying out actions and offering sacrifices which, according to the tradition handed down from generation to generation, propitiate them or make them well disposed toward a mortal. It is a religion of fear". It is the broad contention of Albert Einstein.

"The development from a religion of fear to moral religion is a great step in peoples' lives. And yet, that primitive religions are based entirely on fear and the religions of civilised peoples purely on morality is a prejudice against which we must be on our guard. The truth is that all religions are a varying blend of both types, with this differentiation : that on the higher levels of social life the religion of morality predominates", Einstein writes, and he concludes, "Common to all these types is the anthropometric character of their conception of God". (Albert Einstein, *Ideas and Opinions*, Rupa and Company, 1984, Calcutta, pp. 36-38). With the sense of universal causation, future, to man, "is every whit as necessary and determined as the past. There is nothing divine about morality; it is a purely human affair," observed Einstein. Explaining the reality, he realistically noted that :

"When considering the actual living conditions of present-day civilised humanity from the standpoint of even the most elementary religious commands, one is bound to experience a feeling of deep and painful disappointment at what one sees. For while religion prescribes brotherly love in the relations among the individuals and groups, the actual spectacle more resembles a battlefield than an orchestra everywhere, in economic as well as in political life, the guiding principle is one of ruthless striving for success at the expense of one's fellowmen. This competitive spirit prevails even in school and, destroying all feelings of human fraternity and cooperation conceives of achievement not as derived from the love for productive and thoughtful work, but as springing from personal ambition and fear of rejection" and for its redressal, it demands striving after "rational knowledge". (*Ibid.*, p. 40, pp. 51-52 and p. 49)

"The man who is thoroughly convinced of the universal operation of the law of causation cannot for a moment entertain the idea of a being who interferes in the course of events—provided, of course, that he takes the hypothesis of causality really seriously. He has no use for the religion of fear and equally little for social or moral religion. A god who rewards and punishes is inconceivable to him for the simple reason that a man's actions are determined by necessity external and internal, so that in god's eyes he cannot be responsible, any more than an inanimate object is responsible for the motions it undergoes. Science has therefore been charged with undermining morality, but the charge is unjust. A man's ethical behaviour should be based effectually on sympathy, education, and social ties and needs; no religious basis is necessary. Man would indeed be in a poor way if he had to be restrained by fear of punishment and hope of reward after death." (*Ibid.*, p. 39)

One may take a critical view on the method of analysis but it is only objectivity that leads to the rational thought. Einstein wrote that "the scientific method can teach us nothing else beyond how facts are related to, and conditioned by, each other. The aspiration toward such objective knowledge belongs to the highest of which man is capable", without undermining his achievements and heroic efforts in this sphere. (*Ibid.*, pp. 41-42).

The brilliant observations and comments of Einstein completely demolish subjective idealism and the edifice of the religion and god and raise the premises of dialectical materialism to a new height with more space and illumination to help man understand and analyse nature and development of human society in a systematic way.

During the second half of the nineteenth century there were a number of noble Indian thinkers who made their deep imprint with their contribution to study and expose the contradiction of the Indian society under the British colonial rule.

Bholanath Chandra (1822-1910) presented his radical views on British exploitation of India in a long review of the three volume *A Brief History of Bengal Commerce (1872)* by Krishna Mohan Malik (1801-1883). Bholanath wrote in the Mookherjee's Magazine urging the people to "non-consume the goods of England" to "dethrone the king cotton of Manchester".

Dadabhai Naoroji's *Poverty of India* (papers read before the Bombay branch of the East India Association of London in 1876) brilliantly highlighted[11] the problems of India under the British rule, and showed the interactions and debates he made with the British Government and its theoreticians. He boldly concluded, "The chief cause of India's poverty, misery and all material evils is the exhaustion of its previous wealth, the continuously increasing, exhausting and weakening, drain from its annual production by the very excessive expenditure on the European portion of all its services, and the burden of a large amount a year to be paid to foreign countries for interest on the public debt, which is chiefly caused by the British rule".

"The obvious remedy is to allow India what it produces, and to help it as much as it lies in the power of the British nation to reduce her burden of the interest on the public debt, with a reasonable provision for the means absolutely necessary for the maintenance of the British rule. And for such means Britain must pay its proper share for its own interests".

Arguments on the condition of India (Correspondence between the Secretary of State for India and Dadabhai Naoroji in 1880-81) were put forward with all the earnestness of a noble patriot, but in such form that both skilled economists and practical politicians are bound to take account of them. There he exposed, "In fact, leaving the past alone as a misfortune, the continuance of the present drain will be in plain English, nothing less than plunder of an unceasing invasion, and not a reasonable price for beneficent rule, as the commissioners wrongly and thoroughly endeavour to persuade the public."

"A new danger is now threatening India. Hitherto India's wealth above the surface of the land has been draining away to England; now the wealth under the surface of the land will also be taken away, and India lies prostrate and unable to help herself. England has taken away her capital. That some capital will be brought to take away mineral wealth of the country as it requires the application of large capital and expensive machinery. With the exception of the employment of lower class of bodily and mental labourers, the larger portion of the produce will, in several shapes, be eaten up and carried away by the Europeans, first as servants, and next in profits and dividends; and the poor India will have to thank her stars that she will get some crumbs in the lower employments of her children. And great will be the sounding of trumpets of the wealth found in India, and the blessings conferred on India, just as we have sickeningly dinned into our ears, day after day, about railways, foreign trade etc."

"Every European is isolated from the people around him. He is not their mental, moral or social leader or companion. For any mental or moral influence or guidance or sympathy with the people he might just as well be living in the moon. The people know not him, and he knows not, nor cares for the people. Some honourable exceptions do now and then make some effort to do some good if they can, but in the very nature of things these efforts are always *feeble*, exotic, and of little permanent effect. These men are not always in the place, and their words die away when they go". The writer, thus, in these lucid words pointed out the alienation of man and contradiction in the capitalist society of the late nineteenth century.

As regards India, he continued the argument, "The most deplorable moral loss to India needs most serious consideration, as much as its political as in its national aspect. Nationally disastrous as it is, it carries politically with its nemesis."

"The thousands that are being sent out by the universities every year find themselves in a most anomalous position." There is no place for them in their motherland. ...The nemesis is as clear from the present violence to nature, as disease and death arise from uncleanliness and rottenness.... Heaven only knows what it will grow to! He who runs may see that if the present material and moral destruction of India continues, a great convulsion must inevitably arise, by which India will be more and more crushed under the iron wheel of despotism and destruction or may succeed in shattering the destroying hand and power... Englishmen sometimes indulge the notion that England is secure in the division and disunion among the various races and nationalities of India. But even in this, new forces are working their way. Those Englishmen who sleep such foolish, sleep of security know very little of what is going on. The kind of education that is being received by thousands of all classes and creeds is throwing them all in a similar mould; a sympathy of sentiment, ideas and aspirations is growing amongst them; and, more particularly, *a political union* and sympathy is the first fruit of the new awakening, as all see alike their deprivation and the degradation and destruction of their country. All differences of race and religion and rivalry are gradually sinking before the *common cause*. This beginning, no doubt, is at present insignificant; but it is surely and steadily progressing. Hindus, Mohammedans and Parsees are alike asking whether the English rule is to be a blessing or a curse. Politics now engross their attention more and more."

Dadabhai Naoroji continued, "This is no longer a secret or a state of things not quite open to those of our rulers who would see. It may be seen that there is scarcely any union among the different nationalities and races in any shape or ways of life, except only in political associations, they go hand in hand, with all the fervour and sympathy of a common cause.

"Certain songs (are) now being spread among the people of Western India against the destruction of Indian industry and arts.... The songs are at present directed against English wares, but they are also a natural and effective preparation against other English things when time comes, if the English in their blindness allow such times to come.

"The existing system of British rule is an un-British debasing, destructive, despotic and impoverishing rule. A righteous rule based on true British principles will be a great blessing both to England and India".

Naoroji was abreast of the world's political development and of rise and alignment of forces at that time. Addressing on the condition of India on 2 June 1899 in London, he observed that "the action of the English nation in regard to the people of India was of as vital importance to them as it was to India, and it was not even of less vital consequence to the whole human race. For a new element had already come into existence in the councils of nations. A country which had hitherto confined itself, under its Monroe doctrine, to its own continent was now coming forward to *share* in what was called the *imperialism* of the world, and the question had already arisen which course that country should follow...." He warned of the U.S. imperialism and its "globalisation" in the twentieth century . "The legislative council was simply and solely", he observed, "a delusion and a farce and its working constituted a *worse despotism* than was ever exercised by any native ruler even in the old days". (Italics added).

Thus, Naoroji saw the things and outlined the objective reality of the world situation. He carried and developed the ideas further in a letter dated 12.1.1905 addressed to D.E. Wacha stating that a bad name is given to the Congress that it was slow with no sense of dynamicity. So the persons of modern time were unsatisfied and impatient. But this impatient attitude, he noted, was the best fruit of the Congress activity as it carried the credentials of its evolution and advancement. "The very discontent and impatience it (The Congress) has evoked against itself as slow and non-progressive among the rising generation are among its best results or fruit.... While there is great necessity for informing people here, there is as much necessity that the true knowledge of their condition should widely spread among the Indian people themselves. The coordination of both is necessary to evolve the required revolution—*whether it would be peaceful or violent*. The character of this revolution will *depend upon the wisdom or unwisdom* of the British Government and the action of the British people"[12], Dadabhai Naoroji objectively asserted for the liberation of India.

In the same vein, Romesh Chandra Dutt pioneered the work on the economic history of India during the British colonial period and very cogently exposed the economic exploitation and drain from India to the UK resulting in the acute poverty of the people and harsh reality of India's economic distress and political subjugation. He analysed the economic and financial distress, unequal trade and domination of the British capital exclusively in a vast colonised country like India. He exposed the vilest character of British capital in the exploitation of the country's people and resources and reaping of the maximum tribute at the cost of the labour of the Indian people.

Movements for social reforms initiated by the persons like Jyotiba Phule in Maharashtra for the rights of the socially backward and lower caste people certainly helped to spread some rational ideas and thinking in the traditional and hierarchical Indian society. It played an important role to acquaint the people with the reality of the Indian society. The anti-Brahman campaign was first sounded in Maharashtra in the 1870s by Jyotiba Phule with his book, *Ghulam-Giri* (1872) and his organisation, the Satyasadhak Samaj (1873) which proclaimed the need to save the "lower castes from the hypocritical Brahmans and their opportunistic scriptures". During the same time, Justice M.G. Ranade exposed India's deindustrialisation and rustification. He extolled the cause of India's economic and political interests through many articles and addresses before the meetings of the associations and in public functions. Regarding free trade between the UK and India, he very objectively pointed out that it was just a competition between the giant and the dwarf. He held this view following the German positivist school of thought current at that time.

The writings and practical work of the eminent persons like Raja Rammohan Roy, Pandit Iswarchandra Vidyasagar, Jyotiba Phule, Dadabhai Naoroji, M.G. Ranade and Romesh Dutt showed and well explained the contradiction between the colonial power UK, and colonised India and its people. Their contributions provided the most valuable ingredients for recognising the objective reality and generally formed objective idealism, a basis for materialist understanding of the Indian social condition. This depicted a rational trend of thought—a product of enlightenment—which was pitted against the colonial rule and old Brahminical theocracy as well as the ideas of backward society It was truly secular in character. Materialist philosophy made its appearance general impact through this process in the late nineteenth century. It made its presence felt in the heterogeneous and caste-based Indian society.

The establishment and development of the Congress Party was the direct result of this trend of rational thought and intellectual practice, reform and scores of mass movements including the armed resistance of the Indian people. It founded and shaped the Congress Party as a secular political organisation on a sound ideological basis propounded by the moderate and liberal leadership with their foresight. The organisation had no religious bias or such motive in political activity.

The outstanding success of the earlier leadership of the Congress Party can be outlined in the following characteristics viz., (1) Forming the first all India secular political organisation of public activity in a vast backward society like India, (2) Analysing and exposing the antagonistic contradiction between the British colonial rule and the Indian people; its propagation in books, pamphlets, meetings etc., created public opinion in favour of the demand for reforms in Indian Government. (3) Laying the foundation of a secular political institution generally wedded to the materialist philosophy for understanding the reality of the existing social order which succeeded to forge unity between the majority and minority communities living in the country and made tactics for both constitutional and other means of politics quite open for the country. (4) Its leadership noted the emergence of the USA as a new colonial and imperialist power in the world politics.

In the Allahabad convention of the Congress in 1908, the party constitution was adopted with the objectives of achieving autonomy of India, national unity, advance of nationalism and economic development of the country. It made an obligatory provision that one-fifth of the members of the All India Congress Committee shall be from the Muslim community. (Jogesh Chandra Bagal, *Muktir Sandhane Bharat*, 1960, p. 249).

The Lucknow pact signed between the Congress and Muslim League in 1916 for united struggle against the British colonialism and imperialism was the most outstanding and shining charter of unity and communal harmony that the moderate leaders of the Congress and Muslim League, with their enlightenment, probity and amazing foresight, signed for the people of the Indian sub-continent. Even as late as in 1928, Tej Bahadur Sapru, the old surviving liberal leader warned the Congress Party to accept constitutional amendment proposals of Muhammad Ali Jinnah in order to avoid imminent damage and disaster, which in fact came as the reality in twenty years with the partition of the Indian sub-continent on the basis of religion in August 1947. But this advice fell on the deaf ears of the power-mongering "leaders" of the Congress and Hindu Mahasabha. The situation continued to deteriorate and became so worse that it made communal problem perennial and far more complicated in the country. Irrationality and subjective idealism gripped Indian politics in the 1920s and that continues to have its ever greater toll in the Indian sub-continent through the present time.

NOTES

1. Subodh Chakraborty, ed., *Vidyasagar Rachanabali* (Bengali), Kamini Prakashalaya, Calcutta, 1992, pp. 664-665.
2. *Ibid,* pp. 671-73and pp. 676-77.
3. Achintya Kumar Sengupta, *Parampursh Ramkrishna* (Bengali), Dey's Book Store, Calcutta, 1991, p. 244 and 359. For a detailed account of the rationalist movement in India in the nineteenth century see Sourindramohan Gangopadhyay, *Bengalir Rashtra Chinta* (Bengali), G. R. F. Publishers, Calcutta, 1991.
4. Subodh Chakraborty, ed., *Vidyasagar Rachanabali,* Kamini Prakashalaya, Calcutta, 1992, pp. 1456-57 and p. 1427.
5. Karl Marx *Capital,* Vol. I, Foreign Languages Publishing House, Moscow, 1958, p. 19.
6. Subodh Chakraborty, ed., *op. cit,* pp. 838-39.
7. *Ibid.*, p. 1454, p. 1529 and p. 1531.
8. Bhupendranath Datta, *Bharater Dwitiya Swadhinatar Sangram* (Bengali), Nababharat Publishers, Calcutta, 1983, p. 85, and *Vidyasagar Rachanabali,* p. 1531.
9. Bhupendranath Datta, *op. cit.*, p. 8 and p. 93. For further reference see works of Shambhu Chandra Bandyopadhyay and Chandicharan Bandyopadhyay on the Life of Vidyasagar. P. 518 and others; Golam Murshid, ed., *Vidyasagar Sardha-Shata-Barsha Purti Smark Grantha,* (Bengali) Vidyodaya Library Calcutta, 1970, pp. 3-4, 13, 103, 144-45, 148, 150, 155, and 217.
10. Karl Marx and Fredrick Engels, *On Colonialism,* Foreign Languages Publishing House, Moscow, 1956, p. 304.
11. Dadabhai Naoroji, *Poverty and Un-British Rule in India,* Swan Sonnenchien & Co., London, 1901. p. 207, 624, p. 636 and some other sections.
12. Bipan Chandra, Amalesh Tripathi and Barun De, *Swadhinata Sangram,* (Bengali), National Book Trust, New Delhi, 1983, p. 101, and R. P. Masani, *Dadabhai Naoroji,* New Delhi, 1975, pp. 138-139 (emphasis added).

2

RISE OF IDEALIST PHILOSOPHY IN INDIA

The advance of idealist philosophy actually made its great inroad through the metaphysics and interpretation of Hindu religion on the Indian society in the late nineteenth century and its politics in the latter period. Swami Vivekananda in a paper[1] read at the Parliament of Religions held at Chicago in 1893 observed, "The Hindus have received their religion through revelation, the *Vedas*. They hold that the *Vedas* are without beginning and without end.... By the *Vedas* no books are meant. They mean the accumulated treasury of spiritual laws discovered by different persons at different times. Just as the law of gravitation existed before its discovery, and would continue to exist if all humanity forgot it, so it is with the laws that govern the spiritual world. The moral, ethical and spiritual relations between soul and soul, and between individual spirits and the father of all spirits, were there before their discovery and would remain, even if we forgot them". He continued, "The *Vedas* teach us that creation is without beginning or end. Science is said to have proved that the sum total of cosmic energy is always the same. Then, if there was a time when nothing existed, where was all this manifested energy? Some say it was in a potential form in God. In that case God is sometimes potential and sometimes kinetic, which would make him mutable". He argued, "The idea of a body. Am I then nothing but a combination of material substances? The *Vedas* declare 'No'. I am a spirit living in a body" and "so then, the Hindu believes that he is a spirit".

Thus, Vivekananda emphasised spirit and its pre-existence, precedence and predominance in the universe. The spiritual laws, according to him, govern the spiritual world. He said, "there is spiritual relation between soul and soul and between individual spirits and the father of all spirits."

Vivekananda extended his argument, "Are not all the tendencies of mind and body accounted for by inherited aptitude? Here are two parallel lines of existence—one of the mind, the other of matter. If matter and its transformations answer for all that we have, there is no necessity for supposing the existence of a soul. But it cannot be proved that thought has been evolved out of matter, and if philosophical monism is inevitable, spiritual monism is certainly logical, and no less desirable than a materialistic monism". "Consciousness", he noted, "is only the surface of the mental ocean, and within its depths are stored up all our experiences. Try and struggle, they would come up, and you would be conscious even of your past life." He maintained, "Hindu believes that he is spirit", and that "death means the change of this centre from body to body. Nor is the soul bound by the conditions of matter. In its very essence it is free, unbounded, holy, pure and perfect. But somehow or other it finds itself tied down to matter, and thinks of itself as matter". The human soul is "eternal and immortal, perfect and infinite and death means only a change of centre from one body to another".

But how does the soul in its very essence "free" finds "somehow or other" "tied down to matter"? Who ties down and whom? Why soul is tied down only to matter and to nothing else? Vivekananda was conspicuously silent and turned to be speculative. He provided us with no explanation in this regard and commented that "it cannot be proved that thought has been evolved out of matter". Observation with the instruments like microscope and telescope confirms that matter exists independent of our knowledge. He discovered "two parallel lines of existence of matter and mind," and thereby smuggle in theism through the idea of spirit and soul, body-mind dualism and metaphysics. He observed, "The *Vedas* teach that the soul is divine, only held in bondage of matter; perfection will be reached when this bond will burst and the word they use for it is, therefore, *Mukti*—freedom, freedom from the bonds of imperfection, freedom from death and misery". He recognised the existence of matter but gave primacy to the spirit. This is nothing but fideism.

In a lecture delivered at Lahore in 1897, Vivekananda said, "the time has come for us to gather all our scattered forces to concentrate them into one focus, and through that, to lead the nation on its onward march, which for centuries almost, has been stopped. The house has been cleansed. Let it be inhabited anew. The road has been cleared : march ahead, children of the Aryans !"

"If at present the word Hindu means anything bad never mind; by our action let us be ready to show that this is the highest word that any language can invent. It has been one of the principles of my life not to be ashamed of my ancestors, I am one of the proudest man ever born, but let me tell you frankly, it is not for myself, but on account of my ancestry...children of those ancient Aryans, through the grace of the Lord may you have the same pride, may that faith in your ancestors come into your blood, may it become part and parcel of your lives, may it work towards the salvation of the world" and "Before trying to find out the common ground for our national life, one thing we must remember. Just as one man differs from another in certain peculiar particulars....so with nations (races), there is a certain point where the life of a nation centres, where lies the nationality of the nation, and until that is touched that nation cannot die. In the light of this we can understand the most marvellous phenomenon that the history of the world has ever known...we still stand practically the same race, ready to face difficulties again and again if necessary, and not only so, of late, there have been signs that we are not only strong, but ready to go out, for the sign of life is expansion".

Such concepts of one race, its religion and superiority identified and unified in such an imaginary spiritual world and rank metaphysics is devoid of the historical experience and of general practical life of the society consisting of more than one race and one faith. Clearly, this philosophy is prejudiced with race, religion and spiritualism, which stands in strong opposition to materialism that only has scientifically explained the phenomenon in nature and social development with the secular and universal approach. He asserted, "Therefrom the very start we must have to understand the mission of our own race, the destiny it has to fulfil, the place it has to occupy in the march of the nations, the note which it has to contribute to the harmony of races" and "If a Hindu is not spiritual I do not call him a Hindu. In other countries a man may be political first, and then he may have a little religion, but here in India the first and foremost duty of our lives is to be spiritual first, and then, if there is time, let other things come. Bearing this in mind we shall be in a better position to understand why, for our national welfare, we must first seek out at the present day, all the spiritual forces of the race, as was done in days of yore, and will be done in all times, to come. National union in India must be a gathering up of its scattered spiritual forces. A nation in India must be a union of those whose hearts beat to the same spiritual tune". So said Vivekananda in tune with the ancient *Adwaita Vedanta*.

He elaborated his aphorism with these words that a "man who does not believe in a most marvellous infinite power, from which everything has come, in which everything lives, and to which everything must in the end return, cannot be called a Hindu. If that be so, let us try to preach that idea all over the land. Preach whatever conception you have to give, there is no difference, we are not going to fight over it, but preach God; that is all we want". He held that "*Atman* inhabits body after body until there is no more interest for it to continue to do so, and it becomes free, not to be born again". But why and how does *Atman* "inhabit" in a body, and what interest does it have in it? How can these notions be warranted? On these questions he did not give any reason and material fact but only referred to the idea of *Samskara* and theory of "eternal souls" taught by the *Sastras*.

He continued the arguments, saying that "there is no regeneration for India until you be spiritual. Not only so, but upon it depends the welfare of the whole world". "Here am I, one of the least of the Hindu race yet proud of my race, proud of my ancestors. I am proud to call myself a Hindu, I am proud that I am one of your unworthy servants. I am proud that I am a countryman of yours, you the descendants of the most glorious *Rishis* the world ever saw".

Extending the *Vedanta* philosophy, Vivekananda further observed, "This body is made of particles which we call matter and it is dull and insentient. So is what the Vedantists call the fine body. The fine body, according to them, is a material but transparent body, made of very fine particles, so fine that no microscope can see them. What is the use of that? It is the receptacle of fine forces," and that "Just as this gross body is the receptacle of the gross forces, so the fine body is the receptacle of the fine forces, which we call thought, in various modifications. First is the body which is gross matter, with gross force. Force cannot exist without matter. It must require some matter to exist, so the gross forces work in the body; and those very forces become finer; the very force which is working in a gross form works in a finer form and becomes thought. There is no distinction between them, simply one is the gross and the other the finer manifestation of the same thing. Neither is there any distinction between this fine body and the gross body. The fine body is also material, only very fine matter; and just as this gross body is the instrument that works the gross forces, so the fine body is the instrument that works the fine forces. From where do all these forces come? According to *Vedanta* philosophy, there are two things in nature, one of which they call *akasha*, which is the substance, infinitely fine, and the other *prana*, which is the force." "Whatever, you see, or feel or hear, as air, earth, or anything, if material,—the product of *akasha*. It goes on and becomes finer and finer, or grosser or grosser, changing under the action of the *prana*. Like *akasha*, *prana* is omnipotent and interpenetrating everything. *Akasha* is like the water, and everything else in the universe is like blocks of ice made out of water, and floating in the water, and *prana* is the power that changes this *akasha* into all these various forms. The gross body is the instrument made out of *akasha*, for the manifestation of *prana* in gross forms, as mascular motion, or walking, sitting, talking, and so forth. That fine body is also made of *akasha*, a very fine form of *akasha* for the manifestation of the same *prana*, the finer form of thought. So, first there is this gross body. Beyond that is this fine body, and beyond that is the *Jiva*, the real man.....it is the one body, only the part which endures longer is the fine body, and that which dissolves sooner is the gross.... *Jiva*, according to the *Vedanta* philosophy, is eternal, just as god is eternal...the *Jiva* is not manufactured, either of *akasha* or *prana*; it is immaterial and, therefore, will remain for ever." He further contended that "the fine body will also be decomposed, after a long time, but the *Jiva* is simple, and will never be destroyed".

Hence thought, as this philosophy holds, is the fine force of the fine body, and primary, although it says, "Force cannot exist without matter".

"This *Jiva*, according to the *Vedanta* philosophy, is eternal just as god is eternal," and Vivekananda said, "God is both the material and the efficient cause of this universe. He projects this universe out of himself." But at the same time he declared, "Force cannot exist without matter. It must require some matter to exist". Thus, to Vivekananda, God precedes matter and thought primary in the fast system of *Vedanta* philosophy which Iswarchandra Vidyasagar condemned as "false" from the standpoint of radical thought and modern philosophy. The very attitude of Vidyasagar and Vivekananda towards the fast system of the Vedanta and Sankhya is strikingly different and opposite for obvious reasons. Vivekananda's idea is centred around the *Vedanta* philosophy and theism in the tradition of old religious thinking of India, while Vidyasagar held views in contrast to it, by focussing the life of social man of the modern time.

India, according to Vivekananda, is really a museum of anthropology. "Here are the Persian, the Greek, the Yunchi, the Hun, the Chin, the Sythian and many more, the Jews, Parsis, Arabs, Mongols...are ocean of humanity composed of these race waves, seething, boiling, struggling, constantly changing forms, rising to the surface and spreading and swallowing little ones, again subsiding— this is the history of India".

And further he said[2] that :

The main base, spine or centre of life, in India, is only religion, and spiritualism is the process of its work. This nation is still alive because it has not lost the great treasure like God and religion. Religion, and religion only, is the main base of India's people and national life.

In Asia, specially in India, all barriers regarding nationality, language and society are removed with the co-ordinating power of religion as Indians feel that there is no greater ideal than spiritual thought. It is the main theme of Indian life and its work can be carried with the minimum obstacle.

It is a truism that religion is the highest ideal. Religion is the only means for carrying out the task. "Attaining co-ordination among the different religions is the first programme for building up future India."

Only the holy tradition of our nation—our religion—is the basis of our unity, and only on its foundation national life has to be formed. In Europe politics is the basis of national unity. But in Asia, religion is the root of that unity. So forging the unity of religion is absolutely essential for building up India in future. India's ideal—God, and only God. So long India keeps faith on God, there is hope for survival.

If one nation has to go forward it must have high ideal. Ideal is the *parabrahmo*. But as all of you would not be in a position to be inspired by abstract ideal, you earnestly require an ideal person. You have received that ideal in Sri Ramakrishna. No other person can be our ideal in this age.... We want today such a man, who has sympathy to man of the present time. This necessity of ours has been satisfied with Ramakrishna. Today every one holds him high above. It does not matter anything in which form you accept him, as saint or incarnation.

"Though God exists everywhere, we can know him only through human character. In no other age, any great person became of so sublime a character as Ramakrishna; so centering him, we shall have to get united; but every one will be free to accept him in his own idea—some may call him master, some saviour, some god, some ideal person or some great person—whatever one may prefer."

Yet, Vivekananda was a little liberal and stayed as guest of a Muslim lawyer at Mount Abu. The Private Secretary of Khetri Raj met him there and asked, "you are a Hindu saint. How could you stay in the residence of a Muslim?" Vivekananda strongly opposed this view and said that he himself was above all their social restrictions in the name of religion and that he could dine even with a scavenger.

After a prolonged discourse on religion with many persons, in a railway station of Rajasthan, Vivekananda could not take meal and he felt very hungry. While no other person turned up, a cobler brought some of his own food, and offered bread to him, and he very gladly accepted food from the low caste person. He rebuked there some person, who made a plea against this act, for the sake of human dignity.

Swami Vivekananda's letter to Mohammed Sarfarz of Nainital on 10 June 1898 stated : "I am firmly persuaded that without the help of practical Islam, theories of Vedantism, however, fine and wonderful they may be, are entirely valueless to vast mass of mankind.... For our own motherland junction of two great systems—Hinduism and Islam, Vedanta brain and Islam body—is the only hope. I see in my mind's eye the future of perfect India rising out of this chaos and strife, glorious and invincible".

While touring Almora, Vivekananda once fell critically ill owing to hunger and tiredness on the way. Swami Akhandananda was his companion. A Muslim saint lived nearby. The saint brought some fruits for him. Vivekananda consumed the fruits, saved his life and he became much delighted to see the Muslim saint time and again.

Once a campaigner of the cow protection association went to Vivekananda to ask for monetary help to the organisation. In course of interview with the campaigner he firmly refuted the idea of "*Karma*" and said that "the cows, for obvious reasons, go to the butcher and are slaughtered and we have no necessity to do anything in that affair". This view was in quite contrast to the campaign for cow protection of the Arya Samaj which published pamphlets like "Go-Karunanidhi" in Hindi since the early 1880s.

Basically, Vivekananda with his spirituality and theism, was a great proponent of the Hinduism and Vedanta. But this position, did not prevent him from understanding and joining with the other communities like the Mohammedans, and the lower caste people of the Hinduism. This indicates a certain bent of his mind toward a social democratic thought against social obscurantism, sectarianism and feudal absolutism, especially in the Indian situation. But the foundation of his thought is strongly based and reinforced by the idealist philosophy and spiritualism under Hindu religion.

World history, according to Vivekananda, is the history of a few self-confident persons in themselves. That faith rouses the inner godlines. It is the ideal of self-confidence that can do maximum good to the mankind. It was his firm belief that, if this self-confidence could be propagated and translated into action, "much of the sorrows and sufferings of the world would have been removed". In the history of mankind, if some inspiration transmitted greater power to the great souls, it is the self-confidence.

He advised : Work with firmness. Engage in work

Remember the main theme: "welfare of the people without minutely hurting their religion. Have faith in Lord. What is wanted, is full simplicity, sacredness, great intellect and all conquering will power. If some persons with these qualities engage themselves in work, the world would be shaken.

The creed of *Adwaita*, Vivekananda believed, will be the religion of the enlightened human society of the future. Among nations, Hindus can have the glory to reach that high thought because they are more ancient compared to the Hebru or Arabian nations, but the able and active *Vedanta* that regards itself as the soul of the entire mankind—was never actually nourished among the Hindus.

Thus, a few persons, self-confidence and will-power, according to Vivekananda, can make world history! What a fine and fantastic subjective idealism!

Vedanta would be the religion of enlightened mankind of the future, even though he admits that *Vedanta* actually was never nourished among the Hindus! What a fancied idea of history! Mode of production, condition of the real life of the society and its direct producers, their role in material life of the society and in history, and social antagonism do not find any place in the philosophy of *Vedanta*. Vivekananda speaks of oneness, work and service. But work and service for whom and by whom? Obviously, that is mainly done with the donation of the rich for supporting the existing order of things in the society dominated by the capitalists and landlords. It actually becomes handiwork of the ruling propertied class for their "salvation".

Work or service to the masses of the people in the name of *Adwaita*, is nothing but, mainly practice of charity by the rich, and reformism sanctified by theism and reaction in the society. And that is why Vidyasagar was totally opposed to and decried the system of *Vedanta* and *Sankhya* philosophy as false and recommended for teaching and propagation of the modern philosophy of the west for upliftment of the country. Further, it seems strange that, while leaders like Dadabhai Naoroji, unravelled the contradiction between colonialism and Indian people and warned against the emergence of the USA as the new country in the race of persuing colonialism, Vivekananda declared that his journey to the west specially to the USA "was meant for the common and poor people." (*The Life of Swami Vivekananda*, Vol. I, 1979, p. 379; cf. *Amar Bharat, Amor Bharat* : Bengali) But this is quite possible as the imagination and subjectivism are the hallmarks of religious idealist philosophy.

Ramakrishna, Vivekananda's mentor, viewed that the human body was like a structure made of bamboo ribs and covered with cloth and that moves. "Some one exists inside and so it moves" and "one and undivided Shachhidananda" exists both inside and outside the body. After Ramakrishna's death, Narendranath became leader of his disciples and began to supervise them. On 7 May 1887, Narendranath said in a meeting with this fellow brothers of the first Ramakrishna Math that he felt that there was no God, as in spite of intense prayers, he did not get reply even for once. Mani (Master), one of the disciples of Ramakrishna, stated in a meeting with Narendranath on 8 May 1887 that Vidyasagar did not at all entertain any religion; and was averse to be caned for others upon God and religion. Narendranath flared up and castigated, "He, who has not understood it how can he understand other subjects?" and "If he has not followed this, how can he understand kindness and service to others? How can he know of school? How can he understand that it is right to teach the children by establishing school, have family and beget children?" and "He, who understands the first right, he follows all". In the same meeting, Prasanna, another disciple of Ramakrishna, asked Narendranath, "You say God exists. Again, it is you who say, Charvaka and others held that the world has been created by itself!" Narendranath answered, "Haven't you read Chemistry? See, who will make the combination? It is just as human hand brings together oxygen, hydrogen and electricity for making water". "All regard the intelligent force; there is only one as the consciousness (spirit) who causes all the affairs", and "He (Ramakrishna) said, faith is the essence". Prasanna said to Narendranath, "you sometimes say, there is no God; now you say this; you do not stick to your words, you often change your views". Narendranath said that he would not change his view any more; and added that so long there is desire and attachment, there is disbelief in God. He then began to condemn family life and felt a state of renouncement. [Mahendranath Gupta (Srima), *Sri Sri Ramakrishna Kathamrita*, Vol. 2, Thakurbati, Calcutta, 1978, pp. 237, 245, 246, 252 and 260-61]

Narendranath was actually in dilemma as late as in the middle of 1887 but subjective idealism ultimately had swayed him and he finally embraced *Adwaita Vedanta* in the same year that opposed the materialist view of the world and nascent rationalist though in the society. He became a powerful crusader for *Adwaita Vedanta* which Rammohan had criticised in no uncertain terms and Iswarchandra Vidyasagar, being a great scholar of *Vedanta,* himself challenged and rightly pronounced the system as false as early as in 1853. The *struggle* between the two systems continued on and the staunch proponents of the *Vedanta* and *Sankhya* systems, as Vidyasagar had prophetically apprehended, actually set sail to the conservatism and age-old reaction in the Indian society.

Narendranath Datta (later Vivekananda) was born in 1863. In his earlier life he joined the Brahmo Samaj. He was a staunch Brahmo and enrolled as a member of the Sadharan Brahmo Samaj. He used to sing well in the choir of the Brahmo Samaj. He first met Ramakrishna in 1881. He passed B.A. examination in 1883. He gradually became acquainted with Ramakrishna. Over time, a band of devotees gathered around him which formed the nucleus of the future Ramakrishna sect. Pandit Shivnath Sastri said that Ramakrishna had the capacity to form a group of his own. Haromohan Mitra, a classmate of Narendranath, repeatedly said to his brother. Bhupendranath Datta that Swamiji used to say : "But for Ramakrishna I would have been a Brahmo missionary". (Bhupendranath Datta, *Vivekananda-Prophet-Patriot*, 1954, p. 65 and p. 164).

After his father's death in 1884 Narendranath had to give up the articled clerkship owing to unexpectedly sudden family economic stringency but continued to study law. Later due to Ramakrishna's illness he stayed at Cossipur and absented himself from home for a long time. On account of his continued absence his mother got frightened and went to Cossipur to bring him back. She took her youngest child, six years old Bhupendranath along with her. The mother and the boy were sent upstairs and were ushered before the ailing Ramakrishna. In the midst of the large room he was sitting on his bed but in half-reclining posture; his back was resting on a big pillow. He looked at both of them and said to mother : "The doctor has advised me not to speak but I must speak to you. It is good that you have come. Take Naren back with you. Ghosh and others donned him in *sanyashi's* clothes. But I exclaimed,— how is that you have a widow-mother and an infant brother to look after. It does not befit you to be a *sanyasi*!" Thereupon, Narendranath accompanied his mother and brother on the way back to home. In the carriage mother told him what Ramakrishna had told her. But Narendranath answered, "He (Ramakrishna) tells the thief to steal but warns the house-holder at the same time." (A Bengali phrase which means working both ways). On the way back home, Narendranath got down midway at Baggbazar as he said he had some business there (*op. cit.*, p. 157).

Krishna Kumar Mitra, a member of the Sadharan Brahmo Samaj said the following in his autobiography : "Acharya Keshabchandra, Pandit Shibnath Sastri and other Brahmos brought Ramakrishna out of his unknown room of Dakshineswar and made him public, and gave him the title of 'Paramhansa'.....Narendranath was attracted to him by his simple and devotional life. It is true that Narendranath became disciple of Ramakrishna but this disciple made his *guru* " 'unsectarian' " (*op. cit.*, p. 178).

If Ramakrishna was truthful in his statement to Narendranath's mother, it becomes evident that the sect's pressure and coercion worked in converting Narendranath to a *sanyasi*. It is also surprising that Ramakrishna had initiated Narendranath to monk life although he knew of his unstable family condition very well. There was obviously his own motive behind such act.

Narendranath's statement to his mother is indicative and revealing in this regard and it exposes the very inconsistent and weak position of Ramakrishna. Actually the liberal section of the landed bourgeoisie patronised Ramakrishna sect which emphasised on universalism of religion. It also arranged reception ceremonies for Ramakrishna and Vivekananda. His chief disciple Swami Vivekananda said, "He would eat and dress like a people he wanted to understand, make their initiation and use their language." "One must learn", he said, "to put oneself into another man's very soul." And this method was his own (*op. cit.*, p. 185 and p. 188).

Vivekananda thought that India would conquer "...In the world of ideas. England has the sword, the material world as our Mohammedan conquerers had before her. Yet Akbar the great became practically a Hindu; educated Mohammedans, the Sufis, are hardly to be distinguished from the Hindus.... Their thought has become permeated by ours (*op. cit.*, p. 207).

In Sister Nivedita's words, Vivekananda made Hinduism once more aggressive. His plan was : "The eternal faith must become active and proselytising ... and deliberate assimilation of new elements" (*op. cit.*, p. 215).

In 1900 Swamiji gave two lectures at Pasadona Shakespeare Club on *Ramayana* and *Mahabharata*. In concluding the lecture on *Ramayana* he said "Rama and Sita are the ideals of the Indian nation,... The height of a woman's ambition is to be like Sita, the pure, the devoted, the all suffering. The west says, 'Do show your power by doing'. India says, 'Show your power by suffering'... Sita is typical of India." (*op. cit.*, p. 247).

As regards the delineation of *Mahabharata*, he said, "Thus ends the story of *Mahabharata* setting forth in a sublime poem the triumph of virtue and defeat of vice." Lastly, he viewed, "In fact, *Ramayana* and *the Mahabharata* are the two encyclopedias of the ancient Aryan life and wisdom, portraying ideal civilisation, which humanity has yet to aspire after." (*op. cit.*, p. 247).

Thus Vivekananda idealised the epics for inspirations and development of the Indian society and from Ramakrishna, whom he met in his teens, he learned that God can be worshipped as without form (*Nirakara*), as with form (*Sakara*). This is the teaching of *Vishnupurana*, while the *Brahmasutra*, popularly known as the *Vedanta-Shastra* says that the ignorant can worship through a symbol. Vivekananda's biographers say that, "Brahmo Samaj...seemed too radical to him in the latter period of his life".

This is the psychoanalysis behind the cause that led those who left the Brahmo movement and joined Ramakrishna (*op. cit.*, p. 260).

It is true that Swami Vivekananda like many persons in a transitional period had a "complex character". His biographers say that "Swami Vivekananda was a life of striking contrasts and moods of infinite variety," which confounded even his friends at times. He sought to idealise and accommodate many ideas. As regards his social views, in a letter written in 1894, he said : "We reject none, neither theist, nor pantheist, monist, polytheist, agnostics, nor atheist, the only condition of being disciple is modelling a character at once the broadest and most intense... We have everybody free to know, select and follow whatever suits and helps him... We believe that every being is divine, is God...social laws were created by economic conditions under the sanction of religion. The terrible mistake of religion was to interfere in social matters... We insist at the same time that religion has no right to become a social law-giver. Hands off ! Keep yourself to your own bounds and everything would come out... What business had the priests to interfere (to the misery of millions of human beings) in every social matter." (*op. cit.*, p. 266).

This statement of Vivekananda is full of idealist conception and reveals self-contradiction. In the actual life, theist, pantheist and atheist are always at loggerheads and oppose each other's view and contention, often in the name of religion and divinity. The history of their struggle is well known and that struggle continues on through the end of twentieth century. "Modelling character" in such an atmosphere is not possible as the existing society itself is based on strife, antagonism and violence. Accumulation of private property and estrangement of man is its aim. Vivekananda strived to equate being with the divinity and God. Clearly, it is ecclectical and his emphasis lies on the "predominance of spirit" and not matter—a concept devoid of the real world. He rightly said that social laws were created by economic conditions but he held mistaken idea that the latter were created "under the sanction of religion". Actually, in the society, economics is the primary, basic and fundamental in relation with the social and religious ideas, rituals and institutions.

When it is said that the social laws comes "under the sanction of religion", it obviously follows that religion does interfere in social matters. Under such a situation, religion emerges authoritatively as the social law giver, and hence there is no condition of taking its "hands off". This again assures position of the priests to "interfere" causing misery of the people. They came to dominate the social psychology in the name of religion and culture.

In sum, it believes in theism and preaches its own theology. It protects reaction and slowly and gradually leads the society to theocracy. This is the motion of religious organisation in the society.

Vivekananda observed that "every improvement in India requires first of all an upheaval in religion. Before flooding India with socialistic and political ideas, first deluge the land with spiritual ideas.... In the *Kali Yuga* there is one *Karma* left. *Sacrifices* and tremendous *Tapasyas* are of no avail now. Of *Karma* one remains, and that is the *Karma* of giving. And of these gifts, the gift of spirituality and spiritual knowledge is the highest; the next gift is the gift of secular knowledge; the next is the gift of life, and the fourth is the gift of food" (*Works*, Vol. 3, pp. 221-222). Spiritualism is inseparably bound and based on religion, and strangely, that gets the highest position in the *Karma* of giving. Spiritualism itself is inimical to the rational idea and secular knowledge.

Some may say that "upheaval of religion" means intellectual ferment. But, its actual meaning is quite different. It becomes quite arbitrary and theosophical more especially in the context of religion and precedence of the latter in the practical life of the society.

In other places of his Works, Vivekananda, however, conditionally stressed for spread of education, basic needs of the masses of the people and service to them.

As he declared, "I consider that the great national sin is the neglect of the masses and that is one of the causes of our downfall. No amount of politics would be of any avail until the masses in India are once more well-educated, well-fed and well cared for. They pay for our education, they build our temples, but in return they get kicks. They are practically our slaves. If we want to regenerate India, we must work for them." (*Works,* Vol. 5, p. 152). He further said, "Intelligence must not remain the monopoly of the cultured few; it will be disseminated from higher to lower classes. Education is coming, and compulsory education will follow. The immense power of our people for work must be utilised. India's potentialities are great and will be called forth," (*Works*, Vol. 5, p. 129), and he added,"....first make the people of the country stand on their legs by rousing their inner power, first let them learn to have good food and clothes and plenty of enjoyment—then tell them how to be free from this bondage of enjoyment. Laziness, meanness and hypocracy have covered the whole length and breadth of the country. Can an intelligent man look on all this and remain quiet? Does it not bring tears to the eyes?" (*Works*, Vol. 7, p. 180).

"The peasant, the shoemaker, the sweeper and such other lower classes of India", said Vivekananda, "have much greater capacity for work and self-reliance than you. They have been silently working through long ages, and producing the entire wealth of the land, without a word of complaint. Very soon they will get above you in position. Gradually capital is drifting into their hands, and they are not so much troubled with wants as you are. Modern education has changed your fashion, but new avenues of wealth lie yet undiscovered for want of inventive genious. You have so long oppressed these forbearing masses; now is the time for their retribution. And you will become extinct in your vain search for employment, making it the be-all and end-all of your life." (*Works,* Vol. 7, p. 146). Further he advised, ".....Get yourselves to the tasks of spreading education among the masses. Tell them and make them understand, 'you are our brothers —a part and parcel of our bodies, and we love you and never hate you'. If they receive this sympathy from you, their enthusiasm for work will be increased a hundred-fold. Kindle their knowledge with the help of modern science. Teach them history, geography, science, literature, and along with these the profound truths of religion. In exchange for that teaching, the poverty of the teachers will also disappear. By mutual exchange both parties will become friendly to each other." (*Works*, Vol. 7, pp. 146-47)

On social question, Vivekananda commented, "Now the question before us is this. There cannot be any growth without liberty. Our ancestors freed religious thought and we have a wonderful religion, but they put a heavy chain on the feet of society, and our society is in a word, horrid, diabolical. In the west, society always had freedom, and look at them. On the other hand, look at their religion."

"Liberty is the first condition of growth. Just as man must have liberty to think and speak, so he must have liberty in food, dress and marriage and in every other thing, so long as he does not injure others". (*Works*, Vol. 4, pp. 312-313)

As he elucidated this important subject, "We talk foolishly against material civilisation. The grapes are sour. Even taking all that foolishness for granted, in all India there are, say, a hundred thousand really spiritual men and women. Now, for the spiritualisation of these, must three hundred millions be sunk in savagery and starvation? Why should any one starve? How was it possible for the Hindus to have been conquered by the Mohammedans? It was due to the Hindus' ignorance of material civilisation. Even the Mohammedans taught them to wear tailor-made clothes. Would the Hindus have learned from the Mohammedans how to eat in a clean way without mixing their food with the dust of the streets! Material civilisation, may even luxury, is necessary to create work for the poor. Bread! Bread! I do not believe in a God who cannot give me bread here, giving me eternal bliss in heaven! Pooh! India is to be raised, the poor are to be fed, education is to be spread, and the evil of priestcraft is to be removed. No priestcraft, no social tyranny! More bread, more opportunity for everybody! Our young fools organize meetings to get more power from the English. They only laugh. None deserves liberty who is not ready to give liberty. Suppose the English give over to you all the power. Why, the powers that be then, will hold the people down and let them not have it. Slaves want power to make slaves." (*Works*, Vol. 4, p. 313). Further, he exhorted, "The chief cause of India's ruin has been the monopolising of the whole education and intelligence of the land, by dint of pride and royal authority, among a handful of men. If we are to rise again, we shall have to do it in the same way, *i.e.*, by spreading education among the masses. A great fuss has been made for a half a century about social reform. Travelling through various places of India, these last ten years, I observed the country full of social reform associations. But I did not find one association for them, by sucking whose blood the people known as 'gentlemen' have become and continue to be gentlemen!" (*Works*, Vol. 4, p. 415).

Despite Vivekananda's firm adherence to the *Vedanta* and its spiritualism, these observations amply clarify his patriotic and social democratic view then much applauded by the liberal section of the Indian bourgeoisie. A thin strain of liberty, equality and fraternity—the central theme of the French Revolution—can be discerned from some of his writings and speeches as well.

This radical content concerning the society's practical life and its transformation in Vivekananda's thought can be viewed and related with the activity of his early life. His brother Bhupendranath Datta in the Foreword of his book "*Swami Vivekananda : Patriot-Prophet*", writes, "very few people know that he had political revolutionary ideas in the beginning. He wanted to free the country from foreign yoke. But he failed in his attempt, and seeing the cause of his failure, he tried a different remedy and deflected his attention to another channel. The key to the new venture of his work for India lay here."

It also discloses that, in the year before his death, when two of his foreign admirers (one of whom was his disciple) with the collaboration of some noted citizens of Calcutta started a nationalist group which later on became the necleus of the later revolutionary movement of Bengal, Swami Vivekananda desisted his disciple from joining it. On being questioned by sister Christine as to why he requested the other one to keep aloof from Indian politics, he answered, "What does Nivedita know of Indian conditions and politics. I have done more politics in my life than she! I had the idea of forming a combination of Indian princes for the overthrow of the foreign yoke. For that reason, from the Himalayas to Comrin I have tramped all over the country. For that reason, I made friends with the gun-maker Sir Hiram Maxim. But I got no response from the country. The country is dead." And he narrated further attempt of his at this time in other direction; but he again said, "India is in putrefaction. What I want today is a band of selfless young workers who will educate and uplift the people." Swamiji narrated further of his doings to sister Christine. But she refused to divulge it to Bhupendranath, Swamiji's youngest brother. Here it should be mentioned that the news about the attempt at revolution on the part of the Swamiji was not unknown to the leading revolutionaries of the first batch. It was narrated by the Swamiji himself in the course of a dialogue with Pandit Sakharam Ganesh Deuskar at Belur. Pandit Deuskar himself was an active member of the revolutionary party. On being interrogated by Deuskar regarding the future of the country, Swamiji answered : "The country has become a powder magazine. A little spark may ignite it, I will see the revolution in my life time." All this is revealed in the book's Foreword. Vivekananda's thought thus actually contains two parts, *viz.* (i) theistic *Vedantic* philosophy, and (ii) struggle for people's education, reforms and social work. These are but two conflicting subjects but nevertheless united. The first part, being the rightist, confronts the very rationality and secular content of the other. The second cannot proceed freely and uninterruptedly unless it settles its score with the first. It is the unity of the two opposites. Actually, the first represents theism and religion that is preferred by the exploiting classes in order to protect their class interest. The former being butressed by reaction influences the other and controls the ruling classes' education and other programmes. In fact, the theism and spiritualism, under the garb of Neo-Vedantism, greatly expanded to make the rational part of the Vivekananda's thought as its mere appendage, serving the interest of reactionary classes and the colonial state of India. Fifty years after Vivekananda's death, Bhupendranath wrote in 1954, in the said book, that "an attempt is being made in some quarter to depict him (Ramakrishna) as a conservative Brahman who followed the taboo—prohibitions of neosmriti of Navadvipa Brahmanical orthodoxy in his habits of life. But there are definite recorded testimonies that he was above inhibitive injunctions. It is clear that by casting away the universalism of Ramakrishna, the orthodox Brahmanical priestcraft is engulfing Ramakrishnaism. A religion is judged by the influence it exerts on the society by leading it to a definite goal of life. Hence it is to be said, that unlike the reform movements of the present and of medieval days, Ramakrishnaism has not moulded the society according to its own ideal. It is following the old Brahmanical rut" (*op. cit.*, p. 185). Thus the *Vedanta* system actually works for the existing state of things in the society.

The rational content of Vivekananda's thought has been coaxed and suppressed by the *Vedanta*, against which Vidyasagar warned the people by declaring it as a false system much earlier. That rationality can be freed only by the mighty struggle of the Indian working class, through a protracted war against the ruling comprador bourgeoisie and landlord classes of India.

In *Advaita Vedanta, sat-chit-ananda* (being-intelligence-bliss) means the supreme being, Brahman. Brahmabandhab Upadhyaya (Bhabani Charan Banerji), a friend of Swami Vivekananda, who as a *Sannyasin* in 1894, pointed out that to speak of Brahman as *sat-chit-ananda* means that Brahman knows himself and from that self-knowledge proceeds. The relation of being (*sat*) to itself in self-knowledge (*chit*) is one of perfect harmony, Bliss (*ananda*). In the view of Upadhyaya, the Christian doctrine of God as trinity (father, son and the spirit) is exactly the same as the Vedantic conception of brahman as *sat-chidananda*.

According to Brahmabandhab, *maya* signifies the will-power *(sankalapa)* of God. It means that creation is by the power *(sakti)* of the will *(sankalapa)* of God. He declared that this Vedantic doctrine of *maya* which explains creation and the Christian doctrine of creation are identical.

Regarding his political contributions it can be pointed out that Brahmabandhab made his Bengali daily, *Sandhya* into a popular newspaper which drew the masses into the mainstream of the political movement. Under the *Vedanta* philosophy, he gave Indian nationalism a mass appeal that anticipated Gandhi's own move by decades. It is the ideology that gave tremendous inspiration and strength to the country in general and to its majority community in particular. On 20th September 1906 through *Sandhya*, Brahmabandhab Upadhyaya called independence "......impossible at present. But nonetheless, that is goal we should always keep before our eyes". *Sandhya* declared in 1907 : "We want complete independence. The country cannot prosper so long as the veriest shred of the Feringhi's supremacy over it is left". There came into existence in Bengal many secret societies like Anushilan Samiti which preferred the cult of the bomb and the revolver. They needed a philosophy and *Sandhya* met this demand. The members of the societies avidly read the stirring articles which Upadhyaya wrote.

One of the articles forming the subject-matter of the prosecution for two sedition cases against *Sandhya* was entitled "*Ekhan Theke Gachi Premer Dai*", and this appeared in *Sandhya* on 13th August, 1907. Brahmabandhab Upadhyaya wrote : "We have said over and over again that we are not *swadeshi* only so far as salt and sugar are concerned. What we want is the emancipation of India. Our aim is that India may be free, that the stranger may be driven from our homes, that the continuity of the learning, the civilisation and the system of the *Rishis* may be preserved. ...O mother ! Let us be born again and again in India till your chains fall off. First let the mother be free, and then shall come our own release from the worldly bonds. ....O Feringhi....our power is more than human. It is divine...we have all the advantages of ancient greatness of India on our side. We are immortal.....we hereby summon you to battle."

This shows the intimate relation between the idealist *Adwaita Vedanta* philosophy and Indian nationalism characterized with Hindu religion and spiritualism in the beginning of the twentieth century. It demonstrates the very rise of *Adwaita Vedanta* philosophy with its subjective idealism at large in the Indian politics and exposes its narrow and weak stand to combat the ideology of colonialism.

According to the *Vedanta* philosophy God can become the walls and tables, pig and the murderer and all evil things in the world. How can He become all these degenerated things? Vivekananda says that "God is pure" and "our answer is just as I am a soul and have a body, and, in a sense, this body is not different from me, yet I, the real I, in fad, am not the body. For instance, I say I am a child, a young man or an old man, but my soul has not changed. I remain as the same soul," and "That very thing which we now see at the universe will appear to us God (absolute) and that very God who has so long been external will appear to be internal, as our own self".[3] This is a mere speculation to mystify the progress of the thought and knowledge.

Thus Vedanta philosophy oscillates between metaphysics and theism (absolute). Following metaphysics, it recognises body. It also shows a little tendency to know things in the material world but the strong pressure of the *atman* put it firmly bound and arrested within the ancient religious and spiritual domain. It is in firm opposition and, therefore, antagonistic to materialism, that regards nature as the primary, basic and fundamental in relation to man's sensuousness, his quest for knowledge and development of consciousness. Matter preceded the earth and universe and the matter has been in the eternal cycle. Man himself is at first a being, product of nature; and life is the embodiment of matter organised in a definite form and manner in the whole process of the development of the material world. Idea or thought is but reflection of the material world in the thinking brain. Death is a law of nature.

We do not enter into the details of materialist philosophy here as our immediate object is to show the extension, relationship and deep impact of subjective idealism in which *Vedanta* philosophy is a strong weapon, upon the Indian politics. Later on, the issue on materialist philosophy its conflict and struggle with the subjective idealism and objective idealism will be shown in course of analysis.

Objectively speaking, Vivekananda was not alone to highlight and bloster subjective idealism more particularly through the *Vedanta* philosophy. Earlier, Annie Besant[4] began to champion theosophy and prepared a scheme to establish a college at Benaras as an attempt to provide for Hindu youths an education which shall combine advantages of western knowledge with study of the *spiritual precepts* embodied in their own religion. The Viceroy of India readily agreed to this proposal in 1899. The Viceroy and Governor General wrote to Mrs. Besant that "Light comes from many quarters....and the teachers of the youth of any community can hardly err if they draw the attention of their pupils to that which is best and purest in their national faith." The Lieutenant Governor of Bengal wrote to Mrs. Besant that "any popular movement for the better religious and moral training of Hindu youth must be for good, and I very heartily wish you all success in your undertaking." She also wrote a book (published in 1897 and 1914) entitled *The Ancient Wisdom,* eulogising *brahman, soul, cosmos* etc. She held that "The ideas are in themselves the strongest proof that reincarnation is a fact in nature", and "when soul knows God it is liberated. The intellect is purified by knowledge that beholds him. Knowledge joined to devotion finds the abode of *Brahman*". She was the authority on Theosophy who "adorned" the presidential chair of the Congress in 1917 when its liberal leadership were ousted and a little later it had to make exit from the Congress. The secular character of the Congress Party began to corrupt itself from that time, and fade thereafter, from which it could not get rid over time.

Bal Gangadhar Tilak wrote that it was an indisputable truth that Vivekananda was the first to hold high the flag of Hinduism as a challenge to the material science of the west. Bipin Chandra Pal viewed that Vivekananda's thought originated from *Vedanta* but it was revealed to the people with the ideas of his master; and Vivekananda had to be appreciated in the light of the realisation of Ramakrishna Paramhansa. Gandhi visited Belur Math on 6 February 1921 on the occasion of the birthday of Vivekananda, to pay him respect. He then said that he had read the writings of Vivekananda with great attention, and on reading those, his love for the motherland increased a thousand times. Gandhi asked the youths to appreciate the greatness of the holy place where Vivekananda lived, and exhorted them not to return without some feeling of the holiness or with empty hand. He also developed a close relation with Annie Besant's Theosophical Society.

Jawaharlal Nehru observed that Vivekananda infused energy to the disappointed, debased Hindu mind. He gave it self-confidence and some heritage of the wealth of the past. Nehru also confided that many persons in his times were deeply influenced by his ideology. Aurobindo said that Vivekananda was the representative of "future India and builder of our national life". He was the main leader. So what was his ideal yesterday, Indians are following the path of life with his ideal today. (*Amar Bharat : Amor Bharat*, Bengali, pp. 151-52, 155, 157 and 159)

Religion and spiritualism is its main plank. Real world is casual and secondary to it. Practice and preaching method of *Adwaita Vedanta* is made with the monastic order and worshipping the dreadful image of Kali. (Sister Nivedita, *Swamijike Jaman Dekhachi*: Bengali, 1983).

Earlier developments thus support the fact of the gradual spread and ascendancy of *Vedanta*, the idealist philosophy based on the Hindu religion and spiritualism in the Congress, the main political organisation of the country's freedom movement. Congress under the Gandhian leadership in 1920s became strongly imbued with this idealist philosophy and quite afraid of the class struggle and materialist philosophy. This course of action on the line of militant Hinduism by the Congress created more confusion, suspicion and dissension in the mind of the minority communities. The *Vedanta,* therefore, was of no use to forge communal and caste harmony and united struggle of the Indian people against the British colonialism and imperialism. It had thwarted a consistent united struggle, alienated the basic classes and minority communities and sown seeds of *militant Hinduism* in Indian politics and culture which sprouted abundantly in the later period for class collaboration in order to control and suppress the struggles of the workers and peasants in the country. All this is supported by historical facts and developments.

Annie Besant came to India in 1893 and began theosophical work. In her book *Sri Ramchandra, the Ideal King*, she wrote that he was "not simply a great warrior, a mighty king. He was an *avatara*, a divine incarnation, and a devine incarnation of a special kind". "All men are divine incarnations", she viewed. "But when we speak of an *avatara* we mean more than this. An *avatara*....is a special incarnation, a human form being taken in which divinity veils himself and through which shines forth his glory. Not in germ, in `divine fragments', as in us, but in full radiance of deity, God reveals himself in man to man." That "sometimes He (the *avatara*) is also an example; and as an example for men of the world.... Ramchandra stands supreme, the ideal man in every relation of life...". She stated that in Sri Rama's instance there was the additional mission— "to shew forth the ideal Kshatriya."

Preaching theosophy in such a manner, consistent with the *Vedanta* philosophy had a great effect on the formation of social and political thought on the religious line of the majority community in the country, specially after the Vedantist Vivekananda's successful Hindu religious mission within the country and abroad. This subjective idealism had no doubt corrupted nationalist thought of India but also fragmented it. It is no wonder that persons like Arun Shourie admitted in 1999 that "Her (Annie Besant) contribution in restoring pride in Hindus for their own culture, religion, history was of highest order" and said "we live under that impact to this day" (Arun Shourie, What a Strange Precedent to the Cite, *Asian Age*, Calcutta, 4 June, 1999, p. 12).

Regarding the idealist philosophy and its impact on Indian politics one must refer to the ideas of Sri Aurobindo[5] on revolutionism in the Indian politics. He argued that the feeling for nationalism or patriotism is "a religion" that originates from God. Nobody can prevent it as only God regulates all. Power of motherland is her own. For its growth nobody's action is necessary. He explained *swaraj* with *Vedanta* and said that the nation must acquire *swaraj* on its own strength. In his letter dated 30.8.1904, addressed to his wife he confessed that he paid obeisance and worshipped the country as mother and that while a demon oppressed the breast of mother, a son must go out to her rescue. In the same letter he declared that he had the strength to rescue this fallen nation and that God had sent him to the world for performing this noble duty. Aurobindo, in his speech on 12.4.1908 declared, "We preach the gospel of unqualified *swaraj*". Further, in his booklet *Bhawani Mandir* prepared in the texture of Bankim's *Ananda Math*, he observed: "Bhabani is Shakti.....India needs *shakti* alone".

An anonymous writing entitled "no compromise" earlier sent to the office of *Bengali*, a journal edited by Surendranath Banerjee, was actually authored by Aurobindo. After arrest, he addressed to the British Government, "If to aspire to independence and preach freedom is a crime then you can cast me into jail and there bind me with chains". *(Karmayogin*, 3.10.1909).

Aurobindo in his imprisonment became a changed person. He is the person who said "Whom shall I call enemy? I have enemy no more. It is the enemy who has done much benefit to me.... The wrath of the British Government led me to divinity". He then went on for spiritualism. It changed his opinion and path. After taking shelter at Pondichery for thirty years, Aurobindo finally declared that "India would get freedom without war and bloodshed," because Indian saints made such a prophesy! He further declared that socialism was not at all a good system and it would not be wise to destroy the rich, which the socialists want to do, because they are the repository of nation's wealth. They should be encouraged so that they can spend for the nation, but, if they feel discouraged with the imposition of higher tax without the corresponding rise in production, it would only be a loss for the country (*Talks with Sri Aurobindo*).

"Emboldened" with the power of meditation, on 29.1.1939, Aurobindo surmoned that people should not agitate for socialism, because the English being afraid of that, would back out from the transfer of power. In the opinion of Aurobindo, dominion status for India was not bad and for achieving that, the Indian politicians would have to help the English. Aurobindo did not also support the strong anti-imperialist movement (*ibid*).

In reply to a question of a disciple on Surat Congress (1907), Sri Aurobindo said after a long time, "The facts which bend the course of history from behind, are seldom exposed, as only the part outside in scene is seen. Very few people know (even Tilak also did not know) that it is I who had prevented the delegates from participating in the recognised conference of the moderates, meaning, that I was mainly responsible for the grave consequence". The extremists professing the religious philosophy "sought to capture Congress" from within and oust the liberal leaders. For their purpose Bal Gangadhar Tilak was proposed to be the all India leader.

In Aurobindo's view, everything is the appearance of *Brahma*. This is not just idea of a subject, but realisation. The wall or this book is *Brahma*. Man is seen as not a being but a subject living in God. What excellent, according to Aurobindo, is this experience! Soul is immortal, it survives in re-birth. There is no fear in *yoga*. Aurobindo's effort was to convert his "higher mind" to "super mind" (*Atimanas*). It can be achieved, in his words, through proper realisation (*Sambodhi*) which he had acknowledged to have first received from Vivekananda in the Alipore Jail in 1908-1909, i.e. six years after Vivekananda's death. Being acquitted, he moved along with some followers to quiet Pondicherry, then a French colony, in 1910, and settled therefor practising "*yoga*".

Chittaranjan Das later wrote to Aurobindo asking him to accept leadership in the politics of Bengal. Aurobindo wrote in reply to this letter on 18 November, 1922 that "The real basis of life and work is spiritual—that means, it is *yoga* which can only create new consciousness...so long as I cannot acquire this new power certainly and completely, I am determined not to work in the external sphere. I will not build up until the base, complete in all respects, is established".

These words containing the main trend of Aurobindo's thought clearly show the strong impact of *Vedanta* and spiritualism—subjective idealism—in contrast to the experience of real life of the people. He pointed out the various kinds of experiments on spiritualism and its "startling enrichment" in India. He believed in the 1930s that according to the present condition, there was no delay in descendence of *Satya Yuga*, and with it, as a super man appears, the whole world body would be certainly changed! Aurobindo was not so much concerned to make a hue and cry against imperialism. He thought that the bourgeoisie is the repository of the nation's wealth and they should not be overthrown; and contrary to the idea of the socialists, Aurobindo viewed Stalin as "a wise and self-confident hoodlum. One can say him an incarnate of Demon" "Stalin wants only one thing, power. Nothing else". Aurobindo thought that there was no personal freedom in socialism and "fascism and communism are synonymous. Only Brahmins and thoughtful sages had no place" there.

And this is the philosophy of the "revolutionary" national leaders in India! Is it philosophy of the people or philosophy for supporting the black regime and world reaction? of course, for the latter.

Thought of aggressive Hinduism of Narendranath Datta (Swami Vivekananda) and revival of the Hinduism with the propagation of its scriptures and activity formed the moral basis and theoretical support to the secret societies resorting to violent action in the freedom movement of the country. In the words of Bhupendranath Datta[6], Indian revolutionaries, or the Congressmen —no party could yet built up their philosophy according to their own ideas, and he lamented that the philosophy in India's life was nothing but rumour and imitation. During the Swadeshi movement, the idea of nationalism spread and boycott had set up the idea, "my country, right or wrong". This irrational idea had become imprint in the mind of almost one and all. Nationalism turned into Aryanism or conservative Hinduism of the yore.

Valentine Chirol wrote in his *Indian Unrest* that the object of Hindu nationalists was "Hindu nationalism". Bhupendranath Datta noted that this statement was not utterly false; and, for obvious reasons, revolutionism was confined to the traditional Hindus and many of them belonged to the camp of the revivalists of Hindu religion. As a result, revolutionism turned into Hindu-nationalism. Muslim revolutionaries said that the Hindus at first did not take them in confidence and that they preached Hindu-nationalism and not Indian nationalism. In Bengal especially, though the revolutionaries did never fail to sacrifice their lives, revolutionism took shape within the paradigm of religious thought .

Further, the main weakness was that there was an all Bengal party of revolutionaries, but owing to the lapses of the leaders, it could not be closely centralised, because there was difference among themselves in the formulation of programme and activities.

At that time, this philosophy of revolutionism formed "nationalism". By winning independence one nationality was to be achieved, and for this, Brahmin, Sudra, Prince and subjects would have to be united! Nobody could make a philosophical advance beyond this attitude. One non-Hindu barrister, Apurba Kumar Ghosh who was outside the revolutionary party but was aware of some of its activities and he sympathised and counselled on socialism. He used to advise and explain the ways and means on the implementation of the socialist ideas in the Indian politics. On looking back into past, it can be recognised that there was mistake in philosophy and the same is still being understood by few persons, and they took that objects would remain "static" and brotherly unity of all classes without exception to their interests, would achieve independence of the country. That was "the fundamental defect" in the philosophy of the Indian revolutionaries and the Congress. The mind of the revolutionaries was fixed. All things were thought as abstract and no concrete emerged from a shallow marsh, and as a result, laxity in practical work in all spheres spread, and mind remained very static, unchanging and full of superstition. Aurobindo became disciple of a religious person and viewed revolutionism in the eyes of religion. Many leaders were devoted Hindus and they viewed sociology and politics through the religion. Revolutionaries were very ignorant of Indian society and economics.

Their ideas were rigid, fixed and immutable. In their view, spiritualism became all pervasive, and consequently it dominated the Indian political scene. It built up a firm order in politics of the country.

All this clearly exposes metaphysics in the traditional and religious mind of the Indian leaders, which the present leaders have not yet fully got rid of, over the years.

Non-cooperation movement owed much to the ideas of foreign authors like Thoreu and Tolstoi under the influence of Christian faith, consecrated with the rites and rituals of Hinduism, Datta confides. Indian revolutionaries failed to present a world view on social and economic development to the people, and the entire work was put in a state of flux and turned into smoke although the moderate politicians secretly extended their help to the revolutionaries. Datta further observed that all the ideas were taken in from abroad and those had taken a different course at lightening speed through the hands of the fanciful Bengalee leaders. Revolutionism had *very little relation* with the socio-economic demands of the contemporary period. Actually, nationalism and terrorism were both imported from abroad, and for this reason, mass of the people all along remained away from the revolutionism. The revolutionaries of Bengal were generally attracted to the ideals of bourgeois democracy. Further, the strong current of Brahminism and traditional Islam in India was in force, and against it, modern socialism had to contend. No co-ordination between the two different forces had taken place at that time. The result was the lack of unity between the parts of revolutionary party. Further, there was no conflict between the two trends of thought among the revolutionaries. As the consequence, bourgeois-equalitarian republicanism became the political ideal in the revolutionism. Indian revolutiorusm had its characteristics and grew with the establishment of secret society, political dacoity, organisation of groups, secret propaganda for revolutionary movement, political murder, isolation from mass organisation, students or intellectuals as strength of movement, want of any definite party programme, stress on political issues only with static thought, aloofness from social and economic revolutionism and lack of socio-economic programme, etc.

The Indian revolutionaries were bourgeois-nationalist and they confined themselves in narrow position. The revolutionaries had to no greater political outlook with party programme and they picked up a bitter quarrel with the moderates. "Their knowledge is till now static and they lack social and economic ideas and public activity", wrote Bhupendra Nath Datta in the early 1950s.

In the Indian history, the religious movement of Namdeb, Tukaram, Ramdas, Nanak, Brahmo leaders, aided with the study and teachings of the *Vedanta* by the neo-vedantists created much heat for a moral power. It is this moral power which appeared as great inspiration for self-sacrifice in revolutionism, especially in Bengal. This fire of religion helped the revolutionaries for all their secret activities. Whatever limitation the revolutionaries had; or misfortunes they faced, their role in Indian history can hardly be emphasized. Rather, the reforms of the British Government were much due to the secondary result of their activities.

Subjective idealism ascended and progressed on, and materialism very much lagged behind as it was suppressed by the former school of thought. But, as contradiction between the British colonial power and the Indian people began to manifest in the 1920s and 1930s, struggle of the workers and peasants against the Indian big capitalist and landlord classes—the collaborators—of the British rule made some progress, and materialist thought made a relative advance through the organisation and activity of the exploited and destitute masses of the Indian people, that sought to secularly unravel the social contradiction in the realm of communal politics and colonial reformism. Economic decline conditioned working class struggles and those exposed the internal strife as well as the external contradiction between the British colonialism and imperialism on the one hand and the Indian people on the other. These contradictions were no doubt real and current but could not proceed much and develop in the right direction to their logical conclusion owing the very weakness of the Communist Party and prevalence of subjective idealism or Gandhism and Congress Party wedded to the petty-fogging of colonial constitutional reforms manifest with corruption of the Indian comprador bourgeoisie and landlord classes.

On the political plane, it appeared as the contradiction between the moderate and the extremists. The moderates with their liberal standpoint generally exposed the contradiction between the interests of Great Britain and India in a secular manner and sought to utilise whatever parliamentary reforms that could be made within the colonial system. The extremists with their ideology opposing the British rule in India directly came affront the moderate and liberal leadership of the Congress. But while the extremist leaders confronted the colonial state machinery, they drew their philosophical support and inspiration from the old *Adwaita Vedanta* surcharged with the old Hindu religion and spiritualism. As the government appointed Sedition Committee[7] under S.C. Rawlat recorded, "In 1886 had died the Bengali ascetic Ramkrishna. He was undoubtedly a remarkable and purely religious.... To him the goddess Kali was the goddess of divine strength; although another of her attributes is destruction...after his death his doctrines were preached by...Narendra Nath Dutta, a young *bhadralok*, B.A., subsequently famous as Vivekananda...Vivekananda died in 1902 but his writings and teachings survived...and have deeply impressed the educated Hindus...this influence was perverted by Barindra and his followers in order to create an atmosphere suitable for execution of their projects. So indeed was the teachings of *Bhagwat Gita*...". It continued, "For their own initiates the conspirators devised a remarkable series of books. The *Bhagwat Gita,* the writings of Vivekananda, the lives of Mazzine and Gariboldi were parts of their course". This evidence is quite meaningful and clear.

Valentine Chirol in his book entitled *Indian Old and New* (1885-1925) observed "The old invocation to the goddess Kali, 'Bande Mataram' or 'Hail to the Mother' acquired a new significance and came to be used as a political war-cry of Indian Nationalism"[8]. And J.C. Nicholson's very inportant Confidential Report 1917 reads, "Swami Vivekananda...died in 1902.... Apparently before that date Arabinda Ghosh had attempted to influence the political life of Bengal. From Baroda he had sent Jyotindra Nath Banerjee, a soldier in the Gaekwad's army and later his brother Barindra Kumar Ghosh... They approached Babu Surendra Nath Banerjee, some members of Tagore family, Swami Vivekananda, Mis Saralabala Ghoshal, Messers P. Mitra, C.R. Das, Bijoy Chatterjee and many other barristers"[9]. Nicholson. further added, "To this end *Gita* has always been a favourite.... If the virtue of *ahingsha* comes to

Kshatriya, if you shall say I will not kill, there is nobody to protect your country.... So does Aurobindo expound himself the *Gita*.... The writings of Swami Vivekananda and the novels of Bankim Chatterjee are quoted.... The Goddess Kali, thirsting for sacrifices, was set up as the symbol of this movement"[10]. Charles Tegart, former Commissioner of Calcutta Police, in a speech of 1932 observed, "Barin renewed his efforts...and laid the foundations of the terrorist societies based on perverted religion and equally perverted patriotism" and he noted, "As Kali drove out the demons so should they, strengthened by the worship of Kali, drive out the *Firinghee*, a contemptuous name for the Europeans". Tegart elaborated, "Recent spectacular outrages such as the hurling of bombs in the Assembly at Delhi and the murderous attack on the Governor of Punjab, will suggest the existence of such conspiracies. They were founded by Bengal terrorists and will draw their inspiration from Bengal", and "The groups in Northern India were loosely knit, they have not got the deadly and persistent organisation behind them which exists in Bengal. This is not due to lack of effort on the part of the Bengali terrorists, who have tried to build up the movement in the U.P. and Punjab on exactly similar lines to those in Bengal"[11]. Politics became enmeshed more with religion than economic programme over the years.

What was the impact of the religious thought and spiritualism on the leaders like Subhash Chandra Bose? It can be hardly emphasized that Subhash Chandra himself acknowledged[12] his profuse indebtedness and gratitude to Sri Ramakrishna and Vivekananda in his letter dated 6.3.1936 addressed to a monk of the Ramakrishna Mission from abroad. He had admitted in it that, had Swami Vivekananda been alive, he certainly would have been his mentor.

This philosophy of *Adwaita Vedanta* pervaded the country and influenced activity and thought of many leaders in the Indian National Congress. In fact, many revolutionaries joined the Congress Party and maintained their old ideas, relations and connections. As early as in 1920, in Nagpur Congress, an idea was mooted[13] in the circle of the Congress Reception Committee volunteers to declare that future India would be a *Hindu state*. In fact, Aurobindo, *Yogi* and spiritualist, was asked to be its president in the same year, and when he refused to return to politics, Vijayraghaba Chariya became the president and Gandhi's programme of non-violence and non-co-operation was adopted. Earlier in 1917, Annie Besant, theosophist leader became the Congress President. In 1920, Jinnah was insulted in the Nagpur Congress session. Mohammad Ali, Congress President, was heckled and threatened[14] with censure motion by some of the Hindu members of the Congress Working Committee while he was delivering the presidential speech during the Congress session in Coconada in 1923. After 1924, most of the prominent leaders of the Swaraj Party came to adorn Hindu Mahasabha, earlier founded by Madan Mohan Malaviya, a former Congress President with whom prominent leaders like Lala Lajpat Rai of Arya Samaj and a pseudo-liberal Motilal Nehru had always maintained a very close relationship in "practical politics" of constitutionalism initiated by the British imperialism in its own interest. M.K. Gandhi's statements and writings coached in Hindu religious words, tone and spiritualism, had far reaching influence to consolidate the right wing of the Indian bourgeoisie and its ally and preceptor, the Hindu religious institutions. *Hindutva* thesis was propounded by V.D. Savarkar in 1923. The Rashtriya Swayamsevak Sangh, a militant Hindu organisation was founded in 1925 to preach cultural nationalism under the Hindu religious thought and banner. Organisations of Hinduism grew and advanced unprecedented through the pre-1947 period, with the direct assistance and control of the right reaction in the name of Indian nationalism. Thus the machinery for spread of Hinduism in politics had began to grow and expand through a long period in the past. Today's Hindu fundamentalism in the Indian politics is the continuation, extension, spread and manifestation of its earlier core action plan.Gandhian thought and leadership abjectly failed to check it.

The democratic norms and rules and the old moderates' communal rapport achieved through the Lucknow pact in 1916 and resolution of the Congress party in its Amritsar session in December 1919 for a responsive co-operation with the Constitutional reforms were thrown to the wind, and struggle for communal representation in the "reformed" Assemblies according to the colonial power's whims and dictates, became order of the day. The scramble and machination for representation in the newly introduced parliamentary system became intense in the name of *Swaraj*. The old moderate, S. N. Banerjee, on seeing this desperate mad rush for representation and personal gain, himself expressed doubt over the future of Indian nation. When the communal problem rocked the constitutional boat, Tej Bahadur Sapru, an old liberal, apprehending a grave danger for the country, tried to save the boat by advising the leaders at the all parties' conference in Calcutta in 1928 to accept the main amendments on representation put forward by the Muslim League. But subjectivism, fixation with religion and communalism prevailed to nullify it. Unified struggle against the colonialism and imperialism on the Indian soil turned to be a mirage. Indian politics was left to be plagued with communalism. M. K. Gandhi himself admitted to the infiltration of corrupt leaders into his Congress organisation. The situation became very grave over time. Rajeswar Dayal in his reminiscences writes that in the politics of 1940s, "Politeness of speech gave place to racausness. Not only was Urdu language frowned upon.... The Urdu script in current use throughout the province (U.P) was substituted by Devanagari" and adds that, "Already the nexus between the politicians and corrupt businessmen was becoming evident". Dayal, a former high official of the Indian Government noted that the police seized two large steel trunks from the premises of the RSS and they revealed "incontrovertible evidence of dastardly conspiracy to create a communal holocaust throughout the western districts of the province (U.P.). The trunks were crammed with blue prints of great accuracy and professionalism of every town and village in that vast area, prominently marking out the Muslim localities and habitations. There were also detailed instructions regarding access to the various locations, and other matters which amply revealed their sinister purport". Administrative vigilance brought the massive RSS, a Hindu communal organisation's conspiracy to light. "It was no doubt a matter of political delicacy as the roots of RSS had gone deep into the body politic. There were also other political compulsions as RSS sympathisers, both covert and overt, were to be found in the Congress Party itself and even in the cabinet. It was no secret that the presiding officer of the upper house (of UP)

Atma Gobinda Kher, was himself an adherent and his sons were openly members of the RSS"[15].

The events and facts of history clearly expose the deep import and spiral development of religion in the Indian politics which had far reaching consequences in the country.

NOTES

1. *cf.* Swami Vivekananda, *Hinduism*, Sri Ramakrishna Math, Mylapore, Chennai, 1968.
2. See Swami Lokeswarnanda, ed., *Amar Bharat : Amor Bharat* (Bengali edition from the Works of Swami Vivekananda), Ramakrishna Mission Institute of Culture, Calcutta, 1998, pp. 97-108; and *Works*, Vol. 3, p. 105.
3. See Swami Vivekananda, *Hinduism*, p. 71 and p. 75, *Amar Bharat : Amor Bharat*, p. 97 and 105; *cf.* Julius J. Lipner, Brahmabandhab Upadhyay, Oxford University Press, Calcutta 1998.
4. Annie Besant, *The Ancient Wisdom*, London, 1914, p. 229 and p. 14; and *the Statesman*, Calcutta, 24 January, 1899. cf. Dr. Md. Sahidullah, *Amader Sahityik Daridrata*, 1916.
5. Jogeshchandra Bagal, *Muktir Sandhane Bharat* (Bengali), Ashok Pustakalaya, Calcutta, 1960, p. 241 and Alakranjan Basuchowdhury, *Dui Aurobindo, Matparibartan Na Adarshachuti* (Bengali), Utsha Manush, Calcutta, September-October 1998, pp. 203-207. Niradbaran, *Sri Aurobinder Sange Kathabarta* (Bengali), pp. 13, 28-31, 46-48, 55, 66, 69, 118, and 182; *Sarbajanin Aurobinda*, (Bengali) p. 65; *Sri Aurobinda O Tahar Bani*, p. 34, Aurobindo Ashram, Pondicherry, 1997.
6. See Bhupendranath Datta, *Vivekananda* Patriot-Prophet, Calcutta, 1954. pp. 14, 16-17, p. 21, p. 33, pp. 36-37, p. 42, p. 49 and pp. 55-81.
7. Sedition Committee Report 1918, Government of India, New Delhi, Chapter 2, Para 24 and Para 30.
8. *Cf.* Valentine Chirol, Indian Old and New (1885-1925), London, 1925.
9. J. C. Nicholson, Confidential Report 1917, Government of India, New Delhi, p. 2.
10. *Ibid.*, p. 15.
11. Charles Tartge, *Speech on the Terrorism in India*, November 1932, Royal Empire Society, London, p. 7, p. 8., and p. 19.
12. Subhas Chandra Bose, Letter to the Editor, of *Udbodhan* dt. 6-3-1936, Published in the Independence Number of *Udbodhan*, Calcutta, 1947.
13. B. Vishikar, Dr. *Hegdewar*, Dr. Hedgewar Janma Shata Barsha Utsab Committee (Bengali), Sanghbastu Bhandar, Calcutta, pp. 9-16.
14. Gail Minault, *The Khilafat Movement*, Oxford University Press, Delhi, 1982, p. 199.
15. See Rajeshwar Dayal, *A Life of Our Times*, Orient Longman, Calcutta, 1999.

3

SUBJECTIVE IDEALISM AND INDIAN POLITICS

Facts support and reveal the deep religious content inherent in the philosophy of India's national movement. It worked both within and outside the Indian National Congress more characteristically after the exit of its secular and liberal leadership from the Indian politics. The new leaders embraced and capitalised the growing influence of Hinduism and subjective idealism of the extremists after the eclipse of the moderate leadership representing rationalist thought.

To explain this trend of development it would be quite right to refer to the ideas of Mohandas Karamchand Gandhi which had provided ideological support to this subjective idealism because both originated from the Hindu religion and *Adwaita Vedanta* and they were nurtured by the practice of western metaphysics in the past few decades. Gandhi's thought largely contributed[1] to strengthen religion in the philosophy and politics of the Indian National Congress after 1919.

In his *Hind Swaraj* (1908) M. K. Gandhi concluded the following four propositions which are heavily loaded with the ideals of Hindu religion, viz. (1) true home rule or *Swaraj* is the self-rule or soul-control, (2) its key is the *Satyagraha,* soul force or power of love, (3) it is necessary to use all kinds of indigenous goods for acquiring that force, (4) what we want to do, emanates right from our sense of duty, not being opposed to the English or out of vengeance.

Religious or moral training, according to Gandhi, shall precede other subjects in education. Cow protection is essential for the benefit of all, and India can never be atheist. On the question of conquering political power from the British through protracted guerilla struggle, Gandhi apprehended that, by that means, the holy land of India would be converted into a demon's regime. It would be the act of cowardice, diversion of own power to wrong path and its consequences would never be good, he said.

Gandhi asserted that non-violence was not just a philosophical principle but the trend of his life and respiration; but, no person or society can be made non-violent by coercion. Without non-violence and truth there is "no other way" of living for any of us. To war is wrong and sin. It was also his firm conviction that the independence won through bloodshed and deception would be no independence. No violence, nor untruth, but "non-violence and truth" is the rule of our soul! During the war, he confessed that he was a friend of the Britishers, much more than before, because one of the major causes was that Britain had fallen in "distress." Gandhi sought to utilise the chance of expediency for rapport with the Muslim community of the country! But his cooperation for the Khilafat lasted only for a year. And he withdrew the support unilaterally, although it was a national united front for fight against the British rule in India. Gandhi himself admitted that he had really supported the *Khilafat movement* (1920-21), from the deepest core of his heart with the hope that, by doing so, he would perhaps be able to "protect cow". He was a worshipper of cow. He averred that he and the cow were the creation of the same God. He was even prepared to sacrifice his life for the protection of cow.. Based on these premises Gandhi felt that the Hindu and Muslim "shall have to be united to free themselves from the shackles of imperialism". It was a pious wish on shaky idealism.

Gandhi was a well wisher of the Indian princes. In future India of his thought, Gandhi recognised the place of princes and landlords. He asked them to enjoy life through sacrifice! He held that, by forsaking their ownership in property, they could really become "trustees" of the society. He saw God in man and asked the princes and landlords to declare : "It is the people who are owners and lords and we are your servants". He advised the princes to be servants of the people and account for their services to the people. For long Congress had built up the ideal of non-violence. Non-violent India craved to get back her long overdue, freedom, and Gandhi thought on British conscience and, according to him, India would attain freedom from the unwilling authority only by non-violent means. He vowed in the name of Congress and declared that Congress would do or die!

In Gandhi's ideal the state would not guide the people or it would not enforce its wishes upon them; rather, the state would translate only the wishes of the people into action. He would bring about economic equality through non-violence. Against hatred, Gandhi would convert the people to his outlook certainly by consolidating the power of love. Entire society would move according to this ideal and for this, he would not wait but directly start work. The root of *Satyagraha* lies in prayer. *Satyagraha* worker protects himself from the brutal force by depending on God. So why should one be afraid of the British or of deception by others? If someone dupes, he would be duped most. *Satyagraha* workers would bring the miscreants under control and change their mind.

Even in the violence-affected atmosphere, the hermits of ancient time, who evolved the principle of non-violence, were of "greater genious" than Newton and were more heroic warriors than Wellingdon. Being armed, they felt the inaction of weapons and declared that the path of liberation is non-violence and not violence.

Non-violence always completely protects the honour and dignity of an individual. But it may not always protect ownership of immovable property. But its practical use for defence is more effective than that of armed forces. Non-violence obviously does not help to wrongly collect wealth or in any misdeed observed Gandhi.

Except the narrow and zigjag path of non-violence the pain-stricken world has no other hope. Many persons like me, Gandhi asserted, might fail to share this truth in their lives. That is their inability, not the defect of this eternal principle!

On inquiry it can be found that brutal force has controlled the world for thousands of years and mankind has suffered its bitter fruits. There is much less hope that it would bring good in future. As there can be no light from darkness, love cannot grow in conflict.

Isolated autonomy cannot be the goal of the states of the world. Voluntary mutual dependence is their ideal. In his view, the edifice of world federation can be built only on the basis of non-violence. It is essential to completely banish violence from the activity of the world. Non-violent resistance does not know defeat nor concede defeat. So any nation or community which has accepted non-violence as the absolute principle, under no circumstance, will be defeated or subjugated—not even with the atom bomb. Those who have faith in non-violence, should employ their entire force to "prove" that it is possible to contain violence by non-violence. If the Chinese could rely upon the imagined non-violence, the modern weapons of Japan, according to Gandhi, would become useless, and that Chinese would sacrifice half the population strength but the remaining 20 crores of countrymen would never surrender to Japan. If China did that thing, Gandhi preached, Japan only would be subjugated! And the heroic resistance of the Poles against the German invaders of enormous military strength, organisation and might, according to Gandhi, was comparable to almost non-violence!

While one entire life is spent on material science, then, for acquiring the greatly cherished spiritual knowledge of human life how many lives and re-births are necessary for meditation? If it is necessary for several births, there is no sorrow, Gandhi wrote. The courage of the non-violence is much more preferable to that of the violent person. The means of violent person is his weapon, viz., spear, sword or gun; the religion of the non-violent is his God.

Gandhi continued, "Russia is still absent in the war, but there is one dictator. He dreamt to establish peace and he would achieve it with the making of a path through the sea of blood. It was difficult to foresee what the Russian dictatorship would introduce in the world."

Only the science of non-violence can lead to the path of real democracy!

After atom bombs were dropped in Nagasaki and Hirosima, Gandhi restated his confidence in truth and non-violence as the principal forces of the world, and stressed the greater need for soul power and spiritualism. Atomic weapon, said Gandhi, was "nothing" against it.

Until the causes of war were revealed and rooted out, all efforts to war would be certainly defeated. Was not the inhuman competition and struggle for exploitation of the weaker nations the main cause of war in modern times?

Everywhere the non-violence was being replaced by violence, as if, it was natural and eternal principle. Therefore, the democracy, as we see in England, America and France was only by name because those were also established on violence like in Nazi Germany, fascist Italy and Soviet Russia. Not less in any way. The only exception was that violence in the latter three countries was much more organised in comparison to that of the former three democratic states, Gandhi wrote, as "sermon" to the people.

The path of peace is open. On having patience, achieving of *Swaraj* would be very certain only in this way. The path of peace is the path of truth. Truthfulness is more important than peacefulness. It is not possible for a peace-loving person to be violent for long. He feels from the path of truthfulness that there is no need to be violent and he realises that, even with a grain of violence in mind, truth cannot be achieved.

My conviction, Gandhi wrote, the ideal of India, is different from the ideal of others. India is suitable for establishment of the *supremacy of spiritualism* in the world. The path of self-purification that this country has chosen, is rare in the world. India does not need weapons of iron; it has fought with the aid of spiritualism for eternity and even today, it can avail of that in contrast to other states' faith in brutal force. India can become all conquerer with the spiritual force.

It was Gandhi's firm conviction that it was the responsibility of India to preach the message of non-violence to the world for its translation into action, and it may be subject to meditation for ages. There is no other country, in the opinion of Gandhi, that was in the forefront in this regard.

The message of the East has been appreciated, it cannot be read with the spectacles of the west or with the adoption of atom bomb. East can preach the ideal of love and truth. The increasing number of atom bombs has made west devoid of assurance, because atom bomb means total destruction.

In an address to the fourth annual conference of the Fèderation of Chambers of Commerce, in 1932 Gandhi said that the capitalists can take rein of the Congress Party on one condition that "they would act as the trustees of the society". In his imagined world, the second great principle of equal distribution—originates from non-violence. It means no indiscriminate division of the world's wealth! Everyone would get his demand fulfilled in proportion to his natural need. Everyone would get in proportion to his need, not more than that. How can this ideal of equal distribution be translated into action? Would the rich be deprived of wealth? Non-violence answers that it must not deprive. For violence cannot bring permanent welfare to the society, forcible deprivation of property leads to the society's "deprivation of the values of many persons". According to Gandhi, the rich "knows how to produce wealth" and his activity cannot be allowed to be fruitless. While that is not desired, he must be the possessor of wealth; justifiedly, he shall consume that much which is necessary for his personal needs; and, "he would be the trustee of the surplus and expend for general welfare of the society". In the past, there were many such persons. Today, there are also many. In Gandhi's view, when man thinks himself as servant of the society and earns for the society, his earning becomes honest and industrial enterprise constructive.

But is not the imagination of non-violence subject to the change of comprehensive man's habit? Certainly there are many such persons who gave up their mentality, their petty property, comprehensively accepted society as their own and worked for its welfare. While change of a man is possible, then change of many men must be possible. In this way, Gandhi visioned that there would be no poverty, war, revolution or bloodshed. In that world theism would be wider and deeper than that of any time in the past. The very existence of world in the wider sense, in the opinion of Gandhi, would be based on religion. All efforts for extirpating its root, are bound to fail.

On the demand for economic. improvement, strike which may be called in, cannot have political motive behind it. For as a result of such an unison, the political objective cannot be realised; the striking workers rather face special inconveniences though their livelihood is not jeopardised. Sympathetic strike should not be called in, until all the legal means of the workers participating the strike have been exhausted. Political strikes would have to be judged on their merits and defects. To relate and unite it with the economic strike does no good. Political strike has "a definite place" in non-violent movement. Its indiscriminate use cannot be resorted. Preparation should be made so that it cannot create violence. Strike shall be "spontaneous" and no tactics can be adopted for realisation of its objective, Gandhi concluded.

Thus, the Gandhian framework is based on the tripod of *non-violence, truth* and *satyagraha*, which have their origin right in the religion, especially Hinduism and its spiritualism in India. He propagated this very idealist philosophy forcefully in the politics of the country's freedom movement. He stressed spiritualism and religion of the old world to remove the present evils and abuses of society! This was purely idealism with the heavy weightage of subjective approach. Are not the existing evils and woes of society being the products of economic and social intercourse metamorphosed and transmitted from the past? Were not such intercourse subject to the religious sanction and order that derived its spiritual strength and sustenance in practical life itself?

Gandhi had a typical religious bend of mind and tried to interpret religion in a new way to suit the cause of the rich in politics. He never cared to know the mode of production, composition and development of the civil society and the contradiction inherent therein. With his religious tenet he tried to approach the existing order of things dominated by the owners of private property—the ruling classes in the feudal bourgeois society. He had no question and mind to scientifically inquire into the process of production, generation of wealth and its appropriation in the society—the antagonism of classes—that has actually shaped and determined the course of history and civilisation of mankind. His truth is formed in the old shell of religion and spiritualism, and failed to realise the facts of practical life and activity in the material world which had formed religion and spiritualism. Far from entering into the reality and contradiction of the society, he vainly tried to idealise the existing order of the society with the concept of truth from the hard cast of religion, covering up the contradiction of the society. He sought truth from the scriptures of religion and not from the actual life of the people. His search for truth does not find any difference, variation, conflicts and strifes in the structure of the society. His truth assures the established regime of the capitalist and landlord, and smooth out class struggle and inherent contradiction. Gandhi thus idealised the remote past over the present. He searched for ideal man of religion who would perform non-violence for realisation of truth through abstinence and self-abnegation, while the world itself remains engrossed with self-interest, private property and accumulation of capital. A capitalist or landlord, would become a trustee of society's wealth in Gandhian model, as if non-violence and *Satyagraha* would change his heart! To substantiate this idea, Gandhi referred to examples of such persons through the centuries. But what he pointed out, was the mere exception and weakest strand and not the dominant trend of the property relation in the history of social development. Strains of bourgeois mode of production in fact can be traced back to the much earlier periods of civilisation and those grew and developed into powerful private property and modern dominant bourgeois mode of production. Unless the dominant bourgeois force is suppressed and fully controlled the new one cannot grow and progress. It is distressing that Gandhi carefully avoided this dominant trend and clung to the weakest and decadent force of the minority rich in the society to serve its class interest in the name of truth. Medievalism fogged and fully controlled his perception and thought.

The lesson of history is that the dominant force cannot be influenced or changed with the stance and tantrum of non-violence because the former itself is based on violence and always takes recourse to violence. It knows no other means to ultimately retain its social power. Material force can be practically tackled and overthrown only by material force. The minority of capitalists and landlords is only interested in its authority and dictatorship and never gives right and authority to the innumerable workers and peasants—the vast masses of the people in the society.

All this is attested with the actual developments of history.

Gandhi idealistically distinguished between the economic struggles and political strikes in the society. But actually economics and politics are deeply interwoven, concentrated and integrated in the social life. Every class struggle is a political struggle because the opposite class forces proceed in this method, and confront each other for their class interests. Gandhi sought to cover up the inherent conflict, strife and social antagonism with the so-called non-violence and truth. There is no politics without economics and no economics without politics. Economics with its flesh and wit finds expression through politics. History is replete with this phenomenon in the process of development. Gandhi set sail to the ship of reaction in the historical process of development and sheltered himself under the roof of *Satyagraha* built up above the four-walls of theism, religion, spiritualism and reformism. Gandhi built up his world of theoretical imagination to be realised through *Satyagraha*, a method of old reformism in India. He was a subjective idealist. Religion was interwoven in all his writings which had *long-term adverse effects* in the social and political development of the country. In fact, Hinduism got a sophisticated version in a suitable manner through his writings, which in turn had assuaged, encouraged and ultimately reinforced consolidation of the rightists to combat class struggle and left politics in India. It organised and led a great offensive against secular liberalism, atheism and materialist philosophy in the country.

The basic ideology of consistent, long-term united struggle against the British rule was not much stressed and propagated during the Khilafat-Non-cooperation Movement (1920-22). As Ramananda Chatterji, editor of the *Modern Review* wrote in 1920, "Reading between the lines of the speeches of Maulana Mohammad Ali and Mahatma Gandhi it is not difficult to see that with one of them the sad plight of the Khilafat in distant Turkey is the central fact while with the other attainment of *Swaraj* in India is the object in view". Persons like him of course, usually saw the things as fixed, isolated and separate, thereby demonstrating their lack of an objective world view. Actually, the semi-colonial Turkey and colonial India and their peoples both were then under the attack and domination of the colonial and imperialist forces. Struggle of a particular community in India on that issue was not only related with the plight of Jurkey, but it was also very much inter-related and directed as well as against the hated British imperialism dominating in India. This was dialectically related with the noble cause of freedom movement of the country. It fostered the condition and provided the great advantage for united struggle against the British rule in India. The editor took a narrow, one-sided and sectarian view only to confuse the matter on the whole. But no less casual, blunt and misleading was the reply of Gandhi to the editor's observation. Gandhi wrote in his *Young India* on 20.10.1920 "I claim that with us both, Khilafat is the central fact; with Maulana Mohammad Ali because it is his religion, with me because in laying down my life for the Khilafat, I ensure safety of the cow, that is my religion, from the Musalman knife". Gandhi admitted that he wanted to achieve *Moksha* in his life. He became much eager for self-realisation and said that his patriotism was only a *transitory* one in his journey toward permanent salvation and peace. So he found that there was no politics bereft of religion. They who hate, suppress religion. "Politics bereft of religion is a kind of death trap and that destroys soul". (*Young India*, 3.4.1924)

It becomes quite clear from Gandhi's own writings that the religion was first utilised in the Congress politics for the sake of expediency, which helped to grow the seeds of religious fundamentalism in the country. And more he expressed such views, more the communalism and fundamentalism spread its roots in the Indian soil over the years. Gandhi failed to discern and explain to the intelligentia and mass of the people that the real and central object of Khilafat was the united struggle that was directed solely against the monstrous British rule for freedom of India. His verbosity and petty-fogging mystified the political scenario and demonstrated his subjective idealism at large. British imperialism, the greatest enemy of the Indian people, however did not fail to exploit this major weakness of the philosophy and tactics of the Congress. As a result, people remained to be victim of ignorance, superstition and state repression. Communal riots increased. Gandhi later on clarified, "My Hinduism demands no pacts. My support of the Khilafat was unconditional"[2]. Situation gradually worsened with the sudden withdrawal of the movements. Gandhi himself noted the causes of the communal tension[3] in 1924 as follows : (1) The remote cause of the tension is the Mopla rebellion, (2) The attempt of the Fazl Hussain government to rearrange the distribution of posts in the education department consistently with the number of Mussalmans in the Punjab and consequent Hindu opposition, (3) The Shuddhi movement of the Arya Samaj, (4) The most patent being tiredness of non-violence and the fear that the communities might by a long course of training in the non-violence, forget the law of retaliation and self-defence, (5) Mussalman cow-slaughter and Hindu music, (6) Hindu cowardice and consequent Hindu distrust of Mussalman, (7) Mussalman bullying, and (8) Mussalman distrust of Hindu fair play.

Among the measures for cure, Gandhi mainly prescribed[4] that:

(1) Employment under national government must be according to merit to be decided by a board of examiners representing different communities .
(2) *Shuddhi* or *tabligh* as such cannot be disturbed, but either must be conducted honestly and by men of proved character. It should avoid all attack on other religions. There should be no secret propaganda and no offer of material rewards.
(3) The master-key to the solution is the replacement of the rule of the sword by that of arbitration.
(4) Hindus must leave to the Mussalmans and other minorities the question of representation in elected bodies, and gracefully and wholeheartedly give effect to the findings of such referee.
(5) Ignorant fear of cowardly non-violence, falsely called, taking the place of violence should be dispelled.

It becomes very self-evident that Gandhi did not fight out nor exclude religion from the politics for an united national movement as the peasants organised their own movements, and especially, when the Maharana of Udaipur State was threatened by the peasants of Bijolia, that he would face the same fate like that of Tsar of Russia. Its consequence was disastrous for obvious reasons. Religious revivalism thwarted and countered secular politics and freedom movement in India. Historically, the tension between the two communities (Hindu and Muslim) originated inevitably as a consequence of the relative expansion of the world capitalist mode of production, exploitation of the peasants and artisans, contention for government service and privileges, and accompanied religious revivalism in the colonised Indian sub-continent since the last decade of the nineteenth century. Gandhi's non-violence had no relevance to the society as the society itself was based on the violent private property with immanent contradiction and class struggle being the absolute in the long history of economic and social development.

Hindu-Mussalman conflict related with the economic factors in the colonial India became a great obstacle to the united struggle of the Indian nationalist force against the British colonialism and imperialism. The joint movement had been experiencing a decline since the mid-1920s, but in 1920 and 1921 it was a "serious menace"[5] to British imperialism in India. Many joint struggles were launched during this time. Witnessing the fury of Indian people's struggle, Gandhi withdrew movement on his own without consulting the Congress Working Committee and its other constituent organisations. Gandhi's Congress actually became alarmed with the surging class struggles launched by the workers and peasants of India. Class struggles had exposed his compromising character and so he had to make a retreat for the comprador classes of India.

The notorious Bardoli resolution for instance, said, "(1) The executive committee deplores the inhuman conduct of the mob at Chaurichara, which brutally killed the police officers and senselessly burned down the police station; (2) In view of the fact that mass civil disobedience always gives rise to violence which shows that the country is not yet prepared for the methods of passive resistance, the executive committee of the Congress orders that mass civil disobedience shall cease and instructs the local committees of the Congress to advise the farmers to pay the land taxes and cease all aggressive action; (3) The executive committee instructs the Congress and its branches to inform the peasantry that the refusal to pay rent to the landowners is a violation of the decisions of the Congress and causes harm to the vital interests of the country; and (4) The executive assures the landowners that the Congress movement does not in the least threaten their lawful rights and the committee desires that in all cases where the peasantry put forward any claims a way of settlement may be found through the medium of mutual agreement and arbitration".

This single instance along with the facts of the Mopla peasants (Muslims) against the landlords (Hindu) clearly exposed that the

Congress under the Gandhian leadership was mortally afraid of the class struggles which were developing at that time in India. Congress policy was designed to cover up the social contradiction. Owing to the betrayal by the bourgeois leadership, the revolution suffered a defeat. Gandhi, the "celebrated leader" of the Indian bourgeois national movement, at a time when it was at its height, declared "Everything is born in order to serve God—the Brahmins by their knowledge, the Kshatri by their strength, the Vaisya by their commercial abilities and Shudra by their physical labour". "Congress and the Swaraj Party did not aim at complete independence of India and their aim was home rule on a dominion basis".

"This implied that the Indian nationalists were prepared to cooperate with the British in the Anglo-Indian Government, and this practical programme was the inevitable consequence of the "economic cooperation between British and Indian capitalists in the exploitation of the Indian masses."

"The modern Indian big bourgeoisie is allied with British imperialism. The driving forces of the revolution today are the proletariat, the peasantry and the petty bourgeoisie (the artisans, small traders and the petty bourgeoisie intelligentia),"[6] thus the Communist International concluded in the mid-1920s.

This can be further corroborated from the facts and developments in that particular period of time. It becomes self-evident from the writings of Gandhi. In reply to a reader's query, he wrote in *Young India* in September 1921 that he did not advise any tea garden worker to strike and that there could be no question of non-cooperation or strike against capital and capitalists. This only exposes opportunism and compromising character of an arch revivalist Vedantin fighting for *status quo* in the society.

M.K. Gandhi wrote, "*Satyagraha is pure soul-force*. Truth is the very substance of the soul", but he observed that India was quickly passing through the "mob-law stage",[7] and there was much tendency on the part of the organisers to yield to the rule of the mob. There was mob rule at Amritsar on 10 April 1919. There was mob rule at Ahmedabad on the same fateful day. It represented "undisciplined destruction" and therefore it was "thoughtless, profitless, wicked and harmful". He noted that "the greatest obstacle is that we have not yet emerged from the mobocratic stage". They repent quickly. "Our organised government does not repent of its fiendish crimes at Jallianwala, Lahore, Kasur, Akalgarh, Ram Nagar etc." He wrote, "God has been abundantly kind to me". At the time of Rowlatt Act agitation God had "warned" him, and "Ahmedabad, Viramgam and Kheda erred; Amritsar and Kasur erred". "I retraced my steps, called it a Himalayan miscalculation, humbled myself before God and man, and stopped not merely mass civil disobedience but even my own which I know was intended to be civil and non-violent". "Non-violent attainment of self government presupposes a non-violent control over the violent elements in the country". He also instructed that, "this is a holy war" and that the tales of religion were to be circulated to the volunteers for their training.

Such was his abstraction in defence of idealist philosophy and spiritualism in the Congress politics and freedom movement. It was no doubt typically enmeshed and integrated with the theism and Hindu religion. As he wrote[8] in 1917, "We forget the principle of non-violence, which is the essence of all religions. The doctrine of arms stands for irreligion. It is due to the sway of that doctrine that a sanguinary war is raging in Europe."

"In India also we find worship of arms. We see it even in that great work of Tulsidas. But it is seen in all the books that soul-force is the supreme power."

"Rama stands for the soul and Ravana for the non-soul. The immense physical might of Ravana is as nothing compared to the soul force of Rama. Ravana's ten heads are as straw to Rama. Rama is a *yogi*, he has conquered self and pride. He is 'placid equally in affluence and adversity', he has 'neither attachment, nor intoxication of status'. This represents the ultimate in *satyagraha*. The banner of *satyagraha* can again fly in the Indian sky and it is our duty to raise it. If we take recourse to *satyagraha*, we can conquer our conquerors, the English, make them bow before our tremendous soul force, and the issue will be of benefit to the whole world....

"A *satyagrahi* does not wait for others, but throws himself into the fray, relying entirely on his own resources. He trusts that when the time comes, others will do likewise. His practice is his precept. Like air, *satyagraha* is all pervading. It is infectious which means that all people—big and small, men and women—can become satyagrahis. No one is kept out from the army of *satyagrahis*. A *satyagrahi* cannot perpetrate tyranny on anyone; he is not subdued through application of physical force; he does not strike at anyone. Just as anyone can resort to *satyagraha*, it can be resorted to in almost any situation".[9]

Enough of fantasy, spiritualism, anarchism and rank subjectivism work within the religious realm. Was it politics of freedom movement or preaching religion in order to serve the reaction? Gandhi was of course dominated by the latter, for he himself had "claimed to be a student of religion".

Seeing the spread, gravity and impact of the mass movements and class struggles cutting across the caste and community in Indian society, Gandhi had secretly sought a personal interview with the Viceroy, Lord Reading in 1921 through the affectionate courtesy of Madan Mohan Malaviya, Hindu Mahasabha's supreme leader, and obtained the "invitation letter" for himself from the government for restoration of "law", "order" and "peace". This was Gandhi's "truth" and principled politics ! Understanding the reality of class struggle on secular line and social progress was beyond his thought process and political outlook.

Earlier, the anti-cow slaughter campaign on religious ground made by the Sanatan Dharma Sabha and some other organisations in the country could not influence the principles and political activity of the Congress Party. Politics was then quite free from the religious issues in India, but cow protection became an important subject in both religion and politics in the second decade of the twentieth century generally with the decline of the liberal and moderate leadership in the Congress and its withdrawal from the growing mass movements against the British rule in the mid-1920s.

The issue of anti-cow slaughter under the banner of Hinduism came when Raja Shashisekhareswar of Tahirpur sought to move a resolution in the Indian National Congress in the late 1880s. It then caused much anxiety to the leadership of the party. But the problem was solved on the principle that, if any proposal relating to a particular class or community is condemned by the representative of that particular community, there would be no discussion about it in the Indian National Congress, and, this was made the rule[10] of the party. Occasionally, the Muslim delegates to the Congress session were provided with the fares and also other facilities by the Congress organisation on its own. The problem of Hindu-Mussalman was not very old, but the partition of Bengal certainly had an impact on it, wrote Surendra Nath Banerjee, one of the founder leaders of the National Conference and the Indian National Congress.

Now-a-days, Surendra Nath Benerjee wrote, "what a change has taken place!" Those who sweared to countrymen for bringing *Swaraj* they themselves were resorting to lie and enmity as safeguards and that would remind of the impending cause of downfall of the political life in the country. "*Swaraj*" is first used in the Hindu scriptures and there it means "restraint". "Now some persons have adopted this word for wilful actions and practices with the intention for serving their self- interest." "At the beginning of the national movement this filth introduces a big evil"[11] for the future, he observed in no ambiguous terms.

The Non-Cooperation movement had made a good position in the political history of the country. But, by 1924, it was found to be abandoned. All its means, excepting the boycott of foreign cloth, it had been withdrawn. The hatred of the people against the British rule was also gradually directed[12] against community people and as a result communal discontent and riots spread. Surendra Nath Banerjee viewed that the leaders of Non-cooperation played with fire and said that the leaders and' organisers of this movement openly acknowledged its problem and it was "partially responsible" for increasing the communal tension in the country.

In fact, after the formation of Home Rule league by Annie Besant, which created disruption in the Indian National Congress in 1915 and Khilafat-Non-Cooperation Movement (1919-22), much of the important objective of the Congress "to remove racial, provincial and religious prejudices amongst our countrymen and consolidate the spirit of national unity" was considerably diluted and impaired as necessary perspective and objective of attaining the goal of independence was not clarified and pursued for training of the people in a sustained manner.

Parallel to the Gandhian political activity based on the tenets of *Ahimsa* and Sanatan Dharma of Hinduism, there had emerged and grown militant Hinduism in the Indian political scene and both the trends had interacted and supported each other in ideology and practical work at large over the years. They derived inspiration from the same scriptures and from each other.

The revival[13] of Hinduism in the north-western part of India was marked with the organisation and activity of Arya Samaj and Sanatan Dharma Sabha since the last quarter of the nineteenth century. Arya Samaj began its activity with the Hindu religious reform movement, propagation of Hindi and cow protection. Sanatan Dharma Sabha vigorously engaged itself in cow protection campaign with the patronage of local Hindu landlords and traders in northern India. "Glory to the Sanatan Dharma, Glory to Maharani Victoria", was their slogan and ideology. Loyalty and allegiance to the Hindu religion and colonial rule became identical and was largely equated. Agra was the main centre of its activity, from where it spread to the large areas of the princes in Rajasthan and Central provinces which had long standing relations with the Marathas.

In this background, Binayak Damodar Savarkar, born of a chitpawan brahmin jagirdar family in Nashik (Maharashtra) in 1883 was inspired with the national idea in tradition of Hindu scriptures and Maratha hero king, Shivaji, who was then being remembered and popularised with the observance of annual festival. His book *The Indian War of Independence 1857* on a broad approach, was published in 1908. In its preface he wrote, "The feeling of hatred against the Mohammedans was just and necessary in the times of Shivaji but, such a feeling would be unjust and foolish if nursed now, simply because it was the dominant feeling of the Hindus there". In 1907, year of the diamond jubilee of the 1857 great rebellion, Savarkar himself wrote a leaflet stating, "We take up your voice, we rever your flag, we are determined to continue that fiery mission of 'away with the foreigner' which you uttered"[14] (Savarkar, *Indian War of Independence* 1857; 1970, p. 547) On the occasion of the War of Independence (1857) centenary, in 1957, Savarkar wrote, "It is a matter of gratification that the theory I propounded fifty years back for the first time in my book and which was then accepted only by a few scholars and ardent young men, has now been acclaimed as a rational accepted proportion.....”[15]

Savarkar was a staunch revolutionary in the early years of his life. In his jail life, however, Hinduism shows to have very much influenced his thought. While in jail in the Andamans (1910-1921), he defined *Hindutva* in one of his poems in Sanskrit as follows : “*Asindhu Sindhu Paryanta Yashya Bharat Bhumika, Pitribhu Punyabhushaiba-Sa-Ib Hindurity Smrita*”. This contained the germs of a more militant Hinduism in the subsequent periods.

He was brought back from the Andamans in 1921 and sent to Ratnagiri prison in Maharashtra. Here he expanded his earlier subjectivism and spiritual ideas and wrote his thesis “*Hindutva*” in 1923 in Marathi language that became the philosophical and ideological basis of the concept of the Hindu nation and its organisation, Hindu Mahasabha which was already established in 1914 at Haridwar, U.P., now in Uttaranchal. After his release in 1924 he became interested in building up Hindu Sangathan (Organisation). Within two years Ratnagiri Hindu Sabha was formed and he gave the call, “*Militarise Hindudom*”. He took a leading role in the establishment and organisation of the Rashtriya Swayamsevak Sangh in 1925 and onwards. According to Savarkar: They are all Hindus who respect the land of India and inhabit—it is the land which expands from the Hindukush to the seas and which they regard as fatherland and holy land—their religion originates here itself and it is the place of all their faiths.

To Savarkar, nation is a living soul, a concept, outside and beyond body existence; it is a memory received from the universal rich inheritance, and the recognition in which the will to live together and the determination to preserve the indivisible inheritance transferred to them is revealed. In his concept, the Hindu is a nation, not religion nor any community or clan. *Hindutva* is not a word, it can be called “a complete history”. It is different from Hinduism, as the latter is derived as a word, a small fraction of the former. Hindu is “a nation”, and all others in India, according to Savarkar, are communities. At the beginning of the Second World War, Savarkar, who was president of the Hindu Mahasabha from 1937 to 1943, declared : “Militarise Hindudom and Hinduise all politics”. Before that time, Lala Lajpat Rai, Pandit Madan Mohan Malaviya, and Vijay Raghabachariar—all ex-Congress Presidents, Ramananda Chatterjee; N.C. Kelkar, Bhai Parmanand, and Dr. Munje functioned as presidents of the Hindu Mahasabha. As a result, with its existence Hindu Mahasabha spread its roots all over India and thousands of people became "inspired" with the ideal of the Hindu Sangathan. The subject like military training and discipline all through got sufficient importance in the activity of Hindu Mahasabha. Many Hindu industrialists and businessmen like Birla, Scindhia, Walchand, Pendharkar, Velankar financed Hindu Mahasabha's activities, according to Savarkar's Court statement before the special Judge at the Red Fort in 1948, against the charge of conspiracy to kill M.K. Gandhi. Savarkar was however acquitted by the Court.

The most important fact that stands out here is the emergence of a powerful all-India organisation and religious philosophy which guided the militant activity of the Hindu Mahasabha during the three decades from 1914 to 1947. The Hindu religious axis with strong support of the Indian exploiting classes *viz*, capitalists and landlords grew and expanded over the years and dominated the politics of India's freedom movement. This ideological and organisational base inevitably formed the Hindu fundamentalist parties of the present day Indian politics. This, along with Gandhi's idea of Rama being the soul, conditioned and gave a great fillip to the organisation and growth of other communal parties. Hindu Mahasabha acknowledged its good relationship with the Congress leaders, and the prominent Congress leaders like Gandhi never dissociated themselves from the Mahasabha leaders. Ideologically, they shared common ideas and sentiments of the religious philosophy.

The 1923 Benaras session of the Hindu Mahasabha, based on the spiritual concept of Hindu nation, incorporated in the agenda for conversion to Hinduism in its political programme. The concept of Hindu nation was more strengthened, but of course, on a false ideology.

The vulgar subjective idealism developed in the period of India's freedom movement which drew its inspiration not only from the religious scriptures of the past but also from the writings of

Mohandas Karamchand Gandhi as well. The former RSS chief and its ideologue Guru Golwalkar wrote in "*We or Our Nationhood Defined*" (published in 1939) that "......In Hindusthan exists and must needs exist the ancient nation and nought else but Hindu nation. All those not belonging to the national, *i.e.* Hindu race, religion, culture and language naturally fall out of the real national life......" and "......There are only two courses open to the foreign elements, either to merge themselves in the national race and adopt its culture, or to live at the mercy so long as the national race may allow them to do so and to quit the country at the sweet will of the national race...... From this standpoint sanctioned by the experience of shrewd old nations, the foreign races in Hindusthan must either adopt the Hindu culture and language, must learn to respect and hold in reverence Hindu religion, must entertain no idea but those of the glorification of the Hindu race and culture, and must lose their separate existence to merge with Hindu race, or may stay in the country, wholly subordinated to the Hindu nation claiming nothing, deserving no privilege, far less preferential treatment.....not even citizen's rights. There is, at least should be, no other course for them to adopt. We are an old nation, let us deal, as old nations ought to and do deal, with the foreign races who have chosen to live in our country." His *guru* was a Bengali monk of a particular sect.

Golwalkar continued, "To keep up the purity of the nation and its culture, Germany shocked the world by purging the country of Semitic races—the jews......a good lesson for us in Hindustan to learn and profit by." What lesson? Golwalkar clarified : "They (the Muslims and the Christians) are born in this land no doubt. But are they true to its salt?...... No. Together with the change in their faith, gone is the spirit of love and devotion for the nation." It is nothing but ignorance, crude sectarianism and vulgar subjectism.

Thus Golwalkar preached idea of "nation" and racialism in contrast to the ideas of liberty, equality and fraternity. He had a very biased and arbitrary view on the development of human society. His sectarianism and subjectivism had permanently put him in the marsh, as he made religion and spiritualism as the basis of his nation theory. He failed to oppose the theory of colonialism and colonial powers that dominate the countries and nations still now. He took things as rigid, fixed and immutable over time—a crass metaphysics in the philosophical world. He failed to see the changes and to understand the actuality of conflict, evolution, transformation and development of the different tribes and clans—the reality of dialectical and historical materialism—that has shaped the formation of nations and whole course of world history. The incomplete and inadequate assimilation of different races, tribes and clans, and their very existence in India till the present time, proves his truth at large. Indian society is still in the throes of constant change and evolution in terms of assimilation of castes, ethnic groups and communities.

Gandhism is rooted in religion and spiritualism. And what is the philosophy of a political party preaching the Hindu as a nation and the rest as communities? It seeks no truth from the material life of the people through the centuries The *Hindutwa* or any other religious faith can never become the basis of a nation. The concept of a nation based on religion is atrocious. It only speaks of dogmatic, subjective idealism devoid of all economic characteristics, conflict, assimilation, historical developments and hence the reality, and that smacks of sectarianism and feudal chauvinism directed against others inside and outside the country. The idea of *Hindutwa* has been historically linked with and pampered by Indian and foreign imperialist exploiters for their own class interests against the Indian people. Thus it actually turns to work as the opium of the working people with the speculative ideas, "glory" of past and spiritualism of the imagined world, not the real world. It is of course the condition of life and society in the real world that actually matters to the people at large. For, without human life, there can be no existence of religion.

Political developments cast a deep shadow on the Indian society. The conduct of the Home Rule agitation on the lines it was run, completely changed the aspect of the Indian politics. "For the first time in the history of India", one author observed, "politics had been given a religious tinge. For the first time, the faith of people was used for the realisation of a secular object."[16] The vigorous propaganda made by Mrs. Annie Besant, the old theosophist leader took the colour of a religious appeal. "Home rule has become so intertwined with religion", declared Mrs. Besant in her Congress presidential address at Calcutta in 1917, "by the prayers offered upon in the great southern temples—sacred places of pilgrimage—and spreading from there to village temples, and also by its being preached up and down the country by *sadhus* and *sanyasins*".[17] Mrs. Besant, the Home Rule leader, wrote in her book, "*Future of. India*" in 1922 that, "if we think about independent India, we should bear in mind terribleness of Muslim Rule". When revolutionary movement continued in Bengal Mrs. Besant, the theosophist leader, came forward to counter it by organising the Indian bourgeoisie in her Home Rule League. She openly made speeches abroad opposing India's independence. She spoke against the independence resolution at the All India Congress Session in Delhi in 1929. Apart from this, she influenced the Indians with religious functions to keep this country tied to the British rule.

Religion was infused in Indian politics with the definite motive by the emerging Congress leaders. As M.K. Gandhi wrote in reply to a letter written by one Mr. Irwin, addressed to the *Statesman* in 1917 ".... Rightly or wrongly worship of the cow is ingrained in the Hindu nature and I see no escape from a most bigoted and sanguinary strife over the question between Christians and Muslims on the one hand and Hindus on the other except in the fullest recognition and practice by the Hindus of the religion of *Ahimsa*, which it is myself imposed and humble mission in life to preach. Let the truth be faced. It must not be supposed that Hindus feel nothing about the cow-slaughter going on for the Europeans. I know that their wrath is today being buried under the awe inspired by the English rule. But there is not a Hindu throughout the length and breadth of India who does not expect one day to free his land from cow slaughter. But contrary to the genius of Hinduism as I know it, he would not mind forcing, even at the point of the sword either the Christian or the Mohammedan, to abandon cow-slaughter".[18]

This only shows that Gandhi was so imbued with Hindu religion and cow-protection that he forcefully put for ward and utilised the cause of the majority's irrational anti-cow slaughter demand, which was not at all related to economics and organisation of secular politics for national movement in India. But it came right in the agenda of his political approach and thereby espoused and extended the ideology of the Arya Samaj and Sanatan Dharma Sabha which had been functioning in the country for a long time. He did not improve upon their subjective idealism and religiosity in politics. With this move Congress mass contact and support grew for the time being, but, practically, religion, more particularly Hinduism, got precedence in Indian politics and freedom movement. Subjective idealism prevailed over the objective reality and politics of freedom movement got contaminated with religion and its attendant pernicious communalism. During this time and onwards, Congress under Gandhi's control failed to purge out religion from its political doctrine and attitude in the practical work.

Lala Lajpat Rai, a prominent Congress leader, wrote a series of articles at that time giving a fairly good account of the history of communal trouble. In conclusion of an article in 1924 he emphatically declared, "Let those who demand communal representation with separate electorates in all the representative institutions of the land, honestly confess that they do not believe in nationalism or in a united India. The two things are absolutely irreconciliable. Mr. M. A. Jinnah is the latest recruit to this party and I really cannot understand how he calls himself a nationalist still. ......Once you accept communal representation with separate electorates there is no chance of its being ever abolished, without a civil war. A civil war will again, actually mean supremacy of one community over the other"[19] "I am very strongly opposed to the denominational political organisations" said Lajpat, and he argued, "In my judgment they are harmful to the political evolution of the country on the national lines. But if the Hindu-Muslim problem is to be solved on denominational lines, I can see no justification for the view that while the Muslims should be represented by the Muslim League and the Khilafat committee, the Hindu point of view should be left to be represented by the Congress. For the last five years—even if not before that—the Congress has been a joint organisation of Hindus and Muslims; in fact, it has done more for the Muslims than for the Hindus. Under the circumstances I do not think it is fair to the Hindus, that in a settlement of Hindu-Muslim problem, the Congress should have the deciding voice. The Muslim denominational attitude must inevitably be followed by a similar attitude on the part of the Hindus. Circumstances have forced me to conclude that if Hindus and Muslims are to be considered as two parties to a quarrel, the only organisation that can represent the Hindus is the Hindu Mahasabha. It should be remembered that the Mahasabha is an old institution though it never before grew into vitality".[20]

Hardayal, an important leader, wrote in *Pratap* (published from Lahore) in 1925 declaring that the future of Hindu nation, Hindustan and Punjab depended on four principles, viz., Hindu organisation, *Hindu Raj*, Shuddhi of the Muslims and conquering of Afghanistan and Frontier province. According to Hardayal, unless the Hindu nation completed these four tasks, their descendants would remain in danger and security of Hindu nation would be impossible. Although the necessity of the Hindu-Muslim unity in the fight against the British colonialism in India was stressed on the part of Turkey, it was odd,[21] for instance, to find Jawaharlal Nehru saying that it was the duty of Hindus to "help" the Muslims in Khilafat Movement (1920-21) for if the British succeeded in destroying Islam they would then try to destroy the Hindu religion. The Nehru family also maintained close contact and liaison with spiritualist Kubalayananda-swami and sought solace in Ramakrishna Mission. Some of the family members had even taken *Deeksha* from the Mission. Indira Gandhi remained close to the monks of the Ramakrishna Mission all through her life.

In his *autobiography*, Jawaharlal Nehru writes of his going to attend Mrs. Annie Besant's lectures on Theosophy in Allahabad. "I was deeply moved by her oratory and returned from her speeches dazed and as in a dream, I decided to join the Theosophical Society, although I was 13 then ...Annie Besant herself conducted the initiation ceremony", he wrote, and added, "I was thrilled." For obvious reason, this made some impact on him for Hinduism and he first utilised this background of religious association and teaching on Hinduism in his public speeches at the time of Non-Co-operation Movement in the early 1920s.

Idealisation of Ram and Ram Rajya in "practical politics" by the leaders like Annie Besant and Mohandas Karamchand Gandhi no doubt alienated many political leaders from the freedom movement of India. B.R. Ambedkar attacked Gandhi's reference to the sanctity and infallibility of the *Vedas*, *Smritis* and *Shastras* because there were "the very instruments which has blighted the lives of the untouchables". Surprisingly, the Hindu Mahasabha chief, V.D. Savarkar, upheld the theory that Hindus and Muslims were "two antagonistic nations living side by side in India".

Initially, M.A. Jinnah did not support in two nation theory; but Gandhi's trenchant for mixing religion with politics, drove him to the other extreme. Gerald James Larson, quotes with a tinge of humour, an observation from D. E. Smith's book, *India as a Secular State*, "M.A. Jinnah could have constructed his two nation theory, which led to the demand for Pakistan, on the basis of Savarkar's speech!" How about Jawaharlal Nehru who was known to have been critical of mixing religion with politics? According to Larson, in the light of his various pronouncements, it would appear that he was opposed to Gandhi's Neo-Hindu vision of Indian unity. Yet, Jawaharlal described Gandhi's stress on religious values as one of "spiritualisation of politics". Larson makes a new point that Nehru's views were "Neo-Hindu to the core". He argues that "If Gandhi's vision represented what might be called religioisation of the politics, 'Nehru's secularism represented what might be called 'politicisation of the religions'—that is transformation of the search for ultimate meaning....into the immediate task of political mobilisation and the acquisition of power". (*Cf.* Gerald James Larson, *India's Agony Over Religion,* 1997).

What philosophy does it contain? —Rationality and unity for the noble cause of movement for India's freedom and independence or shows its inherent weakness, decline, sectarianism, narrowness and degeneration? Joint electorate only does not ensure national unity especially when separate communal electorates were being thrusted upon by the British colonial rule, the common enemy of the Indian people, in its petty parliamentary reforms. The rationality in politics could grow out of the united, consistent and resolute struggle against the colonial and imperialist rule in the colonial countries like India. The new Congress leaders, having witnessed the fire of class struggle, in 1920-1922 became afraid, withdrew mass movement against the British and got entrenched in the parliamentarism and communal politics of British colonial constitutionalism in India. They had no systematic and comprehensive radical thought and programme to teach and prepare the people for the freedom movement of the country. Politics flowed in the narrow communal channel with its frivolous subjectivism and crude interest of the Indian capitalist and landlord classes deeply imbued with the religious philosophy.

As Prof. S. Gopal observed in an article in 1988, "The social disharmony between Hindus and Muslims had spread to other spheres with regional imbalance in development under the East India Company, leading to the classes who gained most from British rule being predominantly Hindu. By the time the interior areas of India caught up with the rest, national awareness expressed itself increasingly in a Hindu idiom. The process of divergence between the religious communities was further aggravated by official policy symbolised by the establishment of separate electorates; and as the franchise was broadened periodically on this basis, the communal elements grew correspondingly stronger".[22] Even regional pact agreed towards settlement of the rising communal problem, for example in Bengal, under the initiative of the Swarajist leader C.R. Das was thrown out by the All India Congress leadership in 1923-24. In the same year Hindu Mahasabha in its Benaras session included religious conversion in its programme. In 1925, Rashtriya Swayamsevak Sangh was formed in the name of cultural nationalism under *Hindutva*. All this smacks of sectarianism in religions and a variety of leadership muddled with the ideas of communal thought and attaining *swaraj* through the parliamentary reforms of the notorious British colonial power! A vulgar trend with the orchestra of transcendentalism, religiosity and communalism constituting the pernicious subjective idealism came to dominate the Indian politics.

This marked a great decline in the philosophy of Congress and other major political parties of India, in comparison to that of its enlightened liberal political leadership in the earlier period. Failure to check the religious tone and tenor in the political parties' activity naturally suppressed the rational approach to the development of national self-feeling, national self-respect and national sovereignty on the secular line. It frustrated united national liberation struggle and led the Indian people to the wide marsh of spiritualism and sectarian political ideology. The same trend continued on, and its result has been very disastrous in the decades through the late 1990s.

Such a philosophical stand of the leaders like Gandhi, Savarkar and Mrs. Besant made on the part of the Congress Party and Hindu Mahasabha was dominated by the majority community had very much complicated the political situation in India. For it firmly espoused and actually theorised the very brahminical theistic position with the idealisation of nation as the living soul and of Rama as the soul against Ravana (non-soul) of the epic age, who was revered as the hero of the Dravidian civilisation in South India. "Rama stands for the soul and Ravan for the non-soul," wrote Gandhi on 2 September 1917. This along with other writings on Hindu religion by Gandhi not only failed to draw but alienated[23] the Adi Dravida and non-brahmin lower caste sections of the Hindu community oppressed by the upper caste, better-off minority section of the majority community. On the other hand, Rama as the "soul", was enough to indicate the entry of Brahminical Hindu religion in the Congress politics in the Gandhian era. This no doubt aroused confusion, suspicion and fear as well in the Muslim and other minorities' psychie which thwarted and greatly aggravated the whole political situation of the Indian subcontinent in the later period.

It may be stated that, as a reaction to the age-old upper caste Brahminical rites and oppressive practices, in south India (Madras Presidency), a non-Brahmin manifesto was prepared reflecting the social oppression and class contradiction in the Indian society. It was released in 1916 and a clear-cut battle line was drawn between the Adi Dravidas and non-Brahmin movement on the one hand, and the National Congress and the Home Rule Movement on the other. Annie Besant, the old Theosophist leader, editor of *New India* and patron saint of Home Rule Movement decried the contents of the manifesto as "mischievous and unpatriotic". Though she was "concerned" with the welfare of Adi Dravidas, in consonance with the members of the Varnashram Dharma Sabhas, Annie Besant held that "a pariah had to work out his *karma* now and thereafter to break free from the shackles of untouchability". The non-Brahmins, being scared of their motive, criticised the Home Rule and Nationalism as "it would enshrine Brahmin Rule". Dr. T.M. Nair, chief author of the non-Brahmin manifesto and other critics of the Home Rule were branded as "misguided, ignorant, insincere (and therefore dishonest and above all disloyal to the national cause)". Theagoraya Chetty, another important signatory was also criticised severely by *New India* : "our speakers ask the people to move as 'one'. But the movement led by Rai Bahadur Theagoraya Chetty has split the Hindu community into two and he is carrying on a crusade of hate against the Brahmins who would have been invaluable helpers to him, they being a class, the bureaucracy fears". Editorially, the journal attacked, "the non-Brahmin newspaper *Justice* for carrying of a hate against Brahmins and called upon well-intentioned and right-thinking non-Brahmins to dissociate themselves from justice's guerilla method of warfare".

In fact, the Anti-Brahmin movement started in Madras Presidency much earlier. As early as in 1907 when the Congress brought the message of *Swaraj* and *Swadeshi*, Pandit Iyothee Thass, a Buddhist by conviction and a pariah by birth commented on it by stressing the need of imparting equity and justice among the people of the Indian society in his weekly paper called *Oru Paisa Tarnijhan* published from Madras. The articles published in *Tarnijhan* were definitely anti-Brahmin, anti-caste, Anti-Aryan and anti-Sanskrit. Naturally, it came in conflict with Annie Besant's *New India* which was openly pro-Brahmin and pro-Aryan in thought and approach.

On the issue of boycott, the pundit, stressing the cause of internal strength pointed out "what needed to be boycotted was not foreign clothes but caste hatred, the kind of prejudice that could burn the houses of the poor and damn and destroy their goods and rituals". He also stated that the vast gap which separated the actions of those who, lustily chanted 'Vande Mataram', for their espousal of the cause of their motherland". Without prejudice to the leaders' support and praise for the British Raj, it can be stressed that the Adi Dravida and non-Brahmin movement raised the subject of social oppression and class rule within the age-old caste system of the country.

Dr. T.M. Nair, M. Masilmani and Theagoraya Chetty contributed largely in *Tarnizhan* and in E.V. Ramasami Periyar's journal *Kudi Arasu* and continued to keep the lamp of anti-Brahmin and anti-caste movement burning. In fact due to Theagoraya Chetty and Dr. Nair's persistent efforts ultimately the justice party came into existence in 1916. The leaders of the justice party did not recognise the difference between man and man by birth. They also did not believe in the doctrines of *Varnashram Dharma*.

The Justice Party formed government in 1925 under the constitutional reform scheme and laid great stress on education and in the implementation of the resolution of the first non-Brahmin confederation held at Coimbatore in August 1917, which urged for providing free education to Adi Dravidas and other depressed classes of the Indian society.

However, E.V. Ramaswamy Periyar noticed that all was not well with the Justice Party ministry in the Madras Presidency. As a past President of Tamil Nadu Congress and one of the Vice Presidents of Madras Presidency Association—a Congress forum for non-Brahmins, Periyar felt the reality of the Aryanised, upper-caste Brahminical philosophy propagated by Gandhi under the authority of the Congress Party. He resigned from Congress in 1925 in the Kanchipuram session of the Congress on the principles of proportional representation and against the upper caste politics thrusted with Rama as the soul and supreme of *Satyagraha* in the garb of non-violence and non-cooperation. Periyar left Congress to launch the self-respect movement in 1925 concentrating on caste, culture and religion. Congress under Gandhi could neither properly accommodate the Adi Dravidas and non-Brahmins in the Congress leadership and organisation nor favour any action in support of their just demands, in the reform movement. Gandhi's projection of Rama as the soul force and of Ravana as the non-soul supporting the cause of the upper caste propertied class and many other similar writings alienated the Adi Dravidas and non-Brahmin sections consisting the majority of the Indian people. This exposed the nature and domination of a shallow and narrow speculative philosophy in the Congress politics parading as nationalism.

No wonder, Periyar, in 1931, spoke against the wiles of Congress nationalism with oppositional vehemence, particularly against the Gandhi-Irwin pact. The pact, Periyar noted, resulted in surrendering substantial political demands. Sir A. R. Mudaliar wrote in the editorials of *Justice* that it was pure quibbling unworthy of the man. Varnashramites, Mudaliar noted, believe in the eternal perpetuation of the caste system with divine superiority and inferiority of castes owing to *karmic* conduct and they believe in segregation in matters of eating and drinking and were horrified at the idea of inter-marriage. With commendable courage and frankness Sir Mudaliar asked Gandhi not to expound an imaginary *Varnashrama Dharma* of his own making.

The upper caste Congress leaders of the North opposed the non-Brahmin movement.The Adi Dravida and non-Brahmin movement no doubt unfolded class contradiction and struggle against the economic exploitation and social oppression of the upper caste rich in South India.

During the Non-Co-operation and Khilafat movement class struggle on a wide scale was unleased though the Congress under Gandhian leadership was prepared to lead only a specific type of controlled mass movement. Hindu opinion generally condemned the distressed Muslim peasant movement of Kerala in 1921 as being no more than communal and it is true that about 600 Hindus mostly the landlord, *zamindar* and rich money lenders were killed and 2500 forcibly converted into Islam, according to an Arya Samaj source. In Chaurichaura 22 policemen were killed in clash with the protesting peasant mass. In the trial of Mopla and Chaurichaura incidents, more than 250 peasants were finally awarded capital punishment and hanged in the name of keeping barbarous government's colonial law and order. It is a matter of shame that there was no nationalist protests from the Gandhian Congress against the barbarous government conspiracy to take lives of the Indian peasants. Congress resolution assured the zamindars "that the Congress movement is in no way intended to attack their legal rights...." Thus Gandhi served "truth".

The Non-Co-operation Khilafat alliance made in 1921-22 was possibly the point of "greatest strength and unity" in the entire history of national movement. Despite the breaks, developments in the fourth phase, between November 1921 and February 1922 it "very nearly brought the government to its knees" but the alliance between the Congress and Khilafat leaders was however "weakened by Gandhi's unilateral withdrawal"[24] of the movement in February 1922. True class character and philosophy of non-violence was thus exposed to severe violence, reaction and *status quo* in the colonial India. The "heroes" of nationalism showed their true colour and took shelter in the dark cave of non-violence and opportunism. Actually, owing to their attachment with the reactionary forces, they became very much afraid of the fury of surging class struggles and mass movements of the Indian people to overthrow the British rule.

Subjective idealism and unpredictable move of Gandhi created dissent and fissure in the leadership of the Indian freedom movement. Without appreciating the reason, deep import and consequences thoroughly of the allied forces' attack on Turkey during the First World War (1914-19), Gandhi extended "support" to the Khilafat Movement for a short period without clinching the real issue of the need and agreement after a thorough discussion with the Hindu and Muslim leaders for a long-term united struggle against the British rule in India and imperialism all over the world. Objectively, the two were inter-related and bound in an inseparable whole. The position of Turkey, Persia and China, at that time, Lenin showed, was that they were already reduced to semi-colonial countries[25] by the imperialist forces. As a matter of fact, India was then a vast colonial territory directly under the British rule, while the countries like Persia and Turkey inhabited by the people professing Islam, were transformed into semi-colonies. Naturally, there was very much indignation among the Indian Muslims who historically formed an integral section of the Indian people. At the same time, position of India and the countries of the Middle East, as mentioned, became basically same as all of them fell prey to the colonial and imperialist pillage and domination, from which none of them has yet become free. In fact the Prime Minister of Turkey, under the condition of imperialist seize, issued a *fatwa* from the palpit of Aya Sophia Mosque to the Muslim population of the world to stand by the side of the Sultan Khalif, being the spiritual and temporal head representing sovereignty of besieged Turkey. It appealed for *united struggle* against the British and other imperialist forces in their own countries. The dissent of the Muslim population in India had grown through the first two decades of the twentieth century and they largely responded to the call of the Khilafat Movement. Congress leader,

Bal Gangadhar Tilak earlier made the cause one with them. They unitedly opposed the British rule and colonialism, the hated enemy of mankind.

There was a similarity in the objective condition of India and the Middle East as both were under the colonial rule. The Khilafat was not actually a religious call. Its appeal for the united movement had a genuine anti-colonial and anti-imperialist character, unleashed class struggle on a wider scale in the Indian society which frightened the British imperialism. It was subjective and quite naive to state that the movement was organised in defence of the religious faith and cause of a particular section of population only. The movement had its broad common basis, appeal and purpose of anti-colonial and anti-imperialist struggle in the world.

Gandhi, as noted, unilaterally supported the movement of Khilafat Committee of the Indian Muslims purely from the religious standpoint without going into the root of the matter and withdrew from it on his own just a year after. He also suspended all mass movements on the plea that those turned to be "violent". The imperialist powers had already then divided the territory of Turkey state by force for their own economic and political interests and domination in the Middle East. History records this hard reality.

In India, however, the political development took a different shape in the mould of idealist philosophy and religion. All India Khilafat Committee had earlier adopted for boycott of foreign goods. The special session of the Congress at Calcutta in September 1920 adopted non-co-operation resolution drafted by Gandhi on the request of and in co-operation[26] with Maulana Shaukat Ali, a leader of the mass movement. Gandhi and his followers were in fact opposed by Lala Lajpat Rai, President of the special session, C.R. Das, Bipin Chandra Pal, Annie Besant, Pandit Malaviya, M.A. Jinnah and the Maharashtra people, including C.P. Maharatti. The Muslims stood under the banner of the Congress "not as individuals as before, but as a community". Referring to this session Mohammad Ali commented at a later period that the deflections from non-cooperation could be traced in the ranks of those who opposed the Mahatma and Khilafatists. Bipin Chandra Pal expressed his grief against C.R. Das for supporting Gandhi and he wrote a number of articles from

1920 to 1925 criticising Das's activities in Indian politics. From the Nagpur session in December 1920 Das and Pal moved on different tracks.

Bipin Chandra Pal, an "extremist" leader, could not believe that "such astute politicians as the Ali Brothers did not realise the confusion of thinking which notoriously characterised the whole non-cooperation campaign", and "they were only interested in helping destruction of the present government leading the future to take care of itself." In fact, he said, the Ali Brothers "did not make a secret of their ultimate objective". Bipin Pal further said that their "ideal was not honestly political but essentially theocratic". Of course, the Ali Brothers "never pretended to be nationalists in the sense in which that word is understood all the world over", as they "are Mohammedans first and Indians next". Moreover, "their patriotism is not territorial but extra-territorial". Therefore, "the logic of this extra-territorial patriotism is distinctly anti-national".[27] Such was the "reason" of a senior lawyer and extremist leader in Indian politics!

Quoting long passages from Bipin Pal's article in the *Englishman* of July, 1925, Mohammed Ali gave a sharp reply refuting all his charges in the form of an article entitled. "An Unpleasant Correspondence" published in the *Comrade* on 4 September 1925. Mohammed Ali said that this particular phrase 'extra-territorial patriotism' was not of his own creation. Mr. Montagu, used it in his well-known speech as under secretary of state for India in the House of Commons, on the Indian budget, or the reforms of the Morley-Minto regime, "in which he asked Indian Musalmans not to abate a jot of fervour of their extra-territorial patriotism but only to add to it some elements of territorial patriotism also". Mohammad Ali stated that Pan—Islamism was the same to him as the Islamic Brotherhood and, was, in fact Islam itself. Mohammed Ali also pointed out that he wanted "a government of the people, by the people and for the people, and neither an exploitation of India by the Indian bourgeoisie, to which Mr. Pal also belongs, or by Indian Pan-Islamists like me, nor the realisation of the day-dreams of those, whoever they may be, Hindu, Muslim or Sikh, who, with defeated ambitions, only seek opportunities for re-building their lost empires".[28] These words flow from the pen of

Mohammad Ali who, as president of the Congress, in 1923 at Coconada, was threatened with censure motion by several working committee members of the party in session when he asked on the communal question : "can any party claim that it is totally innocent?" There he criticised both Shuddhi and Sangathan of the Hindus and Tablig and Tanjim activities of the Muslims as partisan narrowness. As one contemporary author comments : "The Khilafat Movement (1919-1922) represented the highest watermark of idealism and altruism on the part of Indian Muslims...represented a definite stage in the evolution of Indian Muslim politics. The movement itself inculcated among Muslims a new spirit of self-reliance and fearlessness, taught them the gospel of jail-going and stout defiance of authority, and above all, led to an unprecedented mass awakening and resurgence, largely broadening (as a consequence) the base of freedom struggle"[29]. This was no doubt an important political development in the Indian sub-continent.

Gandhi thought that the core of any religion lies in Hinduism; and what Hinduism does not contain, is of no substance and so unnecessary. This religion is "most tolerant" and free from harshness. Hinduism have the maximum expression and implementation of non-violence. Jainism and Bhuddhism are not different from the Hinduism. Hinduism reposes faith on unity not only among men but also of lives. Cow worship, wrote Gandhi, has distinct contribution in the evolution of humanity. In the concept of unity and in the holiness of all forms of life, it is the practical implementation of this faith. The direct result of the Hindu faith is the great belief in rebirth. And lastly, the principle of *Varnashrama* is the great discovery of the tireless search for truth, Gandhi observed.

Gandhi worshipped Rama, exclusive of all other things. In his concept, Rama was a complete man; he was not a historical person but the explanation of the incidents of his life changed with the advancement of historical discoveries and research. Listening to the call of heart, if some Aryasamajist or Islamic missionary preached his own faith, and for that reason, Hindu-Muslim unity was endangered, that unity would be very fragile. There was no need to be perplexed with such movements. But those movements would have to be genuine. He said that the Malkan Rajputs (Muslim), if they wanted to return to the Hindu organisation, had the full right to do it at their earnest.

Gandhi recognised and committed himself to *Adwaitavad* but he was prepared also to support *Dwaitavad* owing to the ever changing condition of the world. He thought that all worldly affairs, according to the Hinduism, are His *lila* and *maya* (illusion). Without Him, men are nothing. To be worthy, men always have to praise Him, and act according to His will. They should dance in tune of His flute. Good must come out of that. The very rule governing the lives, including the scientist's discovery about matter in the world, is "God". Rule and its imposer are one and the same. (*cf.* Mahatma Gandhi, *Hindu Dharma Ki :* Bengali, National Book Trust, New Delhi, 1996, p. 2, p. 4, p. 9, p. 17, p. 46, p. 48 and p. 52).

The characteristic features of Hinduism were assiduously reiterated and preached by M.K. Gandhi in the *Young India* and *Harijan* in the 1920s through 1940s.

It is easy to see from these writings how *Adwaitavad* and spiritualism under Hindu religion deeply influenced the philosophy of Congress organisation and freedom movement of India. It pampered Aryanism to serve the ideology of the Hindu uppercaste capitalist and landlord classes at large that spread dissent and caused disunity among different communities and castes in Indian society. But was this subjective idealism and religion really necessary to serve the cause of Congress and freedom movement in India?

Idealisation of the existing order of the class-dominated society was the truth for M.K. Gandhi and the Congress Party in which he became the dictator and priest. Actually he supported and wholeheartedly worked for the old regime of violence and untruth against the truth and consciousness. Gandhi theorized reaction with his nonviolence directly descending from the Hinduism and its spiritualism. He viewed all things as isolated and illusory which was not at all true in the material world. In his view, all were creations of God, the father of all spirits. He thereby preached theism and spirituality in politics. This false notion led him to a philosophical muddle. This sheer subjectivism which patently put Gandhi on the highway of class collaboration, compromise with the imperialism, spiritualism and rank opportunism serving the economic and political interests of the landlord and capitalist classes at large. In Gandhi, the exploiting classes found their own image and supported him to serve their long-term class interest, satisfy spiritual aspiration and have solace. Gandhi's non-violence itself is based on the interest of the properted class; it works in violence and constantly engenders violence amid anarchy in the mode of production. Its motive is to support reaction with old bondages of labour service and wage slave system and perpetuate the human slavery with religion and spiritualism.

Gandhism certainly throws man into utter confusion, dispair, passivity in action, compromise with the enemy and superstition only to support exploitation of man by man and cover up social contradiction. He preached politics with religion and spiritualism in all his writings and speeches of the public meetings from the Congress Party platform. Gandhi excluded the social base *i.e.*, mode of production and economics, intentionally brought in religion and spiritualism and enmeshed them in politics which drastically suppressed even the very nascent bourgeois liberal character of the earlier Congress Party. As a result of this process, the Congress Party grew in number of members but became too flabby, theoretically weaker and short-sighted; it lost its earlier intellectual faculty, rationality and sound philosophy which were all necessary to properly unify and ideologically guide the Indian freedom movement. For this reason the movement lost much of its strength, vigour and goal. No wonder, unity, strength, weight and effectiveness of the organisation to fight against British colonialism and imperialism was much impaired. It marked a philosophical decline and fall as it brought in suspicion and degeneration through communalism and adverse political reaction in contrast to fellow-feeling, mutual reciprocity, unity and solidarity among the workers, peasants and toilers of the sub-continent of India.

In the early 1920s, Gandhi wrote that he could not go to the Muslim community without the help of the leaders like Saukat Ali. Communal strife grew apace as there was no agreement between the Congress and the Muslim League or between the Hindu and Muslim communities, on the future constitution for the government of India. Gandhi, with his utopia, however, thought in that there would be unity after India achieved independence. Clarifying his position, Gandhi said on 9.4.1940. "I still believe that there can be no *swaraj* by non-violent means, without communal unity. And eight crores of Muslims can certainly bar the way to peaceful freedom" and "when India gets the power to frame her own constitution, the Muslims will surely have a decisive voice in shaping their own future. It will be. It cannot be decided by the vote of majority." But the difference between the two parties became so wide that the Muslim League leader Nawabzada Liaquat Ali Khan, as quoted by Gandhi, in the same statement wrote that "the sole objective of the Congress under Mr. Gandhi's fostering care has been the revival of Hinduism and the imposition of Hindu culture on all and sundry." In an interview to *The Hindu* published on 11 June 1942, Gandhi said, "I have been asking myself why every wholehearted attempt made by all including myself to reach unity has failed, and failed so completely that I have entirely fallen from grace and am described by some Muslim papers as the greatest enemy of Islam in India. It is a phenomenon I can truly account for by the fact that the third power, even if deliberately wishing it, will not allow real unity to take place" (*Penguine Gandhi Reader*, 1993, pp. 274-276). The answer to the problem is Gandhi himself who systematically used and made religion to play its role and influence the politics of India. He invoked Rama as the soul and surmoned that the politics bereft of religion is a death trap. The leaders of Gandhi's Congress and Muslim League never taught the people about the secular hard reality that India was not divided between the Hindu and Muslim but between the rich and poor—the main thing of the rational and materialist philosophy. It is Gandhi who wrote in *Hind Swaraj* that, there would be no place of an atheist in free India. He introduced *Ramdhoon* and prayer before the beginning of his political meeting. Little did he think or care that his *Ramdhoon* prayer in public meetings and the writings with religious tone and tenor would help the Hindu zealots to get organised and strengthen their force which in turn, created the condition for the formation of militant organisation by other communities as well. Gandhi also dreamed of "peaceful freedom" from the cruel rule of British imperialism in India!

The untoward developments inevitably favoured the British imperialism to manoeuvre and play the trick. The British Government suggested in the late 1940s that India should have a Constituent Assembly and build up a constitution which the British Parliament would accept. Gandhi is said to have advised the Congress not to accept the Constituent Assembly because it was coming not by virtue of India's own strength but because the British were making "a gift" of it even when the Congress and the Muslim League "had not been able to come to terms" with one another. Gandhi went on to say that, "Even if you accept the Constituent Assembly with the willing cooperation of the British you will be under the visible or the invisible protection of British forces, whether Indian or European". This is how he advised the Working Committee in December 1946. In any case, the alternative in Gandhi's opinion was perhaps another *Satyagraha* movement but the communal situation aggravated and became more tense, permitting little scope for the movement. Some of the Congress leaders argued to Gandhi : "You will have to work through us, the Congress; we are afraid that we do not have any fight left to us". Gandhi virtually said to them, "Then act as you think best. I will go on retirement until the people realise that it is a poor kind of freedom which we have gained. Until then, I will abide my time".[30]

All this glaringly shows the consequence of subjective idealism— the philosophy of compromise and surrender— in the Indian politics, charged with personal ambition, petty, colonial parliamentary reforms and its worthy attendant, communalism.

Prof. Nirmal Kumar Bose, Secretary of Gandhi in Bengal and Bihar in 1946-47 wrote, "He left the stage to the great leaders of India who eventually came to terms with the British".[31] At that moment a strange thing happened. Prof. Bose, reported that Gandhi was travelling in the train. He had just then an interview with Lord Mountbatten, Viceroy of India. While reporting his conversation with the Viceroy, Gandhi said in anger that Lord Mountbatten had said to him that "the Congress was no longer with Gandhi but with him." "What did you say", Prof. Bose asked him. "I said, but India is still with me",[32] was Gandhi's reply.

This exposes the true comprador character of the Congress

carried through the 1940s. The politics of India then had fast 'set into communalism and almost the majority were claiming separation of Hindu from Muslim. Idealist philosophy which largely made its impact through sectarianism and spiritualism in the Indian politics took its heavy toll but it did not also spare Gandhi, who himself being a Sanatan Hindu, was killed by a Hindu fanatic in 1948. But, is it not a fact that the militant Hinduism or *Hindutva* is but a product and manifestation of consistent preaching of Sanatan Hinduism and *Adwaita Vedanta* philosophy which was earlier opposed by Rammohan, Vidyasagar and others tooth and nail? Similar is the case with other religions. Subjective idealism thus stands thoroughly exposed with all its primitive and irrational ideas inimical to the growth and development of even social democracy in the backward and semi-colonial countries like India, Pakistan and Bangladesh. It supports backward social formations and most reactionary forces in the society. At the same time it works as a *strongally* of imperialism to exploit the people and counter the radical forces of social change in the Indian sub-continent and other parts of the world.

To explain the narrowness and rigidity of idealist philosophy and its practice in politics we may refer to the critical views made by Rabindranath, a great poet of India. He no doubt belonged to the school of idealist philosophy. But, with the noble vision, he warned against the narrowness of religion and boldly propagated the necessity of reforms and modernity in the Indian society.

Rabindranath Tagore as early as in 1917 noted[33] that different meetings and reports of the newspapers in India were propagating the call for alms from Montague as great but this call "would not helps us". At the same time, he however, mystified the issue with the preaching to the people of the idea of immortality of soul on the thought of the *Upanishad*. Spinning wheel was then popularised as selfhood and rescue of the country. But if *Swaraj* is viewed first with spinning wheel's thread for a long time, similar would be the condition of the country, he asserted. As a certain section of people had respect on the personal greatness of the Mahatma, they could be influenced to make such a blind practice. Many would find result only on obeying his order. Tagore thought that this attitude was not favourable for achieving *Swaraj*. (*Kalantar*, Viswabharati, 1993, p. 277)

"The flag with spinning wheel at its centre now is hoisted in our country. It is but a flag of narrow inanimate force, of immature mechanical power and of less strong commodity power—appeal does not come from the heart's strength. The call to the whole nation on the way of liberation, cannot be the invitation for blind repetition of some external process. For that, it was necessary for the release of humanism. Is it with the operating of spinning wheel?" (*Ibid.*, p. 346)

Tagore raised this vital question.

"For some time, the countrymen were eager with harbouring the idea that *Swaraj* had come very near to their hands. But it was axiomatic truth that we did not follow the conditions for getting *Swaraj*. It can be hardly emphasized that a big step could be made for *Swaraj*, if the Hindu and Muslim could unite as kith and kin. Days of the calendar pass on, but addiction had not gone. The addiction became the easy way of *Swaraj*. There were only one or two narrow lanes for it. Spinning wheel lies in this path.

"Then the question comes, what was meant by *Swaraj*? Leaders of the country did not fully clarify the definition of *Swaraj*. The meaning of independence was broad and all pervasive.

"Associated cultivation of self-authority, its commencement, the spread of feeling of its glory among the people can only make *Swaraj* a reality on the concrete base. While spinning, a Congress member may think of the heaven of economics but he got the idea by some other means, as the spinning wheel never contained its seed (p. 280). The main thing is that we are not in unison and there is no end of division among ourselves. Division is the sorrow and that is sin (p. 225).

"The work for salvation of the country is very great and its means will be very small! There is certainly a deficiency in such a word of expectation. Faith on falsehood lies in such expectation; not in reality, not on the strength of self (p. 249).

"Politics come first, man afterwards. For enjoying facility without any trouble, they want *Swaraj* first, and only thereafter the persons for whom *Swaraj* is meant for (p. 290)." "One day, the politicians began tinkering with the parliamentary politics in India by imitating the English because the very ideal of politics only became visible among all other things of Europe" (p. 292).

"Good behaviour of the opponent cannot be received unless one does qualify to be a true contestant. Only for this reason, Mahatmaji tried to make the King's government feel by giving a big thrust of the people. Only compromise between the two parties was his objective" (p. 240).

Tagore invoked *Upanishad's* God and His blessings for unity among the people with good thought and action.

"In the Khilafat and Non-Cooperation Movement, the Muslim in fact drew the Hindu more close to his own Mosque and other places than that of the Hindu". (p. 312)

Tagore further observed :

"Long time before, the livelihood in India was enjoined with the religion. That made man quiet. The problem was solved with the hereditary division of labour according to the caste profession. (p. 281)

"The number of persons (*Sudras*) carrying on caste profession is the largest; so judged from this angle, India is a country of *Sudra Dharma*. There are many evidences of history in this regard. The very large deadweight of this clap-trap of docility has made the entire Hindu community to bow forever. As the difference in profession according to caste was put under the religious administration in India, the discontent and efforts for revolt were sapped to the root (p. 283).

"If welfare of India is wanted, the Hindu and Muslim have not only to be united but they also be of same status. That would not be personal physical strength for fight in wrestling, but same status of social power for both of them (p. 240). "On many occasions and without any occasion we always want company, meeting and discourse with each other. If we walk side by side, come nearer, then only it can be found that on being man, it is easy for him to find out man of his own (p. 332).

"For the Congress, corridoor of power is wide open and the government of the *Raj* do not become hesitant to compromise with it. Imperialism or fascism is creating the condition for its own self-destruction. It is doubted that the internally accumulated heat for power mongering, perhaps, has become the cause of its unhealthiness. Those who have well grabbed power at the centre of the Congress their patience has fallen and their intellect and justice did not move in the straight right path at the time of crisis. At the root of the evil practice and distortion in behaviour lies the influence of the audacious power mongering at large (p. 373).

"In our country, Congress did not creatively develop itself on the basis of general social equality. It was planted on such a social inequality that inequality had dug unfathomable ditches after each ten or twenty miles, and those ditches are guarded day and night by the parties in the name of religion"(p. 375).

These sections taken from Tagore's different writings in the *Kalantar* (Bengali) during the period of that time are eloquent in rational thought, humanism and progress, within the arena of idealist philosophy and based on the creative interpretation of the *Upanishad*. At the same time, they exposed the general weakness and contradiction in the philosophy of Congress politics and its practice. Tagore's writings had explained the phenomenon and contained warning of the weak social base and pitfalls of the Indian freedom movement in general and in particular, the very method of functioning of the Congress Party.

"The foreign power is our ruler; this is not fire but ash. If the foreign power is driven 'out, fire will continue to burn; even though the country's ruler assumes the state power, sorrow and burning will not stop". The cause was the blindness of non-intelligence (*Ibid.*, p. 245).

"The country where religion unites man with the unity of religion and no other bond can unite, that country is wretched. That country creates dissent and division with religion, which is the most destructive division than all others. The worth of recognition of affection with good feeling between man and man is the true intellect of religion (*Ibid.*, p. 324).

"Hindu period is an era of reaction—in this reign Brahminical religion was firmly structured with great effort. Raising of impregnable walls of practices made it unreachable. It was not in mind that some living subject is killed, if it is tightly interned in the name of protection. The main thing, however, is that after the

Buddhist period, with the great perseverence and in close association of the foreign clans like the Rajput, Indians made Hinduism like a great barrier in order to fully protect themselves from external relations and influences. Its nature itself means prohibition and refusal. Nowhere in the world, such a barrier to all kinds of intercourse, was built up with such a great efficiency. It is not that the barrier is limited only to the Hindu and Muslim (*Ibid.*, p. 313). "Today, it has to be located where the holes and sins of Hindu community exist; it must be attacked very mercilessly. With this idea in mind, the Hindu community has to appeal and say 'Ailing, we are ashamed, not owing to external attack, but for our internal sin. Come, today we unite all to remove that sin'. This is not so easy on our part (*Ibid.*, p. 320).

"Two broad sections of inhabitants in India are Hindu and Muslim. If we think that the effort of doing good for the country will be successful only by pushing aside the Muslim, we will commit a great mistake. (*Ibid.*, p. 318). Religion has not united us, rather it raised thousands of barriers and made these obstacles reinforced as eternal beyond history (*Ibid.*, p. 326).

"I say on behalf of the Hindu to leave the judgment on the lapses of the Muslims—if we could not draw them near, we should acknowledge our shame for that (*Ibid.*, p. 333).

"Participation of the Muslims was much less in the *Swadeshi* Movement in 1905. Some public leaders became angry at this, and said that they should be completely refused. I know why they did not join. But why didn't they join? The great emotion was confined only to the Hindu society, and it did not touch the Muslim community." "Even on that occasion we did not even have our lesson. We have made the ditch of separation deep for each other on the plea of community," thus Tagore concluded on the Indian political situation in 1926 (*Ibid.*, pp. 318-319).

The degeneration inside the Congress did not prevent Gandhi even to call Rammohan, a great Indian leader of social reforms in the earlier period, whom Tagore revered as the greatest person of modern time, "a pigmy"—and that "cause of internal nature of mind actually assumed such a kind and form in the rules of work of the Mahatma", which Tagore could not accept as his own creed (*Ibid.*,

p. 250 and p. 267). This became the development characteristic of the Congress under the Gandhian leadership during the critical period of India's freedom movement. As the Congress Party was run with the dictation from a certain leader, it gradually became an authoritarian organisation. Objectively, the nascent rationalist thought in India was hounded, victimised and crushed by the anarchy of Gandhism in Indian politics.

NOTES

1. *Cf.* M. K. Gandhi, *Gandhi Rachana Sambhar* (Bengali), ed, Gandhi Memorial Committee, Calcutta, 1977.
2. Rudragshu Mukherjee, ed., *The Penguin Gandhi Reader,* Penguin Books, Calcutta 1993, p. 268.
3. *Ibid,* p. 262.
4. *Ibid,* pp. 262-63.
5. Safdar, *Hindu- Mussalman Strife,* The Communist International, Moscow, March 30, 1927, p. 68.
6. *Ibid.,* p. 70.
7. See Rudrangshu Mukherjee, ed., *The Penguin Gandhi Reader,* p. 125 and p.70.
8. *Ibid.,* pp. 126-127.
9. *Ibid.,* p. 127.
10. *Cf.* Surendra Nath Banerjee, A *Nation in Making,* Paschim Banga Bangla Akademi, Calcutta, 1998.
11. *Ibid,* See also B. Bishikar, *Dr. Hedgewar,* p. 12.
12. *Ibid.*
13. Sumit Sarkar, *Modern India, (1885-1947),* Macmillan India Ltd., Calcutta, 1984, pp. 74-76, 99, 127-29 and 235.
14. V. D. Savarkar, *The Indian War of Independence 1857,* Rajdhani Granthagar, New Delhi, 1970, p. 547.
15. *Cf.* Amalendu Mitra, ed., *Great Revolutionary Thinker Savarkar,* Barabazar Kumar Sabha Pustakalaya, Calcutta; 1985, p. 173 and others.
16. Matlubul Hasan Saiyid, *Mohammad Ali Jinnah : A Political Study,* Published by Shaikh Muhammad Ashraf, Kashmiri Bazar, Lahore, 1945, p. 161.
17. "Citation"in *Saiyid,* pp. 161-162.

18. "Citation" in *Saiyid*, p. 165.

19. "Citation" in *Saiyid*, p. 328.

20. "Citation", in *Saiyid*, p. 333.

21. See Jawaharlal Nehru, *Selected Works,* Vol.I, p. 177 ff. H. Y. Sharda Prasad, Centenary Tribute to a Quiet Heroine, *The Asian Age,* Calcutta, 28 July, 1999, p. 12.

22. S. Gopal, Nehru and Minorities, (Reprint), *Mainstream,* November 1998, New Delhi, p. 18.

23. *Cf.* V. Geetha, and S. V. Rajadurai, *Towards A Non-Brahmin Millennium: From Iyothee Thass to Periyar,* Samya, Chennai, 1998.

24. *Cf.* Sumit Sarkar *Modern India, (1885-1947)*, Macmillan India Ltd., 1984, Calcutta, pp. 205-234.

25. V. I. Lenin, *Imperialism, The Highest Stage of Capitalism,* 1916 (Collected Works, Vol. 22), Moscow, 1968, p. 75.

26. See M. K. Gandhi, *Autobiography* in Gandhi Rachana Sambhar (Bengali), Vol. I, ed., Mrityunjoy Maity, Gandhi Memorial Committee, Calcutta, 1977, pp. 504-505.

27. *Cf.* Bipin Chandra Pal, *Through Indian Eyes: The Problem and the Situation: Extraterritorial Patriotism,* The Englishman, Calcutta, July 3, 1925.

28. Mohammed Ali, An Unpleasant Correspondence, in *The Comrade,* 4, September 1925, pp. 112-113.

29. Sharif Al Mujahid, Unsung Hero of Khilafat, *The Asian Age,* Calcutta, 15 January, 1999, p. 13.

30. *Cf.* Nirmal Kumar Bose, *Gandhiji : The Man and His Mission,* Bharatiya Vidya Bhaban, Bombay, 1966, p. 43.

31. *Ibid.*, p. 43.

32. *Ibid.*, p. 44.

33. *Cf.* Rabindranath Tagore, *Kalantar,* Viswabharati, Calcutta, 1993.

4

REFORMS, OBJECTIVE IDEALISM AND CLASS STRUGGLE

The plight of the Muslim community in India after the first war of Independence in 1857, was sought to be relieved with the launching of the Central National Mohammedan Association[1] on 12 May, 1878, seven years before the Indian National Congress was born. This association was established alongwith that of the Anglo-Oriental College at Aligarh under the aegis of Syed Ahmed Khan in the same period. The Association signified the first Muslim attempt in India to create a political consensus on problems confronted by the community. As an organisation of the educated middle class it grew in strength and popularity to such an extent that by 1888 the number of branches of the association throughout India rose to as many as 72. Syed Ameer Ali, a High Court Judge, an erudite liberal leader and founder secretary described the association in his memoirs thus: "It may be safely affirmed that until the establishment of the Central National Mohammedan Association there existed no political body among the Indian Mohammedans capable of representing to the government from a loyal but independent standpoint, the hope and aspirations, the legitimate wants and requirements of the large body of Muslims in this country, who by their number and homogeneity constitute such an important factor in all questions concerning the welfare of India". Ameer Ali remained its founder secretary for 25 years and succeeded in creating a strong public opinion in favour of the advancement of the Muslim community. It worked for the education and political transformation of the Muslim community in the country under the domination of British colonial power.

A Muslim Memorial to the government which Syed Ameer Ali inspired and drafted in 1883 led to a resolution of the Viceroy Lord Dufferin in Council in March 1885, recognising the association's demands for a separate Muslim electorate which accorded constitutional regulation for the Muslims as a distinct section (*quom*) or a community of the Indian people.

But, in spite of his persistent championing of the cause of his community, Syed Ameer Ali was not sectarian in his thought and works. He believed that the development of India on modern lines depended on cardinal co-operation of Hindus and Muslims. He exhorted the Muslim community to work in unity and harmony with all non-Muslims in the country. As an educated Indian, he advocated wider application of the principles of local self-government, employment of the Indians in higher posts of state service and admission of the Indians to higher ranks of the Indian army. The Central National Mohammedan Association's emphasis on inter-communal harmony won the support of many non-Muslims as well. Raja Inder Chunder Singh of Paikpara, was one of its honorary vice-presidents and Babu Saligram Singh and K. M. Chatterjee were on the committee of its management. The list of honorary members contained such eminent liberal Hindu leaders like Surendranath Banerjee, Kristo Das Pal and Jyotindra Mohan Tagore along with some important British officials. It set up a model of Indian institution, like Anglo-Oriental College organised by Syed Ahmad Khan, with the help of both Hindu and Muslim communities in the country.

Marx's celebrated observation on the Hindu-Muslim unity and joint action against the British Rule in 1881 was quite realistic and valid. For, in India especially, every important aspect and sphere of practical life of the society had been formed and developed with the contribution of both Hindu and Mussalman. It was a joint product of their toil, intellect and foresight. The land system of the country was based on the earlier Hindu system with the ownership vested upon the village council against payment of a certain fixed share of the produce to the authorities; the administration was to a great extent constituted on the Arabian style and the military was organised on the model of Turkestan. In art, architecture, literature, music, mass culture and folk song and form of worship etc., mutual relation, enmeshing and combination of ideas worked in a grand process and made a great synthesis to form and develops the society of the Indian sub-continent for centuries. (*cf.* Kshitimohan Sen, *Bharate Hindu-Musalmaner Jukta Sadhana* : Bengali, Viswa Bharati, 1990). On Hindu-Muslim relations, in 1883, Syed Ahmad Khan observed : "To be a Hindu or a Muslim is a matter of internal faith which has nothing to do with mutual relationship and external conditions". "How good is the saying, whoever may be its author, that a human being is composed of two elements—his faith which he owes to God and his moral sympathy which he owes to his fellow-being. Hence leave God's share to God and concern yourself with the share that is yours.... Thus India is the house for both of us (Hindu and Muslim). We both breathe the air of India and take the water of the holy Ganges and Jamuna. We both consume the products of the Indian soil. We are living and dying together. By living so long in India, the blood of both have changed. The colour of both have become similar. The faces of both, having changed, have become similar. The Muslims have acquired hundreds of customs from the Hindus and the Hindus have also learnt hundreds of things from the Mussalmans. We mixed with each other so much that we produced a new language—Urdu, which was neither our language nor theirs. Thus, if we ignore that aspect of ours which we owe to God, both of us, on the basis of being common inhabitants of India, *actually constitute one nation*; and the progress of this country and that of both of us is possible through mutual co-operation, sympathy and love. We shall only destroy ourselves by mutual disunity and animosity and ill-will to each other. It is pitiable to see those who do not understand this point and create feeling of disunity among those two nations (*quoms*) and fail to see that they themselves will be the victims of such a situation, and inflict injury to themselves. My friends, I have repeatedly said and say it again that India is like a bride which has two beautiful and lustrous eyes—Hindus and Muslims".

Declaring himself "a great liberal" in a speech at Lucknow on 28 December, 1887 he held that "to forget the prosperity of one's nation *(quom)* is not a sign of wisdom"; he alone had opposed the system of election, and said that it was on account of his speech that Viceroy Lord Ripon changed his opinion and made *one-third* of the members in the Council appointed and two-thirds elected. Pointing out the incidence of very uneven spread of education and lower rate of literacy among the different communities of India, he questioned how and to what extent competitive examination would be introduced and suit to the country. He criticised Congress demand for election of a section of the Viceroy's Council by the people. Election, he apprehended, would not guard Mohammedan interest. He assured Mohammedans that "the only thing which can raise you to a high rank is high education" (cf. *Speeches and Writings of Syed Ahmad Khan,* ed., Shan Mohammad, Calcutta 1972).

He took strong exception to the Congress agenda for election and its own propaganda that the Muslims had joined the Congress. He questioned about the character of the future administration and apprehended a communal strife for political domination in the absence of the British rule in India. While Syed Ahmad Khan personally raised certain issues on the Congress movement, the Deoband School of Islam in U.P. issued a *fatwa* for the Mohammedans to join the Congress at its inception, and in the earlier years, there was in fact some participation of educated Muslims in the Congress.

The first session of the Congress was attended by only 2 Muslims, the second by 33 and the sixth by 156 (22 per cent of the delegates). "The bogey of Muslim opposition to the Congress was set up quite in the early years of the Congress and it is curious to note that Sheikh Raza Hossain Khan produced at the fourth session (1888, Allahabad), a *fatwa* supporting the Congress from Shams-Ul-Ulma, the leader of the Sunni community of Lucknow, and declared that "it is not the Muslims, but their official masters who are opposed to the Congress." The third and twelfth sessions of the Congress (1887, 1896) were presided over by Muslims. Regarding the Congress activity, in a speech at Meerut on 16.3.1888, Syed Ahmad Khan advised the Mohammedan community that "the method we ought to adopt is this that we should hold ourselves aloof from this political uproar and reflect on our condition, that we are behind hand in education and are deficient in wealth. Then we should try to improve the education of our nation *(quom)*. If my nation follows my advice they will draw benefit from trade and education. Otherwise, remember that government will keep a very sharp eye on you because you are very quarrelsome, very brave, great soldiers and great fighters". In clarification of the earlier speech at Lucknow on 28 December, 1887, he said "...my Bengali brothers and some of my Hindu fellow-countrymen should be angry with my Lucknow lecture, but to deduce from that lecture the conclusion that I have changed my former opinions and abandoned my desire for agreement and friendship between Hindus and Mohammedans, is wrong. There is no person who desires more than I that friendship and union should exist between the two peoples of India, and that one should help the other. I have often said that India is like a bride whose two eyes are the Hindus and Mohammedans. Her beauty consists in this—that her two eyes be of equal lustre". But he questioned about agitational politics and asked :

"...Can any Bengali honestly say that the schemes which they have advocated in the Congress would benefit anybody except themselves, and next to them the Mahrattas and Brahmans? They are trotting about flattering all Mohammedans to induce them to join them. But in doing this they are actuated only by selfish motives. For they very well know that after succeeding in their schemes, Mohammedans could under no condition derive any advantage from them". (*cf.* Shan Mohammad, ed., *Speeches and Writings of Syed Ahmad Khan*, 1972, Calcutta, p. 159, p. 160, p. 163, p. 194, p. 195, pp. 210, 216, 218, 219 and 252)

Syed Ahmad Khan thus wrote about Muslims' backwardness to participate in the political organisation at that time and pointed out the inherent contradiction in the Congress political approach and colonised Indian society. He pointed out the lack of homogenity in the Indian society. He felt the experiment which the Indian National Congress wanted to make, was fraught with dangers and sufferings for all the nationalities of India, specially the Muslims. The Congress aims and objects, in his view, were based on ignorance of the country's social realities. He thought that the psychology of the backward and unprepared Muslim community would not suit to the ideas of the Congress, and that would affect its nascent movement.

The facts generally confirm that, in feudal and colonial India there was differentiation—a development in the attitude of the Muslim community towards politics of the country. One section readily supported the Congress movement. However, Syed Ahmad Khan's writings and speeches helped to considerably check large-scale joining of the Mohammedans in the Congress for its backwardness and for the obvious reasons of the organisation's philosophical decline and authoritarianism after the end of its old liberal leadership around 1920. (cf. *Syed Ahmad Khan, Akhari Madamin,* compiled by Muhammad Imam Ud-din Gujerat and Maulvi Ahmad Baba Makhdumi, Lahore, pp 46-50; and *Congress President Mohammad Ali's Speech* in 1923, in A. C. Banerjee, ed., *Indian Constitutional Documents*, Vol. 3, Calcutta, 1961, pp. 110-117).

It is important to note that in the earlier period, there was a common base and a political atmosphere of mutual accommodation, cooperation and trust between the Congress and the Muslim League towards realisation of the common goal of self-determination for India.Mutual feeling and respect was its keynote for a long time.

Mohammad Ali Jinnah was formally enrolled as a member of the All India Muslim League with loyalty to the congress cause in 1913. He persuaded the League and the Congress in 1916 to agree upon a common scheme of reforms. At the Muslim League's Lucknow session (over which he presided), Jinnah confessed that he had always been "a staunch Congressman" and had "no love for sectarian cries". He considered the "reproach of 'separatism' sometimes levelled at Mussalmans" as "singularly inept and wide of the mark". In Jinnah's opinion, the League, "this great communal organisation (was) rapidly growing into a powerful factor for the birth of United India". *(Jinnah's address to the All India Muslim League, Lucknow,* December 1916, in M. Rafique Afzal, ed., Speeches and Statements of the Quaid-i-Azam Mohammad Ali Jinnah, 1911-34 and 1947-48, Lahore, 1966, pp 56-62). Being a member of both the political parties, Jinnah attended the Congress sessions until 1920. Hakim Azmal Khan, M.A. Ansari and Mohammad Ali functioned as presidents of the two parties at different period of times.

A.K, Fazlul Haq, a leader of Bengal joined Muslim League in 1912 and in 1914, he became the General Secretary of the Muslim League's Bengal Provincial Committee and its all India Joint Secretary. He alongside joined the All India Congress Committee in 1914. He was elected its secretary in 1918 and in the same year he presided over the annual session of the All India Muslim League at Delhi. He represented Muslim League from Bengal in the joint session at Lucknow and acceded to 60 per cent of the seats in the Bengal Provincial Council to be represented by the Hindus, although Bengal then had more than 51 per cent Muslim in its population. But in other provinces, the Muslim representation was agreed to be a little more compared to the community's population. There was provision of "Special Electorates" for representation of the Muslims in the councils. While the provision may be called a snag, it can hardly be emphasized that the pact marked a major advance for co-operation, unity and harmony between the two communities, and its limitations could have been overcome in the successive rounds of talks and agreement for joint electorate etc., in course of time. This scheme of reforms was passed at the 31st session of the Indian National Congress held at Lucknow on December 29, 1916 and adopted by the All India Muslim League on December 31, 1916. The resolution of the Muslim League recorded, "The All India Muslim League, while adopting the scheme of reforms prepared by the Reform Committee of the League and approved by its council, submits it in conjunction with the Indian National Congress to the Government for its introduction after the war as the first necessary step towards the establishment of complete self-government in India". Tilak attended the Lahore conference and participated in the Lahore Pact between The Hindus and the Muslims in January 1917.

The Secretary of State, Mr. Montague's criticism of the joint Congress-League reform scheme was as follows :"It does not attempt to realise responsible Government, but it leaves an irremovable executive at the mercy of a legislature which can paralyse it but not direct it. I do not believe that this House will ever agree to set up a Constitution in India which will leave an executive that is not removable, at the mercy of a legislature which will leave an executive that is not removable, at the mercy of a legislature which cannot control it." (Speech in the House of Commons, June 5, 1919).

Further, the Montague-Chelmsford Report observed, "They (Indian politicians) could not remain content with an alien executive, and therefore, their policy naturally, and from their standpoint justifiably, must be to weaken and discredit it". (Para 177).

Clearly, the Congress-League scheme became a potentially dangerous thing to the British rule in India.

The year 1916 is thus a specially memorable year in the history of the political movement of India. The famous Lucknow Pact was signed in December of that year between the Congress and Muslim League. On behalf of the Muslim League, Mohammed Ali Jinnah, Mohammad Ali, Mukhtar Ahmad Ansari, Syed Wazir Hasan and Raja of Muhammadabad, and on behalf of the Congress, Ambika Charan Majumdar, Surendra Nath Banerjee, Motilal Nehru and Bal Gangadhar Tilak participated in the discussion between the two parties. Surendra Nath Banerjee presided in the joint meeting and the famous pact was signed by the leaders of the Congress and the Muslim League, forming *the basis* of mutual co-operation and action for the home rule, formation of responsible government, amendment of constitution etc., for the country. Bal Gangadhar Tilak had the main role in achieving unity between the Congress and Muslim League because he realised that political success was possible only with the unity of the Hindu and Muslim. The government felt disturbed with this development, projecting joint demand of the two main political parties for the country. "Congress accepted separate electorates and a bargain was struck over distribution of seats", writes Sumit Sarkar, a noted contemporary author. Historian J.H. Broomfield viewed the Lucknow Pact between the two parties as a memorable diplomatic victory.

It would be quite befitting to outline the main theme of the joint conference. In moving the resolution on self-Government for India, at the Lucknow Congress in 1916, Surendra Nath Banerjee, president of the Joint Reforms Committee, observed : "The scheme is before you, and it is the crowning testimony to the growing unity of feeling between the Hindus and Mussalmans. The solidarity of the two communities has been growing...when the Congress met here in 1899— I was one of the delegates present—the Mohammedan community were opposed to us with the exception of a few here and there. Today the leaders of the Mohammedan community have joined the Congress. Three cheers for them. They received us with open arms and with a greater earnestness and cordiality than might have been expected. We were received by my respected and honoured friend, Raja Saheb of Mahummadabad, whose independence and keen solicitude for good understanding between the Hindus and Mussalmans, have won him in an unstinted measure, the esteem confidence and the regard of both the communities.

"...One weapon in the armoury of the enemies of Indian advancement which they use in season and out of season, which they have often used with such tactfulness and skill, is the alleged cleavage between the Hindus and Mohammedans, which they themselves have been so sedulous in creating..." "...We are the natural leaders of the masses...we are the protectors of their interests and those interests will be safe, far more safe in our hands than in the hands of a foreign bureaucracy." *(Speeches of Surendra Nath Banerjee,* Vol. I, Indian Association, Calcutta, 1970, pp. 160-163)

Elucidating the subject, we can refer to the important speech of Jinnah. This helps one to get an objective view of the political condition of India at that time. In the Lucknow Conference of the All India Muslim League in 1916, Mahammad Ali Jinnah in his presidential address said:

"Freedom, justice, right and public law are pitted against despotism, aggression, anarchy and brute force and the result of this deadly combat will decide the future of mankind—whether the end will come with a stricken and shattered world, lying bleeding and helpless under the iron heel of the tyrant, with the whole of humanity stripped bare off its hope and faith and reduced to bondage, or whether the hideous nightmare will pass away and the world redeemed by the blood of the heroic defenders of civilisation and freedom, regain its heritage of peace and enter a period of vaster and glorious synthesis and reconstruction".

It reflects Jinnah's philosophy and world view based on the contradiction and reality in the period of colonialism and imperialism. It indicates the fact that struggle is the absolute in human history, progress of society and development of the world.

On the Indian situation, he appeared to have a social view emerging out of the reality of the existing communities as sections of the Indian people, and recognised contradictions in their progress and development over the years.

As he observed, "...if we turn to the internal situation in India, we meet with a set of social, ethnological and cultural conditions unparalleled in recorded history. We have a vast continent inhabited by 315 millions of people sprung from various racial stock, inheriting various cultures and professing a variety of religious creeds. This stupendous human group thrown together under one physical and political environment, is still in various stages of intellectual and moral growth. All this means a great diversity of outlook, purpose and endeavour. Every Indian nationalist who has given close and anxious thought to the problem of nation building in India, fully realises the magnitude of this task. He is not afraid of admitting frankly that difficulties exist in his path. Such difficulties have no terrors for him. They are already vanishing before the forces which are developing in the New Spirit."

"Amid the class of warring interests and the noise of foolish catchwords, no cool-headed student of Indian affairs can lose sight of the great obvious truism that India is in the first and the last resort for the Indians". "If the Indians are not the pariahs of nature, if they are not out of the pale or operation of the laws that govern mankind elsewhere...can think and plan and organise together for the common needs of the present and for the common hopes of the future, then the only future for them is self-government.... The cant of unfitness must die. The laws of nature and the doctrines of common humanity are not different in the East." "...If we turn to history, we find that in the past only such people have been declared to have been fit for freedom who fought for it and attained it". And, "Indeed, the person who fails to read in the Hindu-Muslim rapproachment with the last few years, the first great sign of the birth of United India, has little knowledge of the political conditions of a few years ago and has no business to talk of India's future". "In its general outlook and ideal as regards the future, the All India Muslim League stands abreast of the Indian National Congress and is ready to participate in any patriotic efforts for the advancement of the country as a whole. In fact, this readiness of the educated Muslims, only about a decade after they first entered the field of politics, to work shoulder to shoulder with the other Indian communities for the common good of all is to my mind the strongest proof of the value and need of the separate Muslim political organisation at present", and this is subject to "A minority must above everything else, have a complete sense of security before its broader political sense can be evoked for co-operation and united endeavour in the national tasks. To the Mussalmans of India that security can only come through adequate and effective safeguards as regards their political existence as a community."

"It is a matter of infinite gratification to me as well as to all patriotic Mussalmans that the Muslim communal position in this matter has been recognised and met in an ungrudging spirit by the leaders of the great Hindu community. This was so amply demonstrated by the happy and unanimous decision that was arrived at by the committee of the Indian National Congress and the All India Muslim League that met at Calcutta only last November. Our joint conference in Lucknow were marked by the honest efforts on either side to find a lasting solution to our differences, and I rejoice to think that a *final settlement* has at last been reached which sets the seal on Hindu-Muslim co-operation and opens a new era in the history of our country".

"The united Indian demand, based on the actual needs of the country and framed with due regard to time and circumstances, must eventually prove irresistible."

"Towards the Hindus our attitude should be of goodwill and brotherly feelings. Co-operation in the cause of our motherland should be our guiding principle. India's real progress can only be achieved by a true understanding and harmonious relations between the two great sister communities." "Let us remember, whether Hindus or Mussalmans, that new India wants a wholly different type of public workers, of more generous spirit and ampler mould, free from the egoism of sect and the narrowness of bigotry, one who can resist the temptation to crush the weak and yet would not quail before the aggression of the strong, who can rise above the petty preoccupations of the day to the higher plane of devotion and service which alone can give to a people, faith, hope, freedom and power."

"The renaissance of India really lies in our own hands. Let us work and trust in God, so that we may leave a rich heritage to our children than all the gold of the world, *viz.*, freedom, for which no sacrifice is too great." (*cf.* Matlubul Hasan Saiyid, *Mohammad Ali Jinnah : A Political Study*, published by Shaikh Muhammad Ashraf, Lahore, 1945, pp. 860-889).

"It is, however, strange that M.K. Gandhi saw the Lucknow pact as "an agreement between the educated and rich" of the Hindu and Muslim communities for gaining power. (*cf* "citation" in Shantimoy Roy, *Bharater Mukti Sangrame Muslim Abadan :* Bengali, 1994, p. 43) This standpoint of Gandhi cast a shadow on the historic agreement and showed unwillingness of the Congress Party later on to proceed with the common, agreed reform scheme. It exposed the narrow and sectarian attitude and prevalence of subjectivism and rising authoritarianism in the Congress Party. This trend became dominant after the Amritsar Congress Session in December 1919 where all the Congress Leaders including Jinnah resolved the policy of responsible cooperation with the Government's constitutional reforms scheme.

Facts support that communal harmony and common psychological make-up of the Hindus and Muslims of the Indian sub-continent generally developed through the centuries. This trend of thought appeared to have influenced Jinnah all through his life. As a liberal democrat, however he became concerned with the minority question and it does not at all follow that he attached a great deal of importance to Islam as a decisive factor in shaping the Muslim political thought. When asked, in August 1919, "Whether he wished to do away in political life with any distinction between Mohammedans and Hindus", he replied, "Yes. Nothing will please me more than when that day comes." He struck to that position right up to the creation of Pakistan. As he addressed Pakistan's Constituent Assembly on August 11, 1947 : "You are free to go to your mosques or to any other place of worship in this state of Pakistan. I think we should keep that in front of us as one ideal and you will find that in course of time Hindus would cease to be Hindus and Muslims would cease to be Muslims, not in religious sense because that is the personal faith of each individual, but in the political sense as citizens of the state".

But certain major untoward developments occurred after the Lucknow Pact in December 1916, which were suppressed for obvious reasons, but deserve very careful attention and consideration for the sake of objectivity and understanding the present situation in India.

There took place massive riots of October 1917 in Bihar, where crowds of upto 50000 Hindus attacked Muslims in 124 villages in Shahabad (Arrah), 28 in Gaya and 2 in Patna. Cow protection propaganda by Sanatan Dharma Sabha and Arya Samajist agitators organised by the upper caste Hindu landowners played the important role in provoking such riots for Hindi and Annie Besant's Home Rule politics. (Sumit Sarkar, *Modern India*, 1984, p. 157).

The Congress Party, then under the presidentship of the theosophist leader, Annie Besant played up on the situation and failed to justly condemn the violent incidents and the Muslim League took strong exception to the Congress ambivalence and prevarication. Annie Besant, Mohandas Karamchand Gandhi and company continued to play the Rama-Soul-Ramrajya orchestra in full tune, without caring of its impact and future consequences in the politics of Indian freedom movement against the ferocious British colonialism, its cruel rule and exploitation of the country.

During the Khilafat and Non-Co-operation movement Gandhi individually and in a secret manner broached with the Office of the Viceroy Reading, for understanding and compromise after withdrawal from the mass movement. It no doubt roused dissent and suspicion among different sections of the Indian people.

At the Round Table Conference in November 1931 M.K. Gandhi as the sole leader of the Congress said that the Congress claimed to represent over 85 per cent of the population of India comprising the toiling semi-starved millions, princes, landed gentry and educated class. The National Congress, said Gandhi, was a daily growing organisation and demonstrated its influence over and among the masses who inhabited in 7 lakh villages "The Congress is the only all-India-wide national organisation, bereft of any communal basis; that it does represent all minorities which have lodged their claims here.... The Congress, I say, claims to represent all these minorities" (*cf.* A.C. Banerjee, *Indian Constitutional Documents*, Vol. 3, pp. 227-229). Such utterings and claims had no ground reality at all, nor they could reason and provide with the secular basis for the freedom movement. Gandhi had to negotiate with B. R. Ambedkar for an agreement for enlisting support of the backward and depressed classes for unity of the Hindu community for political purpose. Gandhi's assertion of an authoritarian nature in the conference made the minorities and depressed classes alienated and apprehensive of their position and identity in the Indian society.

B.R. Ambedkar asked the Round Table Conference to make separate electorate for untouchables. He alleged that they had been oppressed for centuries by the upper caste Hindus and that Gandhi's programme was of no use to them.

Ambedkar was very much aggrieved with Gandhi's statement before the Minorities Committee on 13 November 1931. "I claim myself in my own person to represent the vast mast of the untouchables" Gandhi said. Ambedkar sought to expose Gandhism and Congress philosophy in these words : "There is caste in Hinduism, there is caste in Gandhism, Hinduism believes in the law of hereditary profession, so does Gandhism. Hinduism enjoins cow-worship. So does Gandhism, Hinduism upholds the law of *Karma*, predestination of man's condition in the world, so does Gandhism. Hinduism believes in *avatars* or incarnations of God. So does Gandhism. Hinduism believes in idols. So does Gandhism," (See Christine E. Dobbin; ed, *Basic Documents in the Development of Modern India and Pakistan*, 1970, p. 112).

No wonder, these developments actually led the British Government to thrust its communal award, stating, "This would mean that His Majesty's Government would have to settle for you, not only your problem of representation, but also to decide as wisely and justly as possible what checks and balances the constitution is to contain to protect minorities from an unrestricted and tyrannical use of democratic principles expressing itself solely through majority power" (*ibid.*, p. 111). Narrow, short-sighted, even stupid thinking prevailed in the Coconada Congress in 1923 and by 678 to 458 votes the Congress threw out C.R. Das's proposal on Bengal Pact for mutual Hindu-Muslim relationship and unity and the Congress President Mohammad Ali was threatened with censure motion.

There was to some extent a redeeming political feature but in December 1926 Motilal Nehru wrote to his son a scathing letter about the mischievous communal propaganda at the election time "under the auspices of the Malaviya-Lala Gang, aided by Birla's money, who are making frantic efforts to capture the Congress." It is revealing to find that the elder Nehru with his secrete relation with the Hindu Mahasabha added in tired tones, "I shall consult Gandhiji but as you know, his hobbies do not interest me beyond a certain point." (J. Nehru, *A Bunch of Old Letters,* Bombay, 1958, pp. 46-47).

At the Khilafat conference in Calcutta in 1928, Maulana Mohammad Ali referred to the Nehru Report's preference for dominion status, and spoke witherlingly, "You make compromises in your constitutions everyday with false doctrines, immoral conceptions and wrong ideas but you make no compromise with our 'communalists' with separate electorates and reserved seats. Twenty five per cent is our proportion of the population and yet you will not give us thirty-three per cent of the seats in the Assembly, You are a Jew, you are a bania" (*India Quarterly Register*, ed, 1928 and Hiren Mukherjee, *India's Struggle for Freedom*, pp. 135-136).

The Aga Khan put it on record that he had asked Gandhi, during 1919-22, to show himself "a real father to Indian Muslims", whereupon Gandhi, usually amiable, showed cold jesture by rejoining, "I cannot in truth say I have any feeling of parental love for Muslims"—a rather strangely un-Gandhian remark which wrote the Aga Khan, had "a chilly effect" on the ensuing conversation (Aga Khan, *Memoirs*, 1954, pp. 227-29).

To put it mildly Congress repelling Muslim League advances for agreement in 1937 was "a grave tactical blunder". The "others must simply line up" diktat brought about most unhappy results, for after the League leaders' overtures in the United Provinces (today's Uttar Pradesh) were rejected, it led to "train consequences which were perhaps incalculable though with a peculiar political myopia they were not at the time discerned". (Hiren Mukherjee,

Was India's Partition Unavoidable? Calcutta 1987, p. 41).

Muslim League also made a fair bid of politics at its Lucknow Session 1937, declaring "full independence in a federation of free democratic states" to be its goal. Maulana Abul Kalam Azad perhaps said the last word on the subject of Hindu-Muslim co-operation and unity in India. As he observed, "If the U.P. League's offer of co-operation had been accepted, the Muslim League party would for all practical purposes be merged in the Congress. Jawaharlal's action gave the Muslim League in U.P. a new lease of life. All students of Indian politics know that it was from the U.P. that the League was reorganised. Mr. Jinnah took advantage of the situation and started an offensive which ultimately led to Pakistan". (M.A.K. Azad, *India Wins Freedom,* Calcutta, 1959, pp. 160-62).

The last quarter of the nineteenth century saw the institutionalisation of the ground work for Muslim community in the founding of the M.A.O. College (1877) at the hands of Sir Syed Amad Khan. It played a great role for Muslim renaissance in India. Though it was established for education of the children of the Muslim community, it was open to the other communities. There was no discrimination in admission and teaching.

In the first of some 25 names, those of the Aga Khan, Jinnah, Iqbal, Hasrat Mohani, Mian Fazl-i-Hussain, Abdullah Haroon, Fazlul Haq, Hidayatullah, Mian Abdul Bari of Farangi Mahal, Mufti Kafayatulla, Moulana Hussain Ahmad Madani, Dr. Ziauddin, Zafar Ali Khan and the Ali Brothers stand out with their major role in moulding the public opinion and history of India's freedom movement.

Among these leaders Muhammad Ali Jinnah played a very important role in the Indian political movement through the 1940s.

Three dominant strands[2] in the first phase (1904-20) of Jinnah's political career were : working for self-government for India; striving for Hindu-Muslim unity since without its consummation India could not possibly put up a united demand for self-government; and bringing about unity in disparate Muslim ranks through the Muslim League, since he felt that given their legacy of reservations about the Congress there could be no Hindu-Muslim unity without the Muslims uniting among themselves first and speaking with one voice.

Jinnah added the last strand to his political programme in 1915.

These strands continued to dominate his activities during the second phase (1920-37) as well, but with the difference that with his Congress platform gone, he concentrated a good deal more on the third strand. This started from 1923 onwards when he revived the Muslim League after its eclipse during the height of the Khilafat Movement (1920-22) and served as its permanent president "to prepare the Muslims for cooperation with the Hindus in the cause of Indian freedom", as any Congress or nationalist leader did at that time.

In May 1924, when Jinnah embarked upon reviving and re-organising the Muslim League after abandonment of the Non-Cooperation Movement, he laid down that League would "not (be) in any way going to adopt a policy or programme which will, in the least degree...be antagonistic to the Indian National Congress". He also came closer to the Congress after it had suspended non-co-operation and sanctioned council entry.

And on the crucial Simon Commission (1927) issue much to the consternation of Muslim moderates, he "aligned himself completely" with the Congress, called for a total boycott, and took the lead "in breaking the back of the Simon co-operators". He considered Hindu-Muslim unity as the condition of Indian Freedom and "*Swaraj*...an almost interchangeable term with Hindu-Muslim unity".

However, on the constitutional plane under the British Colonial Rule in India, as the January 1925 Unity Conference and such other efforts had shown over the years, "the mode and quantum of Muslim representation had proved to be most vexatious question". This Jinnah tried to tackle with the four-point Delhi Muslim proposals of 20 March 1927.

The most outstanding feature of this formula was that Muslim would waive their right to separate electorates on certain conditions and provisions which "could provide them with a sense of security", in view of the rising religious communal tension and violence in the country and *scrapping* of the Lucknow Pact signed between the concerned political parties in 1916, by the new leadership of the Congress Party. The proposals called for reservation of Muslim seats according to population in their most populous provinces viz., Punjab and Bengal, extension of reforms to North-Western Frontier Provinces and Baluchistan, separation of Sindh from Bombay Presidency and one-third Muslim representation at the Centre. One school of thought holds that "In providing these conditions, Jinnah was guided by the consideration that the Muslims should be made to feel that they are secure and safeguarded against any act of oppression on the part of the majority and that they need not feel that during the transitional stage towards the fullest development of national government the majority would be in a position to oppress and tyranise the minority as majorities are prone to do in other countries".

Jinnah's proposals were in fact welcome by the Congress Working Committee on March 21, 1927, accepted by the sub-committee appointed by it to discuss in details, approved of with some minor conditions by the AICC at its May 1927 meeting at Bombay, endorsed by the Madras Congress (1927), and were applauded by its President, Dr. M.A. Ansari. These positive developments can be hardly undermined over time.

Despite these commitments, the Nehru Committee (1928) virtually rejected the Muslim proposals. At the all parties conference for consideration of the Nehru Report in December 1928 Jinnah made a "persuasive" speech appealing to the convention "not as a Muslim but as an Indian". As he said, "What we want is that Hindus and Muslims should march together until our object is obtained. Therefore, it is essential that you must get not only the Muslim League but the Muslims of India...would you be content if I were to say, I am with you? Do you want or do you not want the Muslim India to go along with you? Minorities cannot give anything to the majority. It is, therefore, no use asking me not to press for what you call these small points. If they are small points, why not concede? It is up to the majority and majority alone can give".

The conference, as expected, was dominated by the delegates from the Hindu and Sikh communities in the Congress, Hindu Mahasabha and Akali Dal –all representing the strong comprador Indian big bourgeoisie and landlord classes with their strong religious commitment and alliance with the British imperialism. The Muslim

League represented the disorganised Muslim landlords and capitalists of a weak calibre. Both the sections exploited and oppressed the masses of the Indian people at large.

Gandhi had offered Muslims proportional representation both in the legislatures and in the services in 1924, but gone back on the commitments and compromised with the forces strongly opposing it. The situation gradually turned to be worse over time.

The most important point in reference is the problem of mixing religion and politics in the Indian politics. In reply to Gandhi's letter of October 25, 1920, when Jinnah was invited by him "to share in the new life of the country", Jinnah completely disagreed with Gandhi's mix of religion and politics, and advised, "If by `new life' you mean your methods (exploitation of religion by politics and unconstitutional methods) and programme, I am afraid I cannot accept them; for I am fully convinced that it must lead to disaster...that your methods have already caused *split and division* in almost every institution that you have approached hitherto, and in the public life of the country not only amongst Hindus and Muslims and even between fathers and sons; people generally are desperate all over the country and your extreme programme has for the moment struck the imagination mostly of the inexperienced youth and the ignorant and the illiterate. All this means complete disorganisation and chaos. What the consequence of this may be, I shudder to contemplate..."[3]

As Jinnah's proposals for the solution of minority problem were rejected by the Calcutta Conference in 1928, and having been disowned by the organisation of the majority community, he sought to mend his political fences with the co-religionists' groups and leaders to evolve a unified response to the Nehru Report. In 1929, the 14-point proposal was formulated by him, which was to become the Magna Carta of the Muslim community. The Muslim position had hardened at this time. This had reaction on the Congress Party which had already ossified its stand and made its position more sectarian and ambivalent by parading its own variety of "nationalism" circumscribed with the subjective idealism thrusted by Gandhism. The *Adwaitavad* prevailed and the danger became imminent to the Congress organisation and the country.

As a result of the contradiction, political impasse reached to such a different terrain, that it could not be solved. Politics was thus inexoribly identified and mixed with the community's religion; development of nationalism and united struggle of the Indian people against the British colonialism and imperialism—the common enemy of mankind—was relegated and greatly hampered.

Among the Indian national leaders, Muslims first declared that complete independence was the object of India. Resolution to this effect was moved at the Congress and Muslim League Sessions in 1921 by Hosrat Mohani but could not be passed owing to the strong opposition. In the same year, Azad Sovani moved the issue at the All India Khilafat Conference and was passed against stiff opposition of its President Hakim Azmal Khan and his followers.

The All India Khilafat Conference on 10 July, 1922 passed the resolution that "This meeting proclaims that it is in every way religiously unlawful for a Mussalman at the present moment to continue in the British army or to induce others to join the army and it is the duty of all the Mussalmans in general and the ulemas in particular to see that these religious commandments are brought home to every Mussalman in the army".[4] Politics touched the peasants in uniform!

Mohammad Ali, proposing a change in the constitution of the Muslim League in 1921 addressed, "The existing creed was not up-to-date in view of the existing circumstances when loyalty to British Empire.and self-government within the British empire were out of the question as long as British Government persisted in their anti-Islam and anti-Indian policy.... Mahatma Gandhi and those who shared his religious beliefs maintained that we use peaceful means to fight the Government now and for ever, but the Muslim faith went a step further and said that if the existence of the evil could not be removed without violence it must be removed with violence. Force could be used to defeat force. Today, however, Indian Muslims recognised that they were not in a position to oppose force of Government but if the Government's anti-Indian policy continued and peaceful means were useless then there will be use of force if required".[5]

All India Khilafat Organisation continued its campaign and

organisational activities for Indian freedom movement through the 1920s. As Mohammad Ali declared at its Calcutta Conference in 1928 :

"In the all parties' convention I had said that India should have complete independence and there was no communalism in it. Yet I was heckled at every moment and stopped during my speech at every step. Today, they want to have the whole world admit every letter of the Nehru Committee Report. Today Mahatma Gandhi and Sir Ali Imam would be sitting under one flag and over them would fly the flag of the Union Jack".[6]

"The Nehru Report had at its preamble admitted the bondage of servitude and Pandit Motilal's resolution was the worst of all. Dr. Ansari, the President of the All Parties' Convention, was a mere puppet in the hands of Pandit Motilal Nehru and that Mr. J.M. Sengupta has put on the same garb. Only the other day they passed a resolution for *Swaraj* within the British Government if possible and without it if necessary and the time had come for them to say that *Swaraj* must be without the British Empire and yet he (Motilal Nehru) said it (Dominion Status) was freedom. The link is nothing but a missing link... Freedom and Dominion status are widely divergent things.

"I will declare before you that the goal of the Indian Mussalmans is complete independence of India".[7]

Political developments thus exposed the self-contradiction, prevarication and compromising attitude of the leadership of Congress Party. Congress Party's ambivalent stand indicated the very subjective idealism and opportunism of the top Congress leadership. That Congress equated and substituted Dominion status[8] for independence is also evident from the speech of M.K. Gandhi at the Round Table Conference in 1931. As a result, there came the great divide and suspicion between the two communities. Maulana Mohammad Ali who was prosecuted for sedition and imprisoned and said against the British that "force could be used to defeat force",[9] latter on, had to write to the British Prime Minister Ramsay Macdonald in 1931 declaring that :

"Mahatma Gandhi and Motilal Nehru are following the footsteps of the Hindu Mahasabha. I am ready to help your

Government with all the forces at my command".[10] Maulana Abul Kalam Azad regretted that "The revolutionary groups were recruited from the Hindu middle class. In fact, all the revolutionary groups were actively anti-Muslim".[11] This only exposes the sectarianism in politics.

The leftist writer Gopal Halder wrote : "Revolutionary terrorism failed in one vital matter—it could not enlist active Muslim support".[12] It is Gandhi who wrote in 1922 among all other things, that he preferred his own liberation most and that he was at first Hindu then a patriot. He said in 1924 that we (Hindu community) would have to go on meditation for self-purification to win the hearts of the Muslims!

Thus, religiously differentiating two sections of the Indian people, Gandhi sought to address his politics of non-violence and non-co-operation. Without adhering to the materialist philosophy and comprehensive long-term constructive approach for forging real unity to combat the British imperialism Gandhi's stand proved to be weak, fragile and ambivalent, exposing subjectivism and negation of the idea and principle of social democracy in a vast colonial country like India.

On Hindu-Muslim unity, Gandhi wrote on 8.4.1919 : "I believe myself to be an orthodox Hindu and it is my conviction that no one who scrupulously practises Hindu religion may kill a cow-killer to protect a cow. There is one and only one means open to a Hindu to protect a cow and that he should offer himself as a sacrifice if he cannot stand its slaughter. Even if a very few enlightened Hindus thus sacrificed themselves, I have no doubt that our Mussalman brethren would abandon cow-slaughter. But this is *satyagraha*, this is equity; even as, if I want my brother to redress a grievance, I must do so by taking upon my head a certain amount of sacrifice and not by inflicting injury on him. I may not demand it as of right. My only right against my brother is that I can offer myself as a sacrifice.

"It is only when the Hindus are inspired with a feeling of pure love of this type that Hindu-Muslim unity can be expected. As with the Hindus, so with the Mussalmans".[13]

This demonstrates his extreme subjective idealism, irrationality and nothing else. Even Swami Vivekananda of nineteenth century, did not sanction cow protection for the cause of *Hinduism*.

On the issue of cow-slaughter, Gandhi wrote[14] to Maulana Abdul Bari on 8 November 1921, "Could you not pay a visit, and I am sure that both the Mohammedans and the Hindus of Hosangabad will give you a respectful hearing....will you please convey my thanks to Maulana Sahib of Phulwari for his decision to stop cow killing?"

And it was an expression of the necessity of accommodation that had spelt out at length in his letter to the Maulana Abdul Bari written from the Sabarmati Jail on March 15, 1922. "I have come to the conclusion", wrote Gandhi "that the only conclusive demonstration of Hindu-Muslim unity is the universal adoption by them of the spinning wheel and Khaddar spun and woven by the hand...for me the spinning wheel and Khaddar have *a deep religious significance* because it means Hindu and Muslim sympathy for the poor people who were dying today from hunger and disease". The Mahatma evidently had converted the Maulana, because he wrote later, "I was glad when you told me that you were going to spin regularly if I was imprisoned... May I ask you then to use your great influence (on the) Mussalman brethren on behalf of the spinning wheel and Khaddar". This understanding and cooperation between the two communities grew on certain issues related with the demonstration of unity. This was very evident when Maulana Abdul Bari became one of the first 25 signatories to the *Satyagraha* pledge that Gandhi released on February 24, 1919.

Thus, cow protection, spinning wheel and Khaddar with their religious connection and importance came to be incorporated in the *satyagraha* and Indian political movement. The reality of the broad unity centering around the life the communities formed over the centuries was quietly overlooked. By 1919 Congress of Amritsar was overshadowed with the ominous Hindu religious caucus of Swami Sraddhanand, Annie Besant, Motilal Nehru, Madan Mohan Malaviya and Gandhi in the leadership. Dr K.B. Hedgewar who later formed RSS was also in the delegation. This axis with its characteristic symbols became so much vicious that Gandhi assailed Rammohan as a "pigmy", and his crooked disciples used insulting words against poet Rabindranath Tagore and philosopher Brajen

Sil for their opposition to the idea of *Charka* and *Khaddar*. Development confirms that the old Congress led by the liberals that had been free from religious influence, was gradually transformed into an organisation politicking with the Hindu religious idioms, symbols and spiritualism at large in a very critical period of India.

M.A.K. Azad, on the Hindu-Muslim Pact signed by Chittaranjan Das, observed that this bold declaration moved the base of the Congress Party in Bengal and so many congressmen began smear campaign against Das who was accused of opportunism and partiality to the Muslims. It was a matter of regret that, after Das's death, some of his followers undermined his ideal and this declaration was rejected. As a result, Azad wrote, the Muslims of Bengal left the Congress organisation and seed for division of the country was sown.

It is important to refer to the event that, while defending the pact signed in 1923, Chittaranjan warned that "who were opposing the Hindu-Muslim Pact, they were acting as spies of the foreign Government". On 13 June 1926, Sarat Chandra Bose proposed in the General Body Meeting of the Bengal Provincial Congress Committee, that Hindu-Muslim Pact was not a matter of consideration for the countrymen.

Chittaranjan Das submitted that communal harmony was the *sine qua non* for the united struggle for independence from the British colonial power. But, for its implementation, he did not ask for reforming the attitude of the militant nationalist organisation largely wedded to Hindu religion and its rites, of which he was a great patron. He did not have a broad strategy. His political philosophy was not firmly based on objective reality. It was inexpedient on his part to make a rupture with the old liberal leaders of the Congress who always stood for, and strived to maintain communal harmony at all costs. Surendra Nath Banerjee tried to make Raja of Mahmudabad as President of the Congress in 1917 as a follow-up measure of the Lucknow Pact signed between the Congress and the Muslim League in 1916. Against this move, Chittaranjan supported candidature of Annie Besant, the confirmed theosophist leader, as President of the Congress in the same year. This exposed contradiction in the political thought and attitude of Chittaranjan

Das, who later formed Swaraj Party.

The same contradiction can be found in the activity of Gandhi. He was apparently eager for communal understanding and harmony in the society but actually *invoked* Rama as the soul in the society and in the ethos of Congress politics. He did not at all show interest to accept and implement the Lucknow Pact as the charter of communal harmony and united political action by political campaign among the masses of the Indian people at that crucial time of history and Indian politics. Contradiction in the political approach and action of the new Congress leadership confirms that communalism was reared and brought up inside the political organisation and, after the Amritsar Congress in 1919, Hindu religious axis of a particular shade, became distinct, real and powerful in the leadership of the Congress. Its own resolution of responsive cooperation 1919 made with the assent of Tilak and Jinnah, was foiled with the non-cooperation of 1920.

In general, the function of the old liberal leadership of the Congress was basically confined to the parliamentary reforms in the British colonial regime. They joined the Indian Government under the British rule without prejudice. Gandhi's Congress did the same with much verbiage in the later period.

Gandhi, in his *Hind Swaraj* viewed British Parliament as the prostitute mother of all parliaments in the world. But, on the contrary, he capitulated to the constitutionalism of the same British Parliament for the future Government of India. Congress Party leaders in the Gandhian regime, after making too much smokescreen of opposition and haggling, like the old liberals, had accepted office according to the colonial law and under the authority of the British Crown. Congress resolved for independence of India in 1927 but retreated to the position of Dominion status for India in 1928. Congress also resolved that the Constituent Assembly of India would be formed directly on the basis of free adult franchise of the Indian people but again succumbed to the British manoeuvring and design of indirect representation on restricted franchise conducted by the British rule in India in 1945-46. The vast majority of the Indian people were kept out of the constitutional process. The "largest democracy" of India was thus grafted by the British imperialism with its parliamentary legislaiton to suit its own long-term economic interest.

Such were the gross anomalies and contradictions in the actions of the Congress—the instances of prevarication and compromise—under the leadership of Gandhi and company during the 1920s through 1940s.

All this shows subjectivism, anarchism and opportunism of the Congress Party of the comprador bourgeoisie of India. M.K. Gandhi did not even feel the necessity to keep the issue of cow-protection outside the political organisation by adhering to the secular rules framed by the founder leaders of the Indian National Congress.

On 29 May 1924 Gandhi wrote, "for me the only question for immediate solution before the country is the Hindu-Mussalman question. I agree with Mr. Jinnah that Hindu-Muslim unity means *Swaraj*. I see no way of achieving anything in this afflicted country without a lasting heart unity between Hindus and Mussalmans of India. I believe in the immediate possibility of achieving it, because it is so natural, so necessary for both, and because I believe in human nature... The key to the situation lies with the Hindus. We must shed timidity or cowardice. We must be brave enough to trust, all will be well".[15] This was an open script but not a fine script of his mind.

Why were the Lucknow Pact of 1916 and the Congress resolution for responsive cooperation 1919 were put into the cold storage and abondoned? Why the Bengal Pact showing the intention and practical steps towards Hindu-Muslim unity was not entertained and accepted by the Congress leadership in 1923? Gandhi himself backed out of his promise of proportional representation for the Muslim population. Where was the truth and trust of this "philosopher"? In fact, his philosophical muddle is very wide and unspeakable.

Gandhi sermoned on 26 December 1924 : "I share Maulana Shaukat's robust optimism that the present tension is a mere temporary distemper. The Khilafat agitation in which Hindus made common cause with their Mussalman brethren and the non-co-operation that followed it caused an awakening among the hitherto slumbering masses. It has given a new consciousness to the classes as well as the masses." "...A *Swaraj* government means a government established by the free joint will of Hindus, Mussalmans and others. Hindus and Mussalmans, if they desire *Swaraj*, have perforce to settle their difference amicably... The majority must set the example of self-sacrifice".[16]

Did the majority at all set the example of wisdom by considering some of the reform proposals not to speak of its self-sacrifice? It could not, as the wild centralism, thrust and superimposition from above became the order of Indian politics of the Gandhian clique installed by the comprador capitalists and landlords of the majority community of the country.

The Indian National Congress under Gandhi felt no serious concern for the rational thought, democratic thinking and aspiration of the masses of the Indian people, of the regional and state units and territories and had no democratic centralism in the organisation. As a result, the political situation gradually deteriorated with strong religious and communal tenor which was detrimental to the interest of the country and the people.

There was enough evidence of subjectivism dominating through the idea of constitutional reformism in the Indian politics. The Constitution of the Indian National Congress adopted at Nagpur session (1920) read "The object of the Indian National Congress is the attainment of *Swarajya* by the people of India by all legitimate and peaceful means". The words "*Purna Swaraj*" (complete Independence)" were substituted for *Swarajya* in the amendment of 1939. In his undelivered presidential address of 1921 Chittaranjan Das said, "I am willing to co-operate with England, but on one condition only, that she recognises this inherent right of India" (*cf. Indian Constitutional Documents*, ed., A.C. Banerjee, Vol. 3, p. 91 and p. 365). Clearly, the Congress largely reposed faith on the "conscience and generosity" of the British colonial power. Gandhism spread the illusion of "peaceful *swaraj*" among the Indian people.

But Indian people's struggles in the first quarter of the century no doubt affected and shaken the interests of both the native bourgeoisie and British imperialist capital. M.K. Gandhi, Madan Mohan Malaviya, Swami Sraddhananda, Annie Besant and Motilal Nehru—the leaders of the Congress caucus became so much obsessed with subjective thought and religiosity that they could little see the existence and reality of the *class struggles* which took place at that time. Their idealist view led them to think that *Swaraj* would come out of the British "conscience and justice"! They failed to see class struggle as the objective reality and driving force of history. They viewed the occurrence of the class struggles as "communal" and "irreligious". This attitude helped them only to side with the reaction in the name of "non-violence" and "truth". Actually this idea led some leaders to form Hindu Mahasabha and Rastriya Swayam Sevak Sangh to protect the capitalist and landlord classes in India. They were so much illusioned with the idealist philosophy that they cared little for the basic needs and democratic demands of the Indian people, followed the camp of the exploiters and asked for a "peaceful *Swaraj*" from the oppressive British imperialist power in India by falsely propagating the power of spiritualism among them.

To understand the intent of such a theoretical position of the Indian leaders it would be proper to relate and compare this with the stand of the Communist party of China in the perspective of the earlier leadership of Sun-Yat Sen. The Communist Party of China, the nascent party of the Chinese working class, held its second Congress in May, 1922 and issued a manifesto which raised aloft the battle flag of struggle against imperialism. The manifesto stated that, in the eighty years since the Opium War, imperialist aggression against China had virtually reduced it to *a colony*. It continued, "The process of imperialist aggression against China in the past has fully revealed the true nature of world capitalist imperialism. The mouths of the capitalist powers water as they look at the vast fertile lands of China, its unlimited riches and teeming millions of cheap labour. They fight with one another for the most advantageous privileges, and this accounts for China's present special status in the field of international relations".

It described in detail how Japan, the United States and Britain fought for privileges in China after World War I (1914-1918) and arrived at the conclusion that "The Washington Conference has created a new situation in China. Rival aggression by the imperialist powers, which went on for many years past, has not turned into concerted aggression. Such concerted aggression is bound to deprive the Chinese people completely of their economic independence and reduce the four hundred million oppressed people of China to slaves of the international trusts, these masters of a new type. The time has come when we cannot but rise to give battle, for the Chinese people face a life-and-death struggle." (Hu Sheng, *Imperialism and Chinese Politics*, Peking, 1981, pp. 290-91).

The manifesto explained that capitalist imperialism depended on ruthless exploitation of the colonies for its very existence, and that the scramble for colonies by the imperialist powers had led to the outbreak of World War I. It stressed that "China like other nations of the East, had for many years been trampled under foot by Britain, the United States, France and Japan."

From the facts, it becomes clear that although India was a vast colonial country things took a different turn and character through the ill motive and design of petty parliamentary reforms by the British imperialism and "legitimate and peaceful means" of the Congress Party for attaining *Swaraj*. They were alarmed with the rising tide of people's anti-colonial struggle. Assessment and position of the Congress Party about India was quite opposite to the concrete analysis of the Chinese society by the Communist Party of China. In consequence, communalism and the colonial parliamentarism and compromising philosophy in politics swayed, confirming the vile comprador character of the Indian bourgeoisie.

While this untoward trend persisted in the petty constitutional politics of the colonial India, there began an inspiring endeavour for the secular literature absorbing the economic condition of the people, class struggle and criticism of the social prejudices and developments in the world arena. Its message was quite enlivening and radical to the broad masses of the people fighting for the independence of India.

As early as in 1914 Rabindranath Tagore wrote that "At present, the Hindu, for some particular reasons, have became ferocious to resist with its own *Hindutva*. The bent of his mind in this regard, is not very normal. In building up the world, as if, *Hindutva* would be the ultimate creation of the supreme power and on exerting all his efforts for this work, he could not proceed further by any meansand this had became the Hindu's catch word." (Tagore, *Collected Works*, Vol. 93; 1958, p. 364).

This marked, as earlier stated, the advance of the subjective idealism—the *Vedanta* philosophy and powerful revival of spiritualism in Indian politics which, the liberal and moderate political leaders like Surendranath Banerjee, Mohammad Ali Jinnah rightly apprehended and strongly resisted its infiltration in politics. Tagore opposed spiritual arrogance tooth and nail. He was influenced with Rammohan's rationalist thought and works.

Tagore held that the eminent persons made their faith firm by joining it with the God. That faith as the divine order, proved to the Gandhi's ideal, inspite of the grave mistakes; and there was the necessity of adding many more precious new ingredients in the creative model of the Mahatma. If this addition did not take place through patience and regards, with his own co-operation, it would amount to a total loss. Tagore in his letter dated 20.5.1939 addressed to Amiya Chandra Chakraborty, acknowledged that his view was not in agreement on all subjects, with the view of the Mahatma. Tagore wrote that the faith upon the English nation became so deep that the political leaders of India had thought that the path of independence for a conquered nation would be paved by the generosity of the conquering nation. India was occupied and illusioned in all respects by the English rule. Its distressing want was not merely of food, cloth, education and health care; that problem was the very cruel self-estrangement among the inhabitants of India which had no comparison in the Muslim self-governed countries outside India.

Imperialism, in the opinion of Tagore, is the python's unity policy. There is meeting between one nation and another but they do not unite. By chance, if Britain lost India some day it would sigh : I meet my best servant. The character of Europe is atrocious. It takes time to contain sin internally, but they (western powers) cause no delay to annihilate man. Imperialism or fascism, in itself, creates its *own destruction*. It is impossible to have regard on the eulogy of civilisation of the western nation. The latter has demonstrated only its physical force but not the image of liberation. (*cf.* Rabindranath Tagore, *Kalantar* : Bengali, 1993, pp. 183, 185, 287, 292, 373, 376, 377 and 413-414).

The great October Revolution of 1917 in Russia opened a new

vista of ideas before the people and it made cataclysmic change in India's view of Russia. It made a deep impact on Urdu literature as well. Celebrities like Maulana Hasrat Mohani, Mohammad Iqbal, Saadat Hasan Manto, Krishan Chander, Rajinder Singh Bedi, Faiz Ahmed Faiz, Ismat Chughtai, Sazzad Zahir and many others enriched the literature with the ideas of national feeling, patriotism, secularism, independence and revolution. Tamil Poet Subramaniam Bharati was also very much influenced by the October Revolution. His works bear indelible impact of great social changes in Russia and its adjacent territories. Many other writers in India were influenced by this secular and radical trend of thought in the 1920s through 1940s.

Hasrat Mohani combined a taste for poetry, politics and religion. He is remembered for his Urdu Ghazals which represent refined taste of a literature. He who delved deep into the traditions of Urdu's romantic poetry. He was also a political agitator of great sincerity and faith in his cause. Lokmanya Tilak was his mentor and in his vision Hasrat was ahead of even the Congress radicals. He was a devout Muslim and still affirmed his faith in socialism, which the Soviet leaders were trying to achieve after the October Revolution. He saw no contradiction between his feeling for Islam and Socialism, and he agreed to be the chairman of the reception committee of the first conference of the Communist Party of India held in Kanpur in 1925. Later he also signed the declaration of the Progressive Writers' Association. His faith in socialism survived till the end and as member of the Constituent Assembly he moved an amendment to the effect that India should be called Union of Indian Socialist Republics.

Mohammad Iqbal, it must be said, was very much conscious of the atheistic side of Marxism. He also had a tendency for a Pan-Islamic view and judged things from Islamic standpoint. On one occasion, he described Marx as an unidentified Moses, an uncrucified Christ "whose writing has almost the inspiration of a scripture without the illuminating flash of the divine revelation". Notwithstanding the reservations about Marxism which he spelt out, Iqbal could not restrain himself from expressing his admiration for the Bolshevik concern for the capitalist society's underdog (the workers, peasants and toilers). A good number of his poems bear testimony of the impact the Russian Revolution had in his mind. In one of his poems, God asks his angels to awaken the poor of the world. In another he makes Lenin say things before God which the founder of the Soviet state would have said. "Reading such examples of Urdu verse one can justifiably say that admiration for the Soviet system had made Iqbal, one of the greatest Indian poets of this century. There are others who will dispute this claim. The debate has been going on since the poet's death" (Som Anand, Long Arm of Lenin, *The Statesman,* Miscellany, November 29, 1987). Iqbal wrote the celebrated *Tarana-i-Hind* (Song of India) in 1903 on the occasion of the first anniversary of Lahore's *Youngmen's Indian Association*. That was a period when intense patriotism was the dominant note of his poetry. It preached the ideal of a united and free India where Muslims and Hindus could live together. Iqbal's first Urdu work was a patriotic poem titled *Himala* addressed to the mighty sentinel of the sub-continent. The poet showed as much reverence to Hindu deities and *rishis* as to Muslim saints and sufis. He translated into Urdu the *Gayatrimantra* of the Hindu scriptures along with a detailed elucidation of it from the Islamic point of view. What made Iqbal internationally famous was his six-volume Persian poetry revealing the principles affecting the development of human personality and ideal of universality.

Condoling Iqbal's death, Rabindranath Tagore remarked, "Iqbal's death has created a void in India's literature that would take a very long time to fill" and noted that "India has lost a poet whose work had a great universal appeal" (*cf.* Abdus Subhan, "Poet of the East," *The Statemen*, Calcutta, 18 August, 1998).

As a philosopher Iqbal had a deep insight to the constitution and functioning of the Indian society. In his presidential address to the Muslim League in December 1930, in the surcharged communal situation of the country, he said, "I have no hesitation in declaring that if the principle that the Indian Muslim is entitled to full and free development on the lines of his own culture and tradition in his own Indian home-lands is recognised as the basis of a permanent communal settlement he will be ready to stake his all for the freedom of India. The principle that each group is entitled to free development on its own lines is not inspired by any feeling of narrow communalism. There are communalisms and communalisms. A community which is inspired by feelings of ill-will towards other communities is low and ignoble. I entertain the highest respect for the customs, laws, religious and social institutions of other communities. Nay, it is my duty according to the teachings of the Quran, even to defend their places of worship, if need be. Yet I love the communal group which is the source of my life and behaviour and which has formed me what I am by giving me its religion, its literature, its thought, its culture and thereby recreating its whole past as a living operative factor in any present consciousness. Communalism in its higher aspect, then, is indispensable to the formation of a harmonious whole in a country like India. The units of Indian society are not territorial as in European countries. India is a continent of human groups belonging to different races, speaking different languages and professing different religions. Their behaviour is not at all determined by a common race consciousness. Even the Hindus do not form a homogeneous group. The principle of European democracy cannot be applied to India without recognising the fact of communal groups. The Muslim demand for the creation of Muslim India *within* India is, therefore, perfectly justified. The resolution of the All Parties Muslim Conference at Delhi, is, to my mind, wholly inspired by this noble ideal of a harmonious whole which, instead of stifling the respective individualities of its component wholes, affords them chances of fully working out the possibilities that may be latent in them." (*Basic Documents in the Development of Modern India and Pakistan*' Christine E. Dobbin, ed., 1970, pp. 97-98).

The inability of the Nehru Committee to accept and incorporate in its report (1928) some of the reforms proposed by the Muslim League frustrated the aspiration of the Muslims then comprising nearly a quarter of the Indian population. The Lucknow Pact signed between the two major Indian political parties in 1916 was earlier put into oblivion by the Congress Party under the Gandhian leadership. Later on, Gandhi's role in the Second Round Table Conference turned to be arbitrary and ineffective. As one historian has observed, "He estranged Muslims and untouchables by claiming to represent all India."[17] Indian politics was marked with a great philosophical decline and unprecedent communalism.

Mohammad Ali, who whole-heartedly co-operated with Gandhi and organised Non-Co-operation and Khilafat Movement on a much wider scale, under the circumstances, felt isolated and became receptive to the prevailing mood of his community. He now saw motive of the Congress game, and came out in favour of Jinnah's 14 points and a separate Muslim identity. He then talked of "the deep seated differences that divide the Hindus and Muslims"[18] arguing that a "community that in India alone must now be numbering more than 70 million cannot be easily called a minority in the sense of Geneva minorities".[19] He demanded that "in Muslim provinces, Muslims should be allowed to have their majority.....as the Hindus have everywhere else";[20] and that "the Central unitary government should not over-ride them (Muslims) everywhere".[21]

This was Maulana Mohamad Ali's last political testament as he discussed the Indian constitutional problem on his death bed at the time of the Round Table Conference in January, 1931. Indeed the main issue was typically related with the assignment of power and jurisdiction of the Central and state governments in the vast Indian sub-continent, a major political problem, which is real and remains still current today.

It shows how subjective obsession, despite considerable progress of objective idealism, had prevailed and worked through the arbitrary concept of unitarianism, insistence of majoritarianism and Hindu cultural ethnocentrism in its origin and drawing inspiration from the *Vedanta* philosophy. It failed to assure and accommodate the other important sections of the Indian people in the common struggle against the enemy and for independence and social progress of India. It had created on opposite reaction to rouse the sentiment of the Muslim community in their religious perception and doctrine. Subjectivism prevailed on the rationality and social necessity of humanity only to pamper the politics of religious division, secretarianism and communalism—the characteristics which thwart and stifles the formation and development of a nation. But Gandhi was not the master of himself. In the practical politics, he was advised, nurtured and controlled by the comprador Indian big bourgeoisie mentally steeped at large with the Hinduism and its metaphysics—quite antagonistic to the general aspiration of the people of the country. Whatever equity enshrined in Hinduism and Islam, it was conspicuous with its absence in the economic and social life of the Indian people. That fell before the greed of private property and exploitation of man by man long ago. Exploitation of the people by the weak Muslim capitalists and landlords and merchants was no less severe than that of the Hindu capitalists and landlords in the Indian sub-continent over the years.

This class reality became evident and glaring in the speech of Mohandas Karamchand Gandhi at the Second Round Table Conference in London on 30 November 1931. Stressing that he held no brief for the terrorists and that he shall strain every nerve to achieve an "honourable settlement" for the country, Gandhi advocated, "...It is friendship I crave. My business is not to throw overboard the slave-holder and tyrant. My philosophy forbids me to do so, and today the Congress has accepted that philosophy not as a creed, as it is to me, but as a policy.... Today you have to fight the school of terrorists which is there with your disciplined and organised terrorism, because you will be blind to the facts or the writings on the wall. Will you net see the writing that these terrorists are writing with their blood? Will you not see that we do not want bread made of wheat, but we want bread of liberty; and without that liberty there are thousands today who are sworn not to give themselves peace or to give the country peace".

India's liberty by "friendship" with the exploiters and "honourable settlement" with the British colonialism and imperialism, the common enemy and oppressor of the mankind! No doubt, it is a great demonstration of the *Vedanta* philosophy—the pernicious subjective idealism that finds no contradiction anywhere in the world!

This is quite consistent with the "philosophy" and "truth" of Gandhi. For, as early as in 1915, he bluntly told in his speech at Madras Law Dinner in April 1915, "...It gives me the greatest pleasure...to redeclare my loyalty to the British Empire and my loyalty is based upon very selfish grounds.... I discovered that the British Empire had certain ideals which I have fallen in love and one of those ideals is that every subject of the British Empire has the freest scope possible for his energies and honour and whatever he thinks is due to his conscience.... And I have found that it is possible for me to be governed least under the British Empire. Hence my loyalty to the British Empire" (A.C. Banerjee, ed., *Indian*

Constitutional Documents, Calcutta, 1961, Vol. II, p., 289). How can it be the view of a nationalist leader? He became the "leader" because he held such a stance of compromise between the international capital and exploiting classes of India.

Set us proceed further. Gandhi's oracle revealed that :

Truth would remain unchangeable forever. The *Vedas* revealed truth and were boundless. The faith on God and God's existence leaves no scope of debate. Servants of God could feel Him even in a very small work. It would be possible only when the servant had recognised truth. This realisation was more true and pure than knowledge acquired through the sense perception. Whatever pure may be the knowledge from sense organs, that may be wrong. Sense duped us many a time. There was no mistake in transcendental knowledge. At first did come heart, thereafter intellect. Affirmation preceded proof. Revelation would hold, debate followed the course in its favour. Non-violence is the true subject. *Brahmacharya, Asteya, Aparigraha*—all serve the course of non-violence (*Ahimsa*). These are like forces which make non-violence successful. Non-violence is the life of truth. Without this, man would be like a beast. Body, is also a *dharmakshetra*; conflict continues in it, and the feeler, sage and poet could describe the conflict. Krishna was omniscient. In a clean heart, he is sensed like the sound of watch. If the heart is not cleaned, though the omniscient rested in heart, His location is lost. Every life is incarnation of the God. Krishna today would be full Avatar Chakraborty Samrat in Hindu religion. All religions have revealed that salvation is obtained only by making human body as the temple of God. (cf. *Young India*, 8.4.1926, 12.11.1925, 6.8.1931 and *Harijan*, 5.12.1936; and see also M.K. Gandhi, *Hindu Dharma Ki :* (Bengali) National Book Trust, 1996, pp. 21, 29, 52, 59, 61, 63 and 68).

All these characteristic features and attributes noted from the writings of Mohandas Karamchand Gandhi confirm the continuity, extension and deep impact of the monstrous *Adwaita Vedanta* on the Congress philosophy and Indian politics. These ideas were also at large carried forward in the writings of the philosophers like Bhagaban Das, Sri Prakash and Sampurnananda of the Congress Party, based at Kashi Vidyapith and Benaras Hindu University in the 1920s and 1930s. The political consequence of this idealist philosophy no doubt helped the British imperialist power to rope in the majority of the Congress leadership to its sinister design. "The British conquered the country with the assistance and connivance of Indians themselves, and then ruled it for over a century with their collaboration and tacit consent. The empire was from start to finish far more of a joint Anglo-Indian enterprise and partnership than either party has usually been inclined to admit." (*cf.* Penderal Moon, *The British Conquest and Domination of India,* 1999)

NOTES

1. See Abdus Subhan, The Grand Old Man of Islam, *The Statesman,* Calcutta, 4 April, 1999, p. 7.
2. See Sharif Al Mujahid, "Nehru's Report, Jinnah's Points", *The Asian Age,* Calcutta, 11 January, 1999, p. 13 and M. P. Bhandara, Jinnah's Mission for Minorities, *The Asian Age,* Calcutta, 6 January, 1999, p. 13.
3. "Citation" in M. P. Bhandara, *op, cit.*
4. *Indian Annual Register,* Vol. II, 1921, Calcutta, p. 173.
5. *Indian Annual Register,* Vol. II, 1921, Calcutta, p. 231.
6. See *Indian Annual Register*, 1928, Calcutta, Vol. II.
7. *Ibid.*
8. *Cf.* A. C. Banerjee, ed., *Indian Constitutional Documents,* Vol. III, A. Mukherjee & Co. (P) Ltd., Calcutta, 1961.
9. "Citation" in Bimalananda Sasmal, *Swadhinatar Phanki* (Bengali), Calcutta, 1967, p. 24.
10. *Ibid.* (See also Speeches and Writings of Mohammed Ali). N.R. Inamdar ed., *Political thought and Leadership of Lokmanya Tilak,* Concept Publishing Company, New Delhi, 1983
11. Maulana Abul Kalam Azad, *India Wins Freedom,* 1958, Calcutta, p. 5.
12. Gopal Halder, *Studies in Bengal Renaissance,* Calcutta, p. 257.
13. See Rudrangshu Mukherjee, ed., *Penguin Gandhi Reader,* Penguin Books, Calcutta, 1993, pp. 259-60.
14. See Article, by Sourish Bhattacharya, in *Indian Express* (Magazine Section), Bombay, 7 February, 1999.
15. See Rudrangshu Mukherjee, ed., *op. cit,* p. 265.
16. *Ibid.,* pp. 266-67.
17. Percival Spear, *The Oxford History of Modern India,* (1740-1975). Oxford University Press, Calcutta, p. 353 and p. 361.
18. "Citation" in Sharif Al Mujahid, Unsung Hero of Khilafat, *The Asian Age,* Calcutta, 15 January, 1999, p. 13.
19. *Ibid.*
20. *Ibid.*
21. *Ibid.*

5

MATERIALISM, SOCIAL DEMOCRACY AND REFORMISM

The introduction of western logic and metaphysics, brought some changes in attitude towards social life, in India, in the later period of the nineteenth century. Idea of political institution with definite objective received attention among the western educated liberals. The liberals formed the Congress as a secular organisation under their leadership. The liberal leaders in their writings, exposed the contradiction between the colonial Great Britain and colonised India. Establishment of a political organisation, secularism and exposition of the social contradiction—the most important things—were contributions of the liberal leaders to a hierarchical Indian society. These ingredients certainly formed the basic pre-requisites for spread of radical ideas and materialist philosophy in the country. They set the trend for nearly three decades, upto 1916 through the last decade of the nineteenth century. But after this period, the counteracting idealist philosophy with religion and spiritualism propped up by a powerful section of scholars of metaphysics got ascendancy in Indian politics for obvious reasons. Gandhian ideas and the petty parliamentary reformism contemplated by the British colonial power on communal lines greatly helped the progress of this corrupt trend of idealist philosophy and it gradually undermined and suppressed the nascent secular trend of national feeling with its radical characteristics of materialism. Working class movements could not shake off this idealist standpoint to hold on its materialist base. The fall was so abysmal that in 1921-22, the Congress Party under the Gandhian leadership failed to grasp the grave import in the aggression of the Anglo-French imperialist force in the war, which was determined to reduce countries like Turkey, Iraq and Iran into semi-colonies under its domination. But, in fact, the event turned a considerable section of the Indian people against the naked colonial and imperialist aggression in the Middle East and for this cause they had been expressing dissent and concern from the earlier period.

It was a general political issue for the people of India, that was initially raised mainly by a particular section of the Indian people. Had Congress leaders adopted a broad objective world view like that of the old moderates and liberals and took a consistent anti-imperialist stand and adhered to the inter-communal pact of 1916 achieved under the aegis of the liberal leadership, no doubt, the history of Freedom movement and political history of the Indian sub-continent would have been quite different. The attitude of the Congress under hypnotic trance of subjective idealism with its deep import of Hindu religion and spiritualism actually prevented the development of an united, secular material force to combat the British colonial and imperialist rule in India. The forces against colonialism got divided. Subjective idealism within the tenet of Non-violence, Truth and *Satyagraha* triumphed against objective idealism and materialism, and it later degenerated into strong conformist, ecclectic and sectarian trend of philosophy which gripped the freedom movement in India. And that became the chief obstacle to the country's unity, social movement and progress as well.

Objectively speaking, there were, however, many historical factors and developments which had considerable impact on the philosophy and politics in India, by countering the subjective idealism propagated and practised for a strong determined school of reaction, since the beginning of India's freedom movement against the British colonialism. Bhupendra-Nath Datta observed, "The Indian struggle for freedom is a continuous one. Sometimes it is violent, sometimes it is non-violent.... All worked for the same goal—Freedom of the motherland....It cannot be denied that the revolutionary movement has been a great lever in the fight for independence. Hindu and Muslim, Sikh and Parsi, men and women have given their lives for it" (*Collected Speeches* published by the Committee of Conference of Indian Revolutionaries, 1959). It definitely set a secular trend against the communal frenzy. Many a martyr to the cause of freedom went to the gallows with the Urdu couplets on his lips. The last letter Bhagat Singh wrote, dated 3 March 1931 and addressed to his brother Kultar Singh was in Urdu. He recited a couplet of Poet Iqbal and the one which Wajd Ali Shah recited when the British arrested him from Lucknow.

Materialist thought was not absent in Indian social life. For instance, even as late as nineteenth century, it was the popular idea that the ownership of land was eternally vested with God (nature) and that no landlord or *zamindar* actually had ownership on it. Practically, in the pre-British period, landlord or *zamindar* had no absolute ownership of land in India. They were employees and agents appointed and paid by the Emperor. Village councils played a vital role in this regard. Bitter struggle for acquiring and owning agricultural and tribal forest lands is a well-known fact of the later period. Alienation of the peasants from land was one of the major causes of the armed struggle for independence in 1857.

Despite the drive of the new mode of production, village council in India retained common ownership of land and used to supervise village administration on the basis of natural division of labour in the line of heredity or occupation of the family members and necessity of the village. Many village communities co-existed in places maintaining their respective identities. People used to keep their own arms for self-defence. King was respected and he had authority and implemented the principle that material force is necessary to fight against the foreign power for independence and sovereignty of the country.

Bahadur Shah Zafar, the last Mughal emperor of Delhi in 1857, issued a letter to the Indian princes, asking their conscience to co-operate in the 'Grand Struggle for Independence'. The letter read as follows : "This is my heartfelt wish that whatever be the cost and means employed, the *Firranghis* must be driven out of the country and Hindustan may acquire her independence. After the expulsion of the English '*Kaffirs*', I have no intention to lord over the country myself..... If all the rulers and princes are willing to pool their resources and forces to be used against the '*Firranghis*', I am also prepared to surrender my authority to a body of persons agreeable to all, to take over the reins of administration."[1]

In his proclamation of the establishment of *Swaraj*, Bahadur Shah II, Emperor of Delhi, further said : "Oh, you sons of Hindusthan, if we make up our mind, we can destroy the enemy in no time! We will destroy the enemy and will release from dread our religion and our country, dearer to us than life itself."[2]

In the proclamation issued at Bareilly he declared, "Hindus and Mohammedans of India! Arise! Brethren arise! Of all the gifts of God, the most gracious is that of *swaraj*."

That the object of this uprising was to secure freedom from the alien rule is proved by the proclamation of war issued by Nana Saheb on behalf of the Mughal emperor, Bahadur Shah Zafar. In it he solicited the cooperation of all the princes and *jagirdars* to join in the *Jihad* or "holy war" declared against the British in 1857. The Emperor's proclamation read out by Nana Saheb said :

> "The English who are *Kaffirs* came to the country under the pretence of carrying on trade. Afterwards, by practising treachery, they seized all the Hindu and Mohammedan kingdoms.
>
> "The *Kaffirs* upon the strength of their acquisition of the empire have turned very arrogant, and keeping up outward appearance of justice, have most unjustly destroyed life and acquired wealth and property. They have been endeavouring to delude and convert the population of this country by inducing them to abandon their own religion and caste; but having failed by mild means to do this, they were out to use force".
>
> "Tyranny, wickedness and injustice having been much practised by the *Kaffir* English on the faithful and sin-fearing, I have been commissioned by God to punish the *Kaffirs* by annihilating them and to re-establish the Hindu, and Mohammedan kingdoms as formerly and to protect our country.
>
> "Ye heroes! This is the best time for you to avenge the wrongs and wickedness perpetrated by the *Kaffir* English, on our grandfathers and your kings! By allowing such an opportunity to escape, do not suffer the stain of being effeminate and foolish to attach to the people of the south.

> "At the present time the English, having disagreements among themselves, are quarrelling and fighting and killing each other. The French and the Russians who entertained for a long time a hatred against the English and a design to turn them out of Hindusthan have thought this a proper time to carry it out and with this intention they have been sending armies by sea these three months past. The Chinese also have declared war against these *Kaffirs*.... The Persians, the Afghans and Baluchis moreover are ready with their armies collected to aid us. In short, this is the golden time to root out completely the English from our country.[3]

The fire of revolt in Ayodhya was enkindled by Begum Hazrat Mahal and Wazir Ali Nala Khan. Rani Laxmi Bai became the leader of revolt in Jhansi. Laxmi Bai, a noble personage of the revolt mounted her horse and moved up and down her forces, encouraging and inspiring her soldiers. She died in fighting on l8th June 1858, near Gowalior. Tantyia Tope was captured by the enemy and was hanged on l8th April 1859. Nana Saheb, Begum Hajrat Mahal and Amar Singh of Jagadishpur together fled towards Nepal for organisation of forces for launching fresh attack against the British colonial power and nobody knows what happened to them there.

They fought together against the common enemy of all communities of the Indian people. They unitedly held high the banner of unity, struggle and made supreme sacrifice for the great cause of India's freedom from the atrocious British colonial rule. They lit up and carried on the bright flame of freedom and independence for the people of the country.

"The oppressive demon who has robbed us of it by deceit be able to keep it away forever? Can such an act against the will of God stand for ever? No, no. The English have committed so many atrocities that the cup of their sin is already full. To add to it, they have got now the wicked desire to destroy our holy religion. Are you going to remain idle even now? God does not wish that you should remain so; for he has inspired in the hearts of Hindus and Mohammedans the desire to turn the English out of our country. And by the grace of God and your valour they will so completely be defeated that in this our Hindusthan, there will not remain even the least trace of them", the proclamation concluded.

Thus, Emperor Bahadur Shah II correctly identified the main contradiction i.e., colonialism, which through large-scale commodity production, expanded and developed into modern imperialism, as the main enemy of India and its people. He led the first war of Indian independence in 1857 and paved the tortuous path of national liberation of India.

This great historical movement in association with the other armed struggles must be interlinked and viewed with the rationalist thought of Rammohan Roy, Vidyasagar, Dadabhai Naoroji, Madhab Gobinda Ranade, Jyotiba Phule, Ramesh Dutt and many other persons of the nineteenth century, which unfolded the social, economic and political difficulties showing the contradiction of the Indian society. It is unforgettable that Vidyasagar as early as in the 1850s castigated India's age-old Vedanta and Sankhya system of philosophy as utter false and prescribed the teaching of modern western philosophy for the sake of rationality and secularism in the society.

Since the late nineteenth century symptoms of workers struggle could be witnessed at large. It grew at a faster pace and reached a high peak in 1920-21. But, weak in leadership, it could not move forward with working class's own ideology of materialism. The Communist Party of India was formed but it could proceed very little. It is quite noteworthy that Professor Benoy Kumar Sarkar[4] translated two books on materialist philosophy viz., "Family Clan and State" by Frederick Engels and "Transformation of Wealth" by Paul Lafarge into Bengali and first introduced in 1924, the ideas of scientific socialism to the people of this country. In his introduction to the Bengali translation of Engels' book, he said that by analysing the influence of subsistence for living on the making of history of human civilisation against "subjective exposition", spiritualism and supernaturalism, Marx-Engels *liberated* the present world. He observed that this method, has cleared the thought of the present world. He particularly referred to the Communist Manifesto that expounded the main principles of materialist analysis for the first time in the world. He followed Marxist tenet and stressed that persons who do not discuss the necessities of life or economic condition and pressure on human life are unable to understand fully any subject like philosophy, religion, fine arts, literature, practices, casteism, factionalism, "*zamindari-usury*", habits and custom, law-court and police-military. This is "economic interpretation of history"[5] or "real basis of civilisation", Prof. Sarkar wrote in the preface of the Bengali translation of the books by Marx-Engels and Lafarge. He stressed that the general propositions of the works of Marx-Engels are alike the general propositions of other sciences and there is no history without the effort of understanding the life of man. There is heaven and hell difference between understanding the life of man and collection of some facts of his life.

Prof. Sarkar observed that the ability for analysing the relationship between the economic activity and civilisation had not developed before Marx-Engels. It was very difficult to articulate brain on such a vast world-wide thought. The Indian literature had no tendency to understand to what extent the livelihood of man was related with the social system of *Vedanta* philosophy, crafts, customs and superstition which grew and died out over time. People would enjoy the facility of knowing the world-wide nature of wealth from the works of Engels and Lafarge. Moreover, they would be interested to enquire into the changing character of Indian soul through the economic changes. Thousands of objective and materialist personalities of economic base are pounding upon the fortress of subjectivism built up by the philosophers from Plato to Croce over the long period of history. Their battle cry reverberates "victory, victory for Karl Marx"[6]. He also supported the Hindu-Muslim Pact signed under the aegis of Chittaranjan Das, highlighted and propagated its necessity in the building of a modern nation.

During this period, working class of India was slowly being introduced with the thoughts of Marx-Engels and of social equality. But its sworn enemy was the age-old transcendentalism based on religion, spiritualism and subjective idealism forcefully propagated by Gandhi and the Congr ss Party under his dictatorship and many others. It was the beginning of a very unequal struggle between the powerful idealism and nascent materialism in the Indian politics.

In his colonial thesis adopted by the second Congress of the

Communist International in 1920, Lenin[7] stressed the necessity for formation of Soviet as organ of power for the people and national revolution in the colonial countries like India. It is important to note that Hasrat Mohani moved the resolution for India's independence *i.e.* from the strong British colonial yoke at both the Congress and Muslim League sessions in 1921. But it could not be carried against opposition. A message from the Communist International to the 37th All India National Congress in 1922 at Gaya, was indeed very significant and emphatic : "British rule in India was established by force and is maintained by force; therefore it can and will be overthrown only by a violent revolution. We are not in favour of resorting to violence if it can be helped; but for self-defence, the people of India must adopt violent means, without which the foreign domination based upon violence cannot be ended."[8] Its message was quite clear.

The Sultan of Turkey declared a *jihad* against the invading Anglo-French forces which conspired to dismember the State of Turkey, divide and grab the Middle-East during the First World War (1914-18). The Sheikh-Ul-Islam[9] of Turkey at this time addressed the need for united national struggle of the Hindu and Muslim in India against the British rule. Revolutionaries of other countries as well as friends of India began to sympathise with the Indian freedom movement. Around the same time Lenin asked Bhupendranath Dutta, Indian revolutionary leader to gather statistical facts about peasants' organisation and analysis of economic classes in India. Lenin wrote to Datta, "We should not discuss about the social classes. I think you should abide by my thesis on colonial question, gather statistical facts about peasant's league if they exist in India".[10]

Lenin in 1920, advised Mahendrapratap, another Indian revolutionary, "Religion cannot save the people of India. In Russia, persons like Tolstoy and many people like him made the same effort but they failed. You return to India, and *propagate the idea of class-war* and it will certainly make liberation of India nearer".[11] "Unless revolution triumphs the eastern countries", Manabendranath Roy, an Indian revolutionary leader at the second Congress of the Communist International said that "the Communist movement in the west can be brought to naught.... Therefore, it is necessary to redirect efforts to furthering and raising the revolutionary movement in the East and to accept as basic the thesis that the destiny of world communism depends on the triumph of communism in the East". Disagreeing with Roy's conclusion, Lenin advised with a caution, "Com. Roy goes too far in asserting that the destiny of the West depends exclusively on the degree of development and the strength of the revolutionary movement in the Eastern countries. Despite the fact that there are five million proletarians and seven million landless peasants in India, the Indian Communists have not succeeded yet in founding a Communist Party, and even for this reason alone Com. Roy's views are largely unfounded".[12]

The message was quite educative and revealing in the context of the objective reality and condition prevailing in India at that time.

Stalin, on the basis of Lenin's theses on National and Colonial Revolution, gave an objective assessment and advice to the Communist Parties of the colonies, in his speech to the meeting of the Students of the Communist University of the toilers of the East in May 18, 1925. As for India, he observed :

"In some of these countries, India for example, capitalism is growing at a rapid rate, giving rise to and moulding more or less, numerous class of local proletarians....".

"The situation is somewhat different in countries like India. The fundamental and new feature of the conditions of life of colonies like India is not only that the national bourgeoisie has split up into a revolutionary party and a compromising party, but primarily that the compromising section of this bourgeoisie has already managed, in the main, to strike a deal with imperialism. Fearing revolution more than it fears imperialism, and concerned more about its money-bags than about the interests of its own country, this section of the bourgeoisie, the richest and most influential section, is going over entirely to the camp of the irreconcilable enemies of the revolution, it is forming a bloc with imperialism against the workers and peasants of its own country. The victory of the revolution cannot be achieved unless this bloc is smashed. But in order to smash this bloc, fire must be concentrated on the compromising national bourgeoisie, its treachery exposed, the toiling masses freed from its influence, and the conditions necessary for the hegemony of the proletariat systematically prepared. In other words, in colonies like India it is a matter of preparing the proletariat for the role of leader of the liberation movement, step by step dislodging the bourgeoisie and its mouthpieces from this honourable post. The task is to create a revolutionary anti-imperialist bloc and to ensure the hegemony of the proletariat in this bloc. This bloc can assume, although it need not always necessarily do so, the form of a single workers' and peasants' party, formally bound by a single platform. In such countries, the independence of the Communist Party must be the chief slogan of the advanced communist elements, for the hegemony of the proletariat can be prepared and brought about only by the Communist Party. But the Communist Party can and must enter into an open bloc with the revolutionary wing of the bourgeoisie in order, after isolating the compromising national bourgeoisie, to lead the vast masses of the urban and rural party bourgeoisie in the struggle against imperialism."

"Hence, the immediate tasks of the revolutionary movement in the capitalistically developed colonies and dependent countries are :

(1) To win the best elements of the working class to the side of communism and to create independent Communist Parties.
(2) To form a national-revolutionary bloc of the workers, peasants and revolutionary intelligentsia against the bloc of the compromising national bourgeoisie and imperialism.
(3) To ensure the hegemony of the proletariat in that bloc.
(4) To fight to free the urban and rural petty bourgeoisie from the influence of the compromising national bourgeoisie.
(5) To ensure that the liberation movement is linked with the proletarian movement in the advanced countries."

[J. V Stalin, *Works*, Vol. 7 (1925), p.148, I50, 151]

The intransigence of the Congress Party under Gandhi's leadership to recognise and implement the Lucknow Pact (1916), Congress Resolution of responsible cooperation (1919) amendment to the Nehru report (1928) and proposal to coalition ministry in UP in 1937 wident strife and contradiction with the Muslim Leage in the crucial period of Indian politics. The *charka*, *khadar* and *satyagraha* formed the party's holy spirit, in contrast to a real fighting spirit of an organisation against the common enemy.

The Sixth Congress (1928) of the Communist international[13], under these circumstances, observed that the basic tasks of the Indian Communists consisted in struggle against British imperialism for emancipation of the country, for destruction of all relics of feudalism, for agrarian revolution and for establishment of the dictatorship of the proletariat and peasantry in the form of a Soviet republic. These tasks, according to its approved report, can be successfully carried out only when there will be created a powerful Communist Party which would be able to place itself at the head of the wide masses of the working class, peasantry and all the toilers and to lead them against the feudal-imperialist bloc. It noted that "the union of all Communist groups and individual communists scattered throughout the country into a single, independent and centralised party represents the first task of Indian communists". While rejecting the principle of the building of the party on a two class basis, it said that the communists must utilise the connections of the existing workers' and peasants' parties with the toiling masses for strengthening their own party, bearing in mind that the hegemony of the proletariat cannot be realised without the existence of a consolidated steadfast Communist Party armed with the theory of Marxism. Organisation and conduct of strikes and political demonstrations, special attention to the training of leading party cadres from the ranks of the workers, exposition of the nationalist reformist leaders, conversion of the trade union democracy and putting the trade union apparatus into the hands of the workers' organisation of the unorganised workers, working out a programme of concrete demands for peasants and agrarian programme of action, demonstrations of workers in the towns in support of the demands of the peasants were stressed in the same document of the Communist International.

Following the principles and guidelines of the sixth Congress, the "Draft Platform of Action"[14] was framed and adopted by the newly formed Communist Party of India and sent to and published by the Communist International in the Journal *"International Press Correspondence"* of December 18, 1930. This document observed,

"The National Congress issued the Delhi Manifesto supporting Gandhi's eleven points, which represented the programme of the Chambers of Commerce and similar associations. It carried on negotiations with the liberals in prison trying behind the scenes to come to an understanding with the British Government and so forth", and "National Congress betrayed and disorganised the struggle of the toilers in 1919-21, and that Gandhism, uses "the cloak of statements on subjects viz., "love" and the "special historic mission of Hinduism". It stated, "An agrarian revolution against British capitalism and landlordism must be the basis for the revolutionary emancipation of India", and "the assistance granted to British imperialism, by the National Congress takes the shape at the present time of a consistent policy of compromise with British imperialism at the expense of the people". The party in this document called upon all the pariahs to join in the united revolutionary front with all the workers of the country against British rule and landlordism. It declared to fight for the complete abolition of slavery, caste system and the caste inequality in all its forms (social, cultural etc.). It spoke for the complete and absolute equality of the working pariahs and all the toilers of the country.

Adopting these as its guiding principles, the Communist Party of India at that time advanced the following main objects for the Indian revolution :

1. The complete independence of India by the violent overthrow of British rule. The cancellation of all debts. The confiscation and nationalisation of all British factories banks, railways, sea and river transport and plantations.
2. Establishment of a Soviet Government. The realisation of the right of national minorities to self-determination including separation. Abolition of native states. The creation of Indian Federal Workers' and Peasants' Soviet Republic.
3. The confiscation without compensation of all the lands, forests and other property of the landlords, ruling princes, churches, the British government officials and moneylenders and handing over for use to the toiling masses of peasantry,

cancellation of slave agreements and indebtedness of the peasantry to moneylenders and banks.

4. The eight-hour working day and the radical improvement of the conditions of labour. Increase in wages and state maintenance for the unemployed labour.

In the fight for partial demands of the revolutionary movement in the country, the party put forward general demands, special workers' demands, peasants' demands, soldiers' demands, toiling women's demands and youth demands.

Needless to mention, the draft platform was quite consistent with the need of materialist philosophy for labour and opposed to Gandhi's eleven-point ideal programme representing the interests of the comprador capitalists and landlords of India. The draft platform made a radical departure from Congress standpoint and approach and highlighted the basic issues towards solution of the social problems in India.

The objective situation at that time, in India, can be stated in the words[15] of the Communist International :

In India the policy of British imperialism which used to retard the development of native industry, evoked great dissatisfaction among the Indian bourgeoisie. The class consolidation of the latter which replaced its former division into religious sects and castes, and which was expressed in the fusion of the Indian National Congress (organ of the Indian bourgeoisie) with the Muslim League effected in 1916, confronted British imperialists with *a national united front* in the country. Fear of the revolutionary movement during the war compelled British imperialism to make concessions to the native bourgeoisie which found expression, in the economic sphere, in insignificant parliamentary reforms introduced in 1919. Nevertheless, a strong ferment, expressing itself in a severity of revolutionary outbreaks against British imperialism, was produced among the masses of the Indian people as a result of the ruinous consequences of the imperialist war (famine and epidemics, 1918), the catastrophic deterioration of the position of wide sections of the working population, the influence of the October Revolution in Russia and of a series of insurrections in various colonial countries (as for example, the *struggle of the Turkish people for independence).* This first great anti-imperialist movement in India (1919-1922) ended in the betrayal of the national revolution by the Indian bourgeoisie, which in the main was caused by terror before the rising wave of peasant insurrections, and also by the workers' strike against native employers. The *collapse* of the national revolutionary movement and the *gradual decline* of bourgeois nationalism enabled British imperialism once more to return to a policy of hindering the industrial development of India. The recent measures of British imperialism in India show that the objective contradictions between British colonial monopoly and the tendencies in the direction of the independent economic development of India are becoming more accentuated from year to year, and are leading to a new revolutionary crisis.

The real threat to British domination comes, *not from the bourgeois camp,* but from the growing mass movement of the Indian workers, which is developing in the form of large-scale strikes; at the same time the accentuation of the crisis in the village bears witness to the maturing of an agrarious revolution. All these phenomena are leading to a radical transformation of the political situation in India.

"In India and Egypt, we still observe, for the time being, the typical bourgeois-nationalist movement—an opportunist movement, subject to great vacillations, balancing between imperialism and revolution", Thesis of the Communist International noted in 1928. It advised that "the Communists must unmask the national reformism of the Indian National Congress and oppose all pharases of the Swarajists, Gandhists, etc., about passive resistance, with the irreconcilable slogan of struggle for the emancipation of the country and the expulsion of the imperialists".[16]

In India, in spite of the rise in religiosity and communalism following subjective idealism, there was a growing working class movement in the 1910s and that assumed importance over the years. Of much importance in the political development at that time was the emergence of a radical student group under S.A. Dange, S.V. Ghate, R.S. Nimbkar, V.D. Sathaye and R.V. Nadkarni (later joined by S.V. Despande and K.N. Joglekar), that played a very active role in Non-Co-operation Movement but became increasingly critical of Gandhi, and developed interest in Marxism through literature supplied by a rich person with socialist learnings named R.B. Lotwalla. In his *Gandhi* versus *Lenin*, written in April 1921, Dange attempted a point-by-point comparison of the philosophy of Gandhi (which he traced back to Tolstoy) with that of Lenin, and visualised a *Swaraj* which would nationalise big factories, impose a ceiling on wealth and redistribute *zamindari* land among peasants. While accepting non-violence as an effective tactic, it emphasized the need to use of no-tax and the political general strike—"If we win, we will win only by the help of the proletariat, *i.e.,* the labourers and peasantry". In 1922, an English Marxist weekly named *Socialist* came into circulation under the initiative of Dange and others. In 1920, "Navayug", a Bengali evening daily was published from Calcutta with the joint editorship of Mazaffar Ahmad and Najrul Islam, which generally espoused the cause of the workers and peasants. One group was organised in Lahore under the initiative of Golam Hossain. He was in close touch with Mohammad Ali who returned from Tashkent via Kabul. The monthly Urdu paper was edited and published by Hossain from Lahore. Singaravelu Chettiar formed a socialist group in Madras in 1922 and began to publish Labour Kishan Gazette. These papers turned to be the centres of organisation and propagation of radical ideas and socialist thought among the workers and peasants of India. Earlier, Manabendra Nath Roy and many other Indian nationalist leaders and workers reached Moscow. They met Lenin and other Bolshevik leaders, went through the documents of the second Congress of the Communist International and under the initiative and guidance of the Communist International, Communist Party of India was formed on 17.10.1920 at Tashkent. As the India contingent returned from Tashkent, they were intercepted by the Indian police and sent to prison. In 1922-23, the British-Indian government instituted Peshawar Conspiracy Case against them. In 1924, S.A. Dange, Mazaffar Ahmad, Soukat Usmani and others were arrested and prosecuted on the charge of spreading Bolshevism in India. This is known as the Kanpur Communist Conspiracy Case of 1924. Working class movements gradually spread and the communist groups also were organised in different provinces and industries. The communist groups held their first conference under the presidentship of Singaravelu Chettiar in Kanpur in 1925. The communists decided to meet again in Bombay in March 1929. The British-Indian government however swooped on them on 20.3.1929 by arresting 31 leaders, and instituted the famous Meerut Conspiracy Case. The leaders defended the workers' movement and Marxism in their Court statement. Earlier, manifestos and statements demanding Indian independence and reforms were issued by the Communist groups on the occasions of the annual conference of the Congress organisation in 1921 at Ahemedabad and at Gaya in 1922.

The 1925 conference at Kanpur, E.M.S. Namboodiripad notes in his reminisences, was a heroic effort but it did not bring about ideological and political cohesion among the scattered groups of communists in India. The groups however remained active at different centres.

The Draft Platform of Action 1930 though focused the contradiction and stressed the need for anti-imperialist struggle and agrarian revolution in India, could not solve the problems of building proletarian organisation and its activity at the all-India level. On the advice of Communist International, this crucial issue was addressed in the joint letter[17] of the Communist Parties of China, Great Britain and Germany—important sections of the Communist International—to the Indian Communists in 1932.

This letter noted that the revolutionary struggle of the Indian toiling masses for the national and social liberation had reached a turning point. The national bourgeoisie, it said, had betrayed the revolutionary people and were trying their best to preserve their influence over the toiling masses, to ward off the approaching Indian revolution. It followed the policy of counter-revolutionary compromise with British imperialism and betrayal of the revolutionary people. British imperialism, making use of counter-revolutionary national reformism widely developed the policy of repression and provocation, the organising of the reactionary elements of the country, trying to drown in blood the rising masses of workers and peasants and simultaneously continuing negotiations with the Indian bourgeoisie. Full agreement "is being hindered at the present time by the rapidly developing revolutionary movement under the conditions of the deepening economic crisis".

In spite of the fact that the process of drawing the peasant masses into the struggle was proceeding unevenly, it had already assumed such a powerful character (Guerrilla warfare in Burma and Kashmir, struggles in U.P., etc.) that on the one hand it had compelled the National Congress (which was negotiating an agreement with the imperialists) to continue pretending its sham opposition towards imperialism longer than it wished, to deceive the masses and disorganise the peasant struggle. On the other hand, it forced the British imperialists to hasten in the use of barbarous forms of mass terror to break up the people's movement. On January 7, 1932, the *Bombay Chronicle* was compelled to admit that "a noteworthy feature of the peasant movement in the United Provinces is the fact the peasants are becoming their own leaders....that the peasant movement to an ever increasing extent takes place at the initiative of the peasants themselves, and that they have identified themselves with the Congress because they could not get assistance from other organisations".

The letter observed that the events like demonstration against Gandhi, the Sholapur strike etc. showed the process of drawing the Indian proletariat into economic and political struggle, accompanied by its liberation from the National Congress was growing; and, in spite of the still existing uneven character, it was beginning more and more to assume all-India character. The historical demonstration of Bombay workers on the day of Gandhi's departure to London, and the Sholapur demonstration of textile strikers were very remarkable instances of such a struggle, against the influence of reformism in the National struggle.

The development of a spontaneous working class movement, the growth of the class-consciousness of the proletariat most definitely refuted the theory of reaction among the working masses, of a decline of their fighting spirit, of the low level of class-consciousness of the Indian proletariat outside the city like Bombay. Such theories merely show that some comrades "have not overcome their disbelief" in the power of the working class, are not in contact with the workers outside Bombay, and confuse the question of the literacy of the workers, with the level of their class consciousness.

"These comrades had brought with them, into the workers' movement, the anti-proletarian bureaucratic organisational principles of the National Congress, division into leaders and masses, and practical disbelief in the revolutionary rank and file, therefore they cannot even explain the outbreak of spontaneous economic strikers and tremendous participation of the working masses in the anti-imperialist movement."

".....The general picture of the Communist movement is not satisfactory. On the one hand there is a tremendous unprecedented development of the working-class movement. On the other hand, the Communist Party still consists of a small number (though the number is increasing) of weak groups often isolated from the masses, disconnected with each other, not politically united, and in some places not clearly differentiated from national reformism, adopting a conciliatory policy toward it. Instead of a struggle for a united all-India Communist Party, we find socialism, provincialism, self-isolation from the masses, etc., which though it could be understood to some extent in 1930, now represents the *main* danger to the revolutionary proletarian movement", the letter observed. The letter continued, "The biggest mistake made by Indian Communists consists in the fact that in reality, they stood aside from mass movement of the people against British imperialism. In spite of the fact that the documents of the Communist movement refer to this mistaken policy, no change has yet taken place, and self-isolation from the struggle for independence still exists". "The self-isolation of the communists from the anti-imperialist struggle, alleged to be a purely Congress movement, has created confusion in the Communist ranks. It helped to increase the disbelief in the strength of the proletariat and the growth of its class consciousness among the Communist-intellectuals."

The letter objectively stated that "participation in the anti-imperialist movement is closely connected, and interwoven with the energetic participation of Communists in every struggle for the economic interests of the working masses, with the most energetic support, organisation and development of the peasant struggle, the agrarian revolution and the attraction to their side of all revolutionary democratic elements who are prepared to struggle against British imperialism" and that the prerequisite for a correct policy for communists in the anti-imperialist movement is a definite, sharp, clear and upcompromising struggle and exposure of the National Congress and especially the "left" national reformists". It emphasised the necessity "to participate in all mass demonstrations organised by the Congress, coming forward with our own communist slogans and agitation to support all the revolutionary student demonstrations", and asked to demonstrate that the Communist Party "is the leader of the toiling masses and the only leader of the anti-imperialist and agrarian revolution in practice". It pointed out that "it is also incorrect to consider the slogan of a general strike according to the attitude of the trade union leaders. The majority of the Indian trade unions leaders are bureaucratic, non-mass organisations, acting against the interest of the working masses, without contact with them. At the present time, the strength of these reformist trade unions is the result of the poor activity of the proletarian revolutionaries, of disorganisation in the workers' ranks, and the fact that the national reformists utilise the anti-imperialist sentiment of the working class."

The same document observed "The task of Communists is to come forward in deeds not in words as initiators of the struggle of the workers. To start to organise strike committees, composed of rank and file workers and using the assistance of all revolutionary democratic organisations...".

It clearly advised, "It is time to get rid of bad traditions in the trade unions (the traditions of bureaucratic methods of work from above, the division into leaders and rank and file) and to start to form mass trade unions with elected management committees, consisting of workers from the bench, regularly functioning and in contact with the working masses, boldly promoting workers, supporting them and in every way developing their initiative and self-reliance". Position of self-isolation "must be considered extremely harmful and dangerous to the further development of the communist movement at the present time" and "it must be recognised that the party organisation has not carried out a correct policy; instead of a struggle for the party, it has in reality, taken the line of provincialism. Instead of helping the local groups, it has taken up the position of self-limitation, and reducing the whole party merely to a local organisation, not linked with other local organisations. Instead of rousing and organising the ideological struggle for the party developments it hindered the working out of a united party line, and played a great negative role in the formation of a Communist Party. Communist groups, the letter mentioned, "proved unable to rise above the provincial horizon".

The existence of the party as a number of isolated groups, in the document's words "brings about complaints that there are no forces, no comrades available, that it is impossible to cope with the great tasks facing the revolutionary movement, Hence we often find passivity, despondency, mutual disputes, deviations of all kinds, sectarianism and an opportunist attitude to national reformism, in which the possibility of splits, on an unprincipled basis, becomes very great". It stressed that the only correct form of organisation to secure this contact (with the wide masses), and the fighting ability of the party is the system of factory cells. Particularly in India, under condition of terror and comparatively high concentration of the proletariat; "the formation of factory cells is absolutely essential, obligatory and highly important task of the party". The document concluded that "the Indian bourgeoisie is once more betraying and selling the revolutionary people for a mass of pottage" and that "there can be no greater crime than if the Indian Communists (having their platform of action and agreeing with the present letter) instead of struggle for the greater historical aims of the Indian and world proletariat, follow the path of unprincipled factional struggle, fractions and personal groupings. Unprincipled factional struggle will play *into the hands* of the British imperialists. True communist groups must put the interest of the proletariat above everything else, direct all their efforts towards the rapid formation of the Communist Party, settling all questions of dispute within the framework of the Communist International and if necessary with its assistance" (Italics in the original). What was needed was the sufficient Bolshevist firmness and courage and decisiveness to enter the wide All-Indian arena of struggle for the party—the leader and organiser of the Indian revolution. The letter thus concluded.

One year later, in 1933, the Communist Party of China addressed[18] another letter dated 15 July 1933 asking the Communist

Party of India not to allow any factions and groupings and that it must carry on a consistent struggle against all deviations from the Bolshevik line. It pointed out that the bourgeois leaders of the National Congress were crawling on their knees before the British oppressors only for a few crumbs.

It spoke of the necessity to throw aside the Gandhite policy of non-resistance and protection of the interests of the exploiters and follow the path of revolutionary struggle pointed out by the Communists, and so the task of the Communists was to enter and take charge of all the democratic movements of discontent against the existing order. The letter said that "in India owing to conciliatory position of the bourgeoisie, the tactics of the all-embracing united national front could not find application even at the early stages of the anti-imperialist and agrarian revolution. In India it can only be a question of the policy of the revolutionary block of the workers and the basic masses of the petty bourgeoisie. Of course this means a bloc of the masses and not combinations of leaders." "The duty of the Indian communists is to raise the banner of struggle against the (anti-national) constitution (of Motilal Nehru), develop it on the lines of mass movement, linking it up with the strike movement in defence of the immediate demands of the masses, directing it to support the general strike, non-payment of rent, debts and taxes and the liberation of the political prisoners" and that "there is no apathy among the Indian people". Criticising the Indian Communist leaders, the letter said, "you have not yet learned to build a mass trade union organisation, you do not know how to work well in the factories, you do not organise and attract active workers into the struggle and into the party, you do not carry on everyday organisational preparatory work, you do not take the initiative into your hands in the struggle for the unity of the working class, you do not adopt the tactics of the united front in the workers' organisations and do not carry work in the reformist trade unions", and that "some Indian Communists were unable to understand that the struggle against reformism does not necessarily mean a split in the mass organisations and should not lead to the Communists and the class-conscious workers leaving those trade unions which are headed by reformists and national reformists. Such a sectarian policy has only strengthened the position of the bourgeoisie and their agents. At the same time some other Communists have not understood that the work in the reformist trade unions or unity with the national reformist trade union organisations (which you should not decline even now) presupposes a tireless struggle of the Communists against reformism, for Communist policy, for slogans and proposals".

The letter concluded with the words, "the foremost and most important task of the Indian Communists remains the task of uniting their forces.

"Forward to the formation of the All India Communist Party".

While the process of analysis, criticism and counselling and rectification started in the organisation, the government formally declared a ban on the Communist Party of India on 23 July, 1934. The party, its committees, sub-committees and branches became unlawful associations under the Criminal Law Amendment Act of 1908. In Punjab five associations were declared unlawful, in Bombay it was five, in Madras one and in Bengal thirteen associations were declared unlawful towards the end of 1934.

Philosophy in contrast to the subjective idealism was thus making its inroads and slow advance in the Indian politics during the 1920s and 1930s. We have already referred to the organisation and spread of class struggle, formation of communist party and conspiracy cases instituted by the British colonial power against the new born organisation of the Indian working class.

A major philosophical approach and thrust appears to have been made in an important address by Prof. M. Sharif,[19] president, Logic and Metaphysics section of the Indian Philosophical Congress in 1936. As he realistically stated, "Recently two great social movements have almost shaken the very foundations of the existing social order. By these I mean fascism and communism. The former has its philosophy still in making, but the latter is backed by a complete philosophical doctrine. As you are all aware, this doctrine is called dialectical materialism.....it certainly is a philosophical doctrine, and as such it can be viewed as a theory of existence, a theory of knowledge, a theory of social life and a theory of the fundamentals of economics. Dialectical materialism, as a theory of existence, declares that reality is *material* in the sense that it is fundamentally *concrete* and *objective and not ideal and subjective*. The various forms of idealism (rational, empirical, transcendental and dialectical) propounded by a whole train of idealists from Plato to Hegel and Hegelianism are all false. Reality is essentially in existence. Primarily it consists of just the world of concrete objects which in "scientifically controlled perception" and "ideas induced" thereby we know in their entirety. Our scientific knowledge truly reflects the world of objects and the proof of it lies in human action."

Thus reality being just the world of concrete objects, many of which are reproducible, all religious entities, God, angels, soul and the like, are mere mental fictions and false notions. They have no concrete reality. The objects of the concrete world of objects, *are not fixed, static, external, immutable, "fully fashioned"* entities. Nor are they made of fixed, eternal, immutable entities, like the atoms of Democritus, the numbers of Pythagoras, the monads of Libnitz or the 92 elements of old chemistry. ......The stars, the planets, stones, trees, animals, men, atoms, electrons and the ether are all in a state of interaction and motion, ever changing their qualities and passing from one into another. Everything in the world of objects is perpetually changing and its change is not a mere mechanical change determined by sheer external forces. Objects are self-moving, which means, they are processes and processes are essentially organic, each being "qualitatively more in its totality than the sum" of its parts and involving *development* or ascent from the lower to the higher. They are in time, have a beginning and an end and a history in between. Existence itself is in time and has a history. The doctrine of the evolution of organic species is now universally accepted. Nor is the theory of the evolution of inorganic matter of the universe from original nebulae to the "ever hardening, cooling masses of the stars and the planets is now questioned".

The process of development from the lower to the higher is a process in essence unique. It is movement or development, involving an emergent and a necessary procedure. This procedure is not of *mechanical causation*, for that fails to explain development and account for the laws of organic life as revealed in Biology. Nor is it the evolutionary process of the evolutionists, i.e., evolution by mere struggle for existence. Objects change by *necessity* but not by a mere necessity. They change by more than a mere necessity. They change rather by a dialectical necessity. The world-process develops by a dialectical determination or dialectical causation—causation through contradictions and their synthesis.

The linkage of concrete opposites is not a mere mechanical linkage. In their continuity, they involve reciprocal struggle, interpenetration and inter-dependence. Both the thesis and the antithesis struggle against each other, penetrate into each other, till the antithesis gets dominant and the time is reached when it may result in the antithesis.

But this struggle may take thousands of years, as in nature, or a few centuries or years, as in social life, or even a few minutes, as in experimental science. Where consciousness plays a part, effort is made to reduce this time to the minimum.

In the struggle of the thesis and the antithesis sometimes one may get stronger, sometimes the other. There are ups and downs, when the thesis gets stronger, there is the phenomenon of retrogression, but this is always a temporary and accidental retrogression. Finally the struggle must result in the dominance of the antithesis and culminate in the appearance of the synthesis. Indeed it is by virtue of the inner-struggle, interpenetration and interaction of the thesis and the antithesis that the synthesis results and the dialectical process develops.

What is true of objects is equally true of movements and laws. So far as they are interconnected, they are continuous, and in so far as they are distinct from one another, discrete. Continuity of all systems is expressed in the fact that each higher system contains within itself the lower ones as "accessory forms, as subordinate elements." Their discreteness is expressed in their distinctive qualitative differences. Discreteness and continuity are themselves dialectical opposites and they get their unity in every synthesis.

The natural process being dialectical, its development is not only gradual. It is a development by 'leaps' rather than by gradual succession. The opposites struggle with each other, act and react upon each other, penetrate into each other and when gradually the antithesis gains dominance, which by dialectical necessity it must gain, at once with a sudden leap comes into being a new entity, the synthesis. ...Dialectical materialism is not only a theory of being—"a science of nature and History". It is also a theory of knowledge—a "science of thought and its laws". As an epistemological theory it declares that to consider reality and thought as separate is a mistake; to take reality as active and thought as passive or thought as active and reality as passive, is a blunder. Neither plays a passive role, knowledge is not something apart from reality...

...This account of dialectical materialism as a theory of knowledge is not complete. It reveals only one aspect of it and there is another aspect, no less important. And that is this, that thought is dialectically related to its opposite, action, and of the two, action is primary.

...That theory alone is true which, on the basis of principles, can forecast events and its predictions come out true. In the establishment of communism and in the recurrence of crisis in the capitalist world, the predictions of the founder are said to have come out true and, therefore, the doctrine stands established.

Nature gives birth to human life with an impulse to maintain evolution. This impulse develops itself dialectically into various forms of "productive forces". These forces cause "production of the means of life" and thus determine maintenance of life. Dialectical development in the production of the means of life ultimately determines the dialectical development of the relations into which human beings necessarily and inevitably enter. These relations are thus at bottom productive relations and "the totality of these productive relations constitutes the economic structure of society". This economic structure of society is "the real basis upon which a legal and political superstructure arises". The dialectically developing modes of production of the material means of life thus determine, in general the social, political and intellectual processes of life. "At a certain stage of their development", the material productive forces of society, "come into conflict with existing productive relationships, or, what is but a legal expression for the same thing, with the property relationships within which they have hitherto moved". Far from being the source of growth to the productive forces, "these relationships turn into their fetters"; and the more they become so, the greater is the effort of these forces to free themselves of them. After a zig-zag struggle, which may last for centuries or years and after accidental and temporary regressions they free themselves from their shackles with a jerk or a leap, taking, like all jerks and leaps, a comparatively very small period of time. This leap or jerk is a "change in the economic foundation of society and with this the whole gigantic superstructure is more or less rapidly transformed" into a qualitatively different and new social order. And this process of social life repeats itself at higher and still higher planes and forms, the great ever-rising spiral of social development. All phenomena of social life, government, private property, capital, freedom and the like, are supposed to illustrate this scheme of things.

Struggle between the productive forces and property relationships takes the form of class struggle for control and ownership of the means of production between the propertied and the propertyless, between the oppressor and the oppressed. The dynamic factor in history is the struggle for dominance between social classes, themselves set in motion by economic conditions. This struggle goes on dialectically, giving structures, each more developed than the preceding one.

Dialectical Materialism as a philosophy is chiefly used to back dialectical materialism as a social theory.

Dialectical Materialism, brief as it is, brings out the fact that the doctrine combines within itself elements drawn from several currents of thought. It is a synthesis of the nineteenth century Hegelianism, post-Hegelian Humanism, Materialism, revolutionary Socialism, classical economics and natural sciences.

Thereafter, Prof. Sharif shows its limitations as to an average dialectical materialist it is an article of faith. "It is based on prediction and has no practical lasting value, in contrast to that of mathematics as the subject of science. As regards the relationship between the thought and existence, between spirit and nature, philosophers are divided into two great camps, according to the way in which they have answered this question. Spirit or nature?" Continuing, he says that, in human society, class struggle in class interest is not the only relation that counts. Human affections and loyalties and co-operation play as a great role in social life as human antagonism, and one will not be far wrong in saying that the former as much responsible for social development as the latter. In classless society "class-struggle ceases and if it ceases", the dialectical process must come to an "end" and "thus if classless society is possible, historical dialectic is impossible and if historical dialectic is possible, classless society is impossible". In point of fact everything has *everything* else as its different. Apart from its *mere others everything* has a *correlative other*. Life and death, matter and thought are indeed correlatives, but what, one may ask, is the correlative of space, time, the sun, the moon, the earth, the Peacock Throne or the Taj?"

It is out of place here to deal with the issue of theoretical criticism as truth is relative to nature. But in passing it is important to stress that organisation, integration, disorganisation and disintegration of things have all along been within the stronghold of materialist philosophy which regards nature as the primary. Things exist in relation with the nature. Time is the independent variable and infinite. Space has its existence and meaning with reference to the constantly changing character and motion of matter. Terrestrial objects and stars, planets and their sattelites in the solar systems of the universe are inter-related and have all been in the state of motion, development, decline and change, and destructions since their origin and formation. Everything in the expanding universe actually exists in a state of flux.

In 1929, Edwin Hubble discovered that the universe is expanding. That was based on the theory that the matter in the universe was once concentrated in one small spot and was blown outward in the Big Bang that marked the beginning of the universe. His discovery was revolutionary but his all observations were not correct. He said the universe was expanding so quickly that it was only 2 billion years old. Geologists especially thought he was wrong because they had dated rocks on earth at more than 4 billion years old. Later research put the age of the universe at 10 to 20 billion years. Those who said it was 10 billion years old were faced with the dilemma of stars older than 10 billion years old. Very recently a team of astronomers led by Wendy Freedman of the Carneige Institute of Washington said their observatories discovered pulsating stars that revealed an expansion of the universe corresponding to an age of 12 billion years. Nature evolved and transformed itself. Species originated and developed out of matter. Man appeared in the process of development as a being long last.

Rational thought discounts subjective idealism and religious fundamentalism originating from Pan-Hinduism, Pan-Islamism and Pan-Christianity or any such institution. It is totally opposed to their content, object and manoeuvring as their activities artificially divide people on religious line, preach spiritualism and isolate them from the hard reality of life and above all, serve the interests of the landlord and capitalist classes by intensifying and covering up the condition of labour and miseries of the masses of the people under the existing mode of production and social order. Religious fundamentalism preaches idea of a creator and does not see the existence of and distinction between the social classes in the actual life of society, exploiter and the exploited classes and, oppressor and oppressed nations. It concurs to, class collaboration, exploitation and inequalities in the society. It idealises the values, rites and practices of the old world indiscriminately and absolutely, to which mankind and society would never return. To support the existing social order based on private property, generation of surplus value and its private appropriation is the real motive of religious fundamentalism propounded by the mentors of exploiting classes moneybags and the reactionary forces all over the world.

Idealist philosophy actually neglects and conceals the material facts of nature, life and society, condition of labour and contradiction of society. Materialist philosophy contemplates to know the things and show their inter-relations in a rigorous and systematic way. The objects of the two schools are different and opposite to each other.

And this exposes and confirms the existence of contradictions in the actual world, which religious theory can hardly suppress and hoodwink the people. Dialectical materialism stands to study of the contradiction in the essence of the matter and unravel the contradictions in the society. To it, contradiction leads the way forward.

This is enough. Let us come back to the social contradiction and its development in the world of twentieth century.

The Resolution[20] on the Report of Georgi Dimitroff, adopted on 20 August, 1935 by the Seventh Congress of the Communist

International said, "In the colonial and semi-colonial countries, the most important task facing the Communists consists in working to establish an anti-imperialist people's front. For this purpose it is necessary to draw the widest masses into the national liberation movement against growing imperialist exploitation, cruel enslavement, for the driving out of the imperialists, for the independence of the country; to take an active part in the mass anti-imperialist movements headed by the national reformists and to strive to bring about joint action with the national revolutionary and national reformist organisations on the basis of a definite anti-imperialist platform". The Seventh Congress of the Communist International emphasized that only *the further all-round consolidation of the Communist Parties themselves*, the development of their initiative, the carrying out of a policy based on Marxist-Leninist principles, and application of correct flexible tactics, which take into account the concrete situation and the alignment of class forces, "can ensure the mobilisation of the widest masses of toilers for the united struggle against fascism, against capitalism". It added that, "in order that the united front may be really brought about, the Communists must overcome the self-satisfied *sectarianism* in their own ranks which in our day, is in a number of cases, no longer an 'infantile disorder' of the Communist movement but an ingrained vice".

According to this thesis, the Anti-Imperialist People's Front for Indian struggle was formulated by R. Palm Dutt, Ben Bradley and others of the Communist Party of Great Britain and sent to India in 1936. Ben Bradley was sent by the Communist Party of Great Britain to help organise working class movement in India. The party, continued to the illegal during 1934-1941. The imprisoned leaders of the Communist Party of India in 1941 however strangely concluded that the character of the world war "changed fundamentally" with the attack of the Soviet Union by the fascist Germany of Hitlar, although just one year before the leaders of the Communist Party of Great Britain particularly advised the Indian Students Federation in Britain that the Anti-Imperialist Front would be the correct line. But almost all the imprisoned leaders of the Communist Party of India thought it necessary to change the tactical line as the war was "no longer" imperialist and the imperialist war was transformed into the people's war against fascism. A great "discovery" that the war ceased to be imperialist! This abrupt change in the position of the Communist Party of India marked a great deviation from the general line of the Communist International, which was certainly broad, general and universal in character and content.

This stand of the Communist Party of India certainly gave a theoretical concession to the oppressive British colonial and imperialist rule in India. The alien government made the party legal sometime just before the start of the Quit India Movement in August 1942. The party opposed the movement instantly on the "plea" that such a mass movement would weaken the proposed anti-fascist movement. As a result of strong movement, the anti-imperialist front of the people would have become stronger and that could combat the fascist force in time. Without this approach and standpoint, what is the meaning, role and significance of people's war? In absence of this feature, people's war concept does not at all stand. It actually becomes a fiction and misnomer to the people who are capable of making history in their favour by positive action for revolution.

The emergence of advanced thought in Indian politics can be traced in and related with the observations of Dadabhai Naoroji, a great rationalist thinker, reflecting the general antagonistic contradiction between colonialism and imperialism on the one hand and , on the other, people of India. Regarding man as a being, and his social organisation free from any sort of religious prejudice, Dadabhai boldly contended in a speech on 2 June, 1899. "Moreover, the action of the English nation in regard to the people of India was of as vital importance as to themselves as it was to India, and it was not even of less vital consequence to the whole human race. For a new element had lately come into existence in the councils of nations. A country which had hitherto confined itself, under its Monroe doctrine, to its own continent, was now coming forward to share in what was called the Imperialism of the world and the question had already arisen which course that country (USA) should follow". In his speeches of 6 and 27 July 1900 Naoroji observed, "We have not the slightest voice. The Indian Government are the masters of all our resources and they may do what they like with them. We have simply to submit and be bled........" "Here is India with a perfectly free trade entirely under your control" and "The fact was that Indian natives were mere helot. They were worse than American slaves, for the latter were at least taken care of by their masters, whose property they were". (Naoroji, *Poverty and Un-British Rule in India*, 1901, p.,637, p. 646 and p.652). These words clearly express the true philosophy of the Indian National Congress before religions Gandhi's rise in the 1920s. Modern agents of globalisation think and do just the opposite.

How brilliantly did Dadabhai Naoroji observe the world contradiction in a few words and expressed doubt on the motive of the US, and the antagonistic contradiction between the Indian people and the British imperialism evolving in the beginning of the twentieth century. The objective reality and rational thought under materialism contained in his writings indeed stands in the test of time and still shines in the political spheres of the present day world. It actually set the secular theme and correct ideology for Indian freedom movement and future politics of a vast backward and colonial country like India.

Some two decades later, Humbert Droze, Secretary of the Presidium of the fourth Congress of the Third Communist International expressed solidarity with the Indian people in its anti-imperialist struggle and drew attention to some basic subjects for consideration of the Congress Party in 1922 for organising national liberation struggle in India, *viz.* (1) without complete destruction of the colonial power there would be no certainty for improvement of the lives of the people, (2) any kind of compromise with the British rule would not help in any way, to improve condition of the greater proportion of the country's people, (3) without the violent revolutionary path, British rule cannot be overthrown, and (4) only the workers and peasants could lead the revolution to the path of victory and national liberation. The social basis of national revolutionary movement, Communist International stressed, could not be formed with the combination of all classes because all could not come forward in the movement for economic reasons. The axis of national revolutionary movement would be constituted with the industrial workers, poor peasants and different strata of the lower middle class who formed the greatest proportion of the Indian people.

The parliamentary reforms of the British Government for India in 1919-35 came in contradiction with the existing social structure and conditions on which the political parties like the Congress and the Muslim League grew up and moulded their organisations for gaining concessions. The issue of majority rule came in sharp conflict with the consensus rule with the effective preservation of the rights and status of the minorities in the future constitution of India.

It was in this context, the International Press Correspondence (Vol. 15 No. 10 of 9-3-1935) of the Communist International stressed that the Communist Party as such would develop outside the Congress Organisations as a wide independent mobilisation of the masses for the struggle against imperialism, and would consistently put into effect the tactics of the United Front when organising any anti-imperialist action. *Its struggle against national reformism* in close and inseparable contact, with the mobilisation of the masses against the principal enemy, against imperialism, must not be weakened down, even a movement, when applying the tactics; but on the contrary, will have to be deepened and widened. "At this crucial moment, it must not give the conciliators of national reformism the possibility to triumph again over the deceived masses". "It must throw itself into the thick of the masses under its militant banner" and "must not give the conciliators of national reformism the possibility of triumph over the masses"

The same document noted that the policy adhered to by the Indian National Congress headed by the block of the national reformists, bourgeoisie and liberal landlords, proved to be a clearly unfit weapon for defending India against the attacks of the British Imperialism. The Congress Party attempted to hamper and weaken these attacks, "especially in view of the fact that they affected the interests of the Indian bourgeoisie"; however, the duplicity and the conciliatory nature of this policy merely served to pave the way for fresh attacks of the imperialism. The tactics of the united front in the struggle against imperialism must be based on the real relationship of forces in the mass movement. "The tactics of the United Front in the struggle against imperialism must be based on the rallying of the broad masses to this struggle". The document also warned that unless "the sickness of sectarianism is immediately overcome in a determined war", the Communists would not be able to extend its influence over the masses, will not be able to lead the masses of workers.

Rajani Palm Dutt and Ben Bradley wrote a similar thesis entitled "Anti-Imperialist People's Front" published in *The Communist* (Vol. I. No. 12, September, 1936). It said, "Every Indian patriot will recognise that the first need for the powerful advance of the Indian national struggle, the key need of the present situation, is the common struggle. This is the indispensable condition for the successful fight against the existing and ever sharpening reaction and oppression. It is evident that all elements, including from among the liberals, who are prepared to break with imperialism and accept the programme of the national struggle, are welcome to the Common Front." But not much headway could be made with organisational weakness and increasing communal tension. As World war II continued, the fascism advanced and conditions changed, though in a relative sense. In December 1941, a Note from Jail leaders of the CPI noted that the proletariat would accomplish "a big victory if it succeeds in pursuading the national leadership to declare in favour of war" and "the proletariat must come forward with its slogan of "Win the People's War". Resolution of the Party's Polit Bureau circulated in the party letter No. 56 dated 15 December 1941, observed that *"peoples of the world are moving into action with common will not only for the victory over Hitler but also for the victory of all the people's unity with the Soviet people and for a new and higher world order, based not on a new imperialist re-division but on the independence and democratic liberties of all the peoples. Such is the revolutionary importance of the new period"*, and that *"The Communist Parties in all countries were required to recognise that Hitler-fascism as the main enemy and the war waged by the USSR in alliance with Britain and America, was a war which had to be won by all the people in the interests of defending the base of the world revolution. This duty and attitude was imposed by the internationalism of our Party. No national or local conditions could render it invalid". (Communism in India:* 1935-1945, ed., Subodh

Roy, pp. 283-90. Italics in the original). Enough verbiage for no action and doing nothing!

Mao-Tse-Tung, on behalf of the Central Committee of the Communist Party of China sent a letter dated 5.4.1943, supporting the efforts of the Communist Party of India in working for the National Anti-Fascist United Front and striving for independence and liberation of India. It rightly expressed the feeling that "under the concerted efforts of the Communist Party of India and the Indian people, a way will certainly be found out of the present difficult situation so that both the objects – to vanquish fascism and strive for Indian independence would be attained". Another letter of date written by Mao-Tse-Tung and Chu Teh together was sent to the Indian National Congress, stressing the same content and objective (*Ibid.,* pp. 353-54).

The political stand supporting the imperialist bourgeoisie was not an isolated factor or exceptional stand of a particular party or leader in Indian politics at that time. Jawaharlal Nehru peculiarly harboured a kind of socialism which would be growing within the parliamentary democracy and based on India's genious and ideas like *Abhaya* and *non-violence*, supported the British power in the war. The Congress, after wavering, supported the British war efforts. Subhash Chandra Bose wandered between the nationalism and communism – the two opposite ideologies of the bourgeoisie and proletariat – and sought to strike their synthesis. M.K. Gandhi, chanting *Ramdhun* and *Ahimsa*, extended his sympathy with the British in war with the object to bargain for the comprador Indian bourgeoisie and establish its rule over the oppressed Indian people.

These developments were but result of the predominant idealist philosophy of *Vedanta* which taught its adherent about *atman* and its salvation. In the west, idealist philosophy had passed through characteristic change and evolution but in India it has changed very little till now. As Frederick Engels, one of the founder philosophers of scientific socialism as early as in 1878, wrote, "The Kantian theory of the origin of all existing celestial bodies from rotating nebular masses was the greatest advance made by astronomy since Copernicus. For the first time the idea that nature had no history in time began to be shaken. Until then the celestial bodies were believed to have remained in the same permanent orbits and states from the beginning; and even though individual organisms on particular celestial bodies died out, genera and species were nevertheless held to be immutable. It is true that nature was conceived as obviously being in constant motion, but this motion appeared as incessant repetition of the same processes. Kant made the first breach in this conception, which corresponded exactly to the metaphysical mode of thought, and indeed he did it so scientifically that most of the proofs furnished by him still hold good today" and "since irrefutable spectroscopic proof of the existence of such red-hot gaseous masses in the starry heavens, the scientific opposition to Kant's theory has been silenced". He further observed, *"Motion is the mode of existence of matter.* Never anywhere has there been matter without motion, nor can there be. Motion in cosmic space, mechanical motion of smaller masses on the various celestical bodies, the vibration of molecules as heat or as electrical or magnetic currents, chemical decomposition and composition, organic life—at each given moment, each individual atom of matter in the world is in one or another of these forms of motion, or in several forms at once. All rest, all equilibrium is only relative, only has meaning in relation to one or another definite form of motion". (Frederick Engels, *Anti-Dühring*, Peking, 1976, p. 70 and p. 74 italics in the original)

Actual developments in India indicated sheer subjectivism and self-exile in the party's theoretical line and practical movement. In the name of following the line of proletariat internationalism, it just did withdraw from the struggle to spread confusion among the people. It speaks of the continuation of their self-exile in the 1930s.

In fact the two (anti-imperialist front and anti-fascist people's front) are inter-related and enmeshed with each other. The idea of Anti-Fascist Peoples Front remains an abstract faith and a figure of speech unless it really becomes anti-imperialist with people's support and action because fascism is the rule of the more aggressive finance capital and imperialism in the world. The anti-imperialist content and character is the pre-requisite, primary and fundamental to the anti-fascist people's front. Without the former, the determinant, latter cannot exist and develop. Communist International formulated the anti-imperialist and anti-capitalist line of action in 1935 correctly foreseeing the danger of the advance of fascism in the world arena. A firm anti-imperialist stance is the very kernel of the anti-fascist people's front, with the independence of the Communist Party. P.C. Joshi, Secretary of the Communist Party of India (1943-47) had observed later, that "the communist decided not only to adopt the policy of the anti-fascist peoples front but also to recommend the tactics of the Anti-Imperialist United National Front for colonial countries like India", and admitted "we Indian Communists again decided to go back to the Congress and build up as our effective instrument of united national struggle against imperialism".[21] Joshi said that unfortunate fissures caused during the war. Nehru who had "succumbed" to the Congress High Command pressure in 1928, was idealised and he "again succumbed", Joshi noted, "to the Gandhian pressure. Reviewing the course of developments, P.C. Joshi observed, "The right-wing had seen for itself that the Congress-Communist United Front, on the basis of joint work inside the Congress, was making them look like creatures of a bygone past and they did not miss their chance especially when transfer of power was in sight to take up the banner of anti-communism and rid the Congress of Communists". Nehru followed suit with the right to become this idol in the government. All this exposes the true character of the comprador Indian big bourgeoisie and landlord class, serving the interest of imperialism. And such a policy of combining the class interests of the bourgeoisie and the working class within the organisation of the exploiting class ultimately favours the enemy and its international ally, imperialism.

The workers, peasants and toilers of India and their political organisation, Communist Party, could neither gain or advance with such compromising United National Front led by the party of the exploiting classes. The Communist International never said for the formation of such a United Front by sacrificing the independence and activity of the working class and Communist Party. All this marked a lack of class approach and action, theoretical weakness and philosophical decline in the life of the Communist Party of India, which left an indelible adverse impact on its activity and developments in future.

The fall can be viewed more characteristically in the context of the advice of the Communist Party of China—a section of the Communist International—sent to the Communist Party of India after the German fascist attack on the Soviet Union in 1941. Mao-Tse-Tung, Chairman of the Communist Party of China sent a telegram asking the Communist Party of India and Indian National Congress to address the situation to the basic masses of the people so that a line could be evolved in consultation with the workers and peasants of India. But the leadership paid no heed to it. The first party Congress took place in 1943 and many Communist leaders, Joshi writes, joined Congress Party in the name of forming Anti-imperialist United National Front. The party began to lose its philosophical moorings and appeal to the workers, peasants and toilers. Anti-imperialism is the core and basis with anti-fascist stance as the point of emphasis during a certain period. Experience shows that the leaders of the C.P.I. did not actually break off their class origin and attitude. But P.C. Joshi wrote to sermonize, "The historic tragedy of Indian revolution was that the Indian communists were too blinded by Stalinist dogmatism to make positive contribution in shaping the course of events and our most progressive nationalist leader like Nehru was too soft towards his reactionary colleagues. Consequently, the main aims of the Indian revolution have not yet been successfully achieved".[22] While the party failed to act and reaction consolidated for attack on the people, Joshi discovered "Stalinist dogmatism" of the Indian Communists! The accusation is false and opportunistic as Stalin or Communist International never hindered their work. The main thing and lesson is that the reactionary class and its political party as a rule, staunchly oppose revolution and in general stand for counter-revolution. It was pernicious for the Communist Party of India to sacrifice its independence and broach class compromise with the party of exploiters. Revolution is the logical culmination of class struggle, action of the people and not words of the reactionary circle and its survitors.

This attitude of the party was manifested as the time for the transfer of power in India became near. The statement by the cabinet mission and the Viceroy of India dated May 16, 1946, generally acknowledged that the bulk of evidence submitted, had shown "an almost universal desire 'for the unity of India and added consideration of a possible partition of India', since we were greatly impressed by the very genuine and acute anxiety of the Muslims lest they should find themselves subjected to a perpetual Hindu-majority rule." In a memorandum submitted to the cabinet mission, the Communist Party suggested that India should be divided into "linguistically and culturally homogeneous national units," each of which should have "the right to decide freely whether they join the union (of India) or form a separate sovereign state or another Indian Union," and it added : "The Communist Party stands for a free voluntary democratic Indian Union of sovereign units. It is firmly convinced that the best interests of the Indian masses will be served by their remaining together in one common union..." (A.C. Banerjee, ed., *Indian Constitutional Documents*, Vol. 4, pp. 214-15). The stand was quite fair.

But after a very short period, the party distressingly changed its position and came forward to support creation of Pakistan as a separate dominion quitely forgetting to say and demand that its two far flung territories could remain well within the Union of India with the broadest possible regional autonomy protecting the unity, interest and aspiration of the working class without causing loss of human life and property and a very large-scale migration unprecedented in human history. It thus later on set sail to the ship of the reaction and maintained the existing social order.

One may be an opponent of federation and become a partisan of democratic centralism. But still he can prefer federation to national inequality at a certain time as the prerequisite towards complete democratic centralism. It can be stressed in this regard that Marx in 1869 demanded the separation of Ireland from England and added "....although after separation there may come federation". Only by putting forward this demand, did Marx really educate the workers in the spirit of internationalism (See Marx's letter to Engels of November 30, 1867 in Marx and Engels, *Selected Correspondence,* International Publishers, New York, 1942, pp. 228-231; and Lenin, *On the National and Colonial Questions*, Foreign Languages Press, Peking 1975, p. 6, p. 8 and p. 10)

The Congress Party, however assumed power from the British Crown, accepting dominion status of India within the British

Commonwealth of Nations in 1947—the same condition—for which Congress of the liberal leaders were accused and condemned in the 1910s. On 10 May, 1947 Pandit Jawaharlal Nehru rejected the plans proposed by the Viceroy and approved by the British Government. Within six hours the government made a plan for partition which became the basis of the creation of the two dominions of India and Pakistan. Nehru accepted it within 24 hours. Gandhi's Congress and Akali Dal accepted and written undertakings were sent by them. No written undertaking was sent to the government from the Muslim League. (See Jogesh Chandra Bagal, *Muktir Sandhane Bharat* : Bengali, p. 493; and F.S. Aijazuddin, Art in *The Asian Age*, 19 August 1999, Calcutta)

The Communist Party of India earlier tried to follow up its activity in accordance with the Draft thesis of 1930. But the same could not be properly pursued in the following years for obvious reasons of its weakness. War broke out in 1939, and the party's characterisation of the war as a people's war in 1941 and withdrawal from the movement on this plea had faced strong resentment from the Indian people. The experience of "swimming" against the main current of Indian politics had to be reviewed and properly assessed. At the first Congress of the Communist Party of India in Bombay in 1943 the main report delivered by the General Secretary, P.C. Joshi and the speeches that followed, gave the line of "struggle against the Japanese agents",[23] increase in the industrial and agricultural production, etc. In plain language, it appeared to be somewhat an attempt for softening of the party's opposition to the British Government in political and militant economic struggles. The party Congress, according to E.M.S. Namboodiripad, did not have any discussions on the correctness of the line. The Congress Party also supported the British war effort against the axis power.

The internal Polit Bureau crisis arising out of the party line led to the basic corrections made at the Second Party Congress at Calcutta in 1948. The essence of the change in the political-tactical line could be seen in the slogan reverberated in Calcutta and was picked up by the organisation after the Party Congress : "Telengana way is our way". The effort of the party would, in other words, be not only to learn from but repeat Telengana all over the country, establish everywhere the Telengana-model organs of state-power through which the Nehru government would be overthrown.

It was a total reversal of the line pursued by the leadership for half a decade ending February 1948. P.C. Joshi was excluded from the Central Committee and there was apprehension of maltreatment by many members. The delegates went back to their states with "mixed feelings", though the overwhelming sentiment was one of "relief that a break had been made with the earlier party policy". Dissent however persisted and gradually serious differences arose between the new Polit Bureau and the Andhra state leadership which, as is known, was organising and leading the Telengana struggle. The Polit Bureau interpreted the Calcutta Congress line as nothing but preparing the country for a revolutionary uprising of the Russian type. The Andhra leadership continued it, saying that the Telengana way meant something different, more or less similar to what developed in China; they maintained that the Telengana experience itself showed that the Chinese path was more suited to the Indian conditions. The Andhra State Committee's view was, in the end, overruled[24] by the Central leadership. The Polit Bureau proceeded to carry out its line with determination. A planned inner-party campaign was launched to educate comrades on the incorrectness of the line advocated by the Andhra Committee. Preparations were made to organise the railway workers to go on a strike and to lead it on militant lines, making it the starting point of a countrywide working class upsurge. This, as was subsequently proved, was a complete over-estimation of the actual situation in the background of lack of organisation, psychological setback of the masses, communal politics, blood bath and partition of the country.

The fiasco of the planned strike and the large number of cases of disciplinary actions created "an explosive situation" in the party. Many felt uneasy, though the middle ranks did their best to carry out the directives given by the Polit Bureau. Then came the well-known editorial in the organ of the Communist Information Bureau which advised the party to go for a change in the line.

After initial resistance, the Polit Bureau of the Party organised a full meeting of the Central Committee. For full two months (from March and to May end, 1950) nearly 30 leaders discussed among themselves underground on the prevailing situation in the country.

The elaborate discussions in the end, culminated in the repudiation of the line followed by the Polit Bureau and adoption of the Andhra line. This was accompanied by a sharp critique of the organisational measures adopted by the Polit Bureau. Those who were responsible for the political organisational line of the Calcutta Congress were not only removed from the leadership but suspended from the Party, with a commission appointed to investigate into the violations of Party norms by leaders. The entire Central Committee was reconstituted and reduced in size with a majority of those who had stood by the Andhra line. From among such a reconstituted central committee (12 to 13 members), a Polit Bureau of three was elected, with Rajeswara Rao as General Secretary and M. Basavpunnaia as one of the Polit Bureau members.

The line of the new leadership did not receive the same response in the party as the earlier Calcutta Congress (1948) line did. Those who had followed the pre-Calcutta Congress line (Joshi, etc.) said that this was a new version of the sectarian line adopted at the Calcutta Congress. The criticism from the other end was that the new line amounted to the abandonment of the proletarian line. The former were more vociferous and mounted a frontal attack on the new line and its proponents. Three leading members of the party, Dange, Ghate and Ajay Ghosh—prepared a note and had it circulated in the party. This and other documents opposing the Polit Bureau (and its Andhra line) received extensive circulation, the open party headquarters in Bombay itself becoming the hub of these activities. In the entire process of the inner-party struggle, E.M.S. Namboodiripad, one of the party leaders, took a middle course. He writes that he wholeheartedly supported the 1946 change in the party line and admits "I had faithfully followed the Joshi line. So did the leading comrades in Kerala"[25]. The inner-party struggle continued on, with no good result to the organisation.

This made it necessary for the new Polit Bureau to convene a meeting of leading Comrades, including the three who had prepared and circulated their critique of the Polit Bureau and its line. After protracted discussions it was agreed that (I) the entire controversy over the path of the Indian revolution—the Russian and the Chinese should be resolved for which the assistance of the CPSU should be sought; and (2) the Polit Bureau and Central Committee should be reconstituted and party unity restored.

With this aim in view, the General Secretary was removed from the post, and a new Polit Bureau formed, with Ajoy Ghosh discharging the functions of the General Secretary. A four-member delegation of the party, with two each representing from the two contending trends, was selected to go to the Soviet Union (of course clandestinely) and have discussions with the CPSU. Dange and Ajoy Ghosh representing one and Rajeswar Rao and Vasavapunnaiah the other, were the leaders selected to go abroad. E.M.S. Namboodiripad who welcomed the change in line at the Calcutta Congress, was asked to look after the party centre till they came back. He was not sure whether he would be able to implement the Calcutta Congress line or the Andhra line. Unlike many other states, Kerala "did not have any leader who could be said to have consistently fought any of the three lines" which dominated the party under Joshi, Ranadive and Rajeswar Rao.

The party delegation returned from Moscow after having detailed discussion with the CPSU delegation headed by Stalin. The conclusions that emerged out of the "discussions between the two delegations were incorporated into two draft documents—a party programme and a perspective Tactical Line." The two documents were reported on to the entire party after which a special conference was clandestinely held in October 1951 for approval of the documents. After "approving" the two documents the conference elected a new Central Committee which elected a Polit Bureau with Ajay Ghosh as the General Secretary of the party. After this conference the party programme was published and circulated, but the approved perspective Tactical Line did not see light of the day and in lieu of it, surprisingly, a very brief, much mellowed statement of policy was put into circulation among the workers and masses! "The programme and statement of policy" Namboodiripad writes, "had resolved all existing differences, drawing attention to the immediate issues". The original document was suppressed by the leadership.

This was quite contrary to what to the leader of the Soviet

delegation, Stalin had told to the Indian delegation in 1951. Stalin told to the leaders of the Indian delegation, as Namboodiripad quotes him, "Now that you have agreed on the problems under discussion, you go back and implement the line along with your comrades. You, the members of the delegation (meaning those who represented the two trends) remain united, unify the central committee and then the entire party on the basis of the agreed line".[26] Namboodiripad notes that it was a fact that the "comrades" who came back from Moscow "had been mentally prepared to have a critical eye on all subsequent developments" and that "they refused to dogmatically stick to the formulations contained in the two documents (the programme and the perspective Tactical Line)". Here Namboodiripad discovers "dogmatism", "critical eye" sticking to the formulations, and writes to cover up, "Stalin's active participation in the formation of the party programme did not stand in the way of our party unanimously declaring, within a few years *i.e.*, (after Stalin's death) that many ideas contained in the programme were incorrect, making it necessary to keep the entire document in abeyance",[27] and conceals the muddle and opportuinism by stating that "the great merit of the 1951 advice of the Soviet Party was (that our party should independently add to, delete from, amend from, amend or even reject the Moscow documents) that it gave us courage and confidence to have our independent views on whatever comes from the Soviet, Chinese or other fraternal parties".[28] By this statement Namboodiripad smuggles in corruption, liberalism and revisionism. Independent views from which philosophical standpoint? From the standpoint of Marxism or social democracy, proletarian internationalism or petty bourgeois reformism, class struggle or class compromise? Parliamentarianism for dictatorship of the bourgeoisie or people's democracy? Namboodiripad conspicuously remains silence on this most vital question of philosophy and history of the working class movement in India. His reformist stand is quite understandable.

What Namboodiripad and other Indian leaders contend, however, is contrary to the position of proletarian internationalism and general tactics favourable to the working class movement in India. Cominform in its organ, *For a Lasting Peace and for a People's Democracy* (January 27, 1950) wrote, "The task of the

Indian Communists, drawing on the experience of the national liberation movement in China and other countries, is, naturally to strengthen the alliance of the working class with all the peasantry, to fight for the introduction of the urgently needed agrarian reform and on the basis of the common struggle for freedom and national independence of their country against the Anglo-American imperialists oppressing it and against the reactionary big bourgeoisie and feudal princes collaborating with them, to unite all classes, parties, groups and organisations, willing to defend the national independence and freedom of India".[29] The task was indeed quite clearly stated.

Inevitably, as a result of the "independent" tinkering, in the words of Namboodiripad himself, "the three trends in our party, which fought against one another from 1946 to 1951, appeared in new forms"clearly. This showed signs of class compromise and degeneration of the leadership. Proletatiat was thus "supported" by the Indian Communist Party, and Namboodiripad adds, "In fact, every time some new development took place internationally or nationally, comrades holding different positions earlier made their own assessments which came into conflict with one another. That was why, though the party unanimously agreed by the mid-1950s that the programme of 1951 should be basically revised, sharp differences arose on how and on what lines the revision should be made. That was the beginning of a deep inner-party crisis which in the end led to the 1964 split in the party and a further split in the CPI(M)—formation of a number of Naxalite groups followed by the formation of the Dange group out of the CPI"[30]. Why did they fail to work unitedly for the cause of the Indian workers and peasants and people for the country's revolution? What did actually prevent them to work for the class struggle and revolution? There is no answer from them to the Indian people.

The revision and abrogation of the 1951 programme and suppression of the perspective tactical line and blatant pursuit of "independent views" however, caused havoc in the politics of working class movement, and greatly hampered growth and expansion of the communist party in India. Namboodiripad writes, "one reason for these developments beginning in the latter half of the 1950s was that the CPSU advice regarding party unity was not acted upon. Instead of the four delegation members remaining united and proceeding to unify the Central Committee and then the entire party, they themselves began to fight one another. These, however, were developments which took place later".[31] But why did they subvert the agreed 1951 programme and suppress the perspective Tactical Line? And without adherence to and pursuasion of the ideology contained in the documents, how can there be party unity? These are inter-related things in science and social organisation which can never be separated or denied in the working class movement.

The consequence of "independent views" and dilution of the 1951 programme was more anarchic and disastrous to the development of working class movement in India. It caused a great setback to the progress of the objective idealism and emergence of militant materialism in the transformation of Indian politics.

Later developments were but extension and continuation of the same old process though of a much greater import and wider dimension in the late 1960s through 1970s and onwards. Revisionism, acute sectarianism, rank opportunism, and parliamentarianism with their dominant trend at present rule the roost in the name of left politics in India. In the present canvas it would be out of place to discuss this subject in detail. Its history would be quite long, complicated and more distressing. But, suffice here to mention that a growing force of the militant movement of the Indian people is also trying very hard to rise its head outside the parliamentary arena against the oppression and domination of the comprador Indian ruling classes and their government of different colours faithfully serving the interest of the international finance capital warring the flag of globalisation.

The object of writing such an account is to provide the facts and show the attitude and ideological trend in Indian political process. Concisely, two philosophic trends are discernible, *viz.*, (1) Subjective idealism strongly in favour of the existing reactionary social order, and (2) Objective idealism, a relatively weak movement for social change with the materialism on the tortuous Indian field at the end of the twentieth century.

In the practical world, antagonism is the absolute and driving force of history in which the class struggle proceeds uninterruptedly with its characteristics and varying intensity over time. In India, contradiction between the people and the feudalism, especially in the Nizam's state of Telengana had grown over time and it burst out in the Second World War period.

During the whole period of 1940-44, the Communist Party and the left cadre of the Andhra Mahasabha carried on agitation and made representations to see that whichever *firmans* of reforms of the Nizam favoured the people were put into practice and not sabotaged by the landlords and corrupt officials. This enabled the Andhra Mahasabha to gain a wide popular image; the left wing led by the Communist Party took over the leadership of the Andhra Mahasabha. From the beginning of 1944, the Andhra Mahasabha under the leadership of the party conducted many militant struggles against *Zamindars* and *Deshmukhs*, against the practice of *Vetti* (a kind of bonded labour) against illegal exactions and eviction of peasants from their lands.

The movement gradually developed into armed struggle and as many as 3000 villages in Telengana (Andhra Pradesh) were liberated. The movement spread under the leadership of the Communist Party and the Andhra Mahasabha into a powerful people's armed struggle for the liberation against feudal exploitation and against the hated Nizam's rule. As a result, one-third of the Telengana area came under the people's *gram raj* and their fighting committees were established. *Vetti*, illegal exactious, eviction from the land, usurious loans and torture and dishonouring by corrupt officials and village oppressors were put to an end ; waste lands, surplus lands of the landlords to the extent of a million acres along with the necessary cattle and agricultural implements were distributed to the rural poor. Fair wages for agricultural labourers were enforced and grain distributed. The people used to say that, for the first time in the contemporary history, they could have two full means a day. Regular guerrilla squads and village defence squads were organised; the Nizam's police and army and the village oppressors were confined to the big camps; only from there could they go on their forages during certain hours of the day. Even the press had to admit that the Communists were the kings at night (*Cheekati dovalu*).

This was the situation at the end of 1947. Nehru, true to his philosophy to serve the reaction, ordered despatch of army and smash the Telengana struggle by brutal force. With the mounting attack of the Indian Government's army, the crucial question posed before the fighting Telengana pesantry and the Communist Party was whether they should continue the armed guerrilla resistance against the attacks of the union armed forces, in defence of the peasants' land and other democratic rights. Alternatively, should they surrender their arms to the Congress government's armies and betray the trust placed in the party by the fighting people of Telengana? Were they to continue the partisan armed resistance or adopt legal forms of struggle and agitation, by leave of the military rule of Congress governments in the state?

Over this life-or-death question, two sharply opposed views emerged among the leaders of the Communist Party. Struggle or surrender!

One section advocated the abandonment of partisan armed resistance against the armed attacks of the Indian Union armies and the adoption of open and legal forms of struggle and agitation. The main arguments of those who took the slogan of abandoning the partisan resistance were:

(1) a large section of those who were supporting the Telengana armed struggle till the entry of the Indian armies (including the rich peasantry and liberal landlords) would turn hostile to the partisan struggle;
(2) the people would look upon the armies of the Congress not as oppressors but as liberators;
(3) the armed struggle in a small area like Telengana could not defend and sustain itself until countrywide armed struggles, for which there was no possibility, broke out;
(4) Peasants' armed squads were either poorly armed or virtually unarmed and could not resist the well-equipped Indian armies and their superior numbers.

The Vishalandhra Communist Committee opposed this view of withdrawal, and advocated the slogan of armed partisan resistance against the attacks launched by the union armies on the gains of the Telengana peasantry. Its arguments were :

(1) The big gains of the Telengana peasantry, in particular, the 10 lakhs acres of land distributed among them must be defended. These gains should not be allowed to be snatched away by the class enemies without a bitter resistance and fight;

(2) The national and international situation was favourable to the armed partisan struggle. The Telengana struggle was the beginning of the liberation struggle against the bourgeois-landlord government of the Congress Party. It demonstrated that the Indian revolution was more similar to the Chinese Revolution than the classical Russian Revolution. The Andhra Secretariat of the party put it in its May 1948 document : "Our revolution in many respects differs from the classical Russian Revolution, but to a great extent is similar to that of the Chinese Revolution. The perspective likely is not that of a general strike and armed uprising leading to the liberation of the rural side, but of dogged resistance and prolonged civil war in the form of agrarian revolution culminating in the capture of political power by the Democratic Front. Keeping all this in view, in areas where we are a good proportion in the masses as in parts of Andhra, Kerala and Bengal, the time has come to think in terms of guerrilla warfare (Chinese way) against the military onslaughts of the Nehru government which is bent upon mercilessly liquidating us".[32]

(3) The Andhra theses advocated a United Front which included the rich peasantry and the middle bourgeoisie as the allies of the proletariat in the people's democratic revolution.

They asserted that such a wide front of armed struggle could take shape under the leadership of the Communist Party and that the objective conditions for the materialisation of these issues were rapidly maturing. A prolonged armed resistance like that of Telengana alone would bring about such favourable conditions. On the contrary, the Polit Bureau of the Communist Party of India, elected at the second Party Congress "had rejected the entire theses of the Andhra Secretariat as gross reformism and had launched an attack on the concept of the Chinese path, characterising it as a deviation from Marxism-Leninism".[33] The Polit Bureau had maintained that there was only one path and that was the path of the Russian Revolution—the political general strike and the armed uprising of workers in the cities to capture power.

While entirely rejecting the Andhra theses outright the Polit Bureau "had strongly advocated the slogan, of armed resistance in Telengana as this might hasten the working class general strike and armed uprising in the anticipated post-war revolutionary crisis".[34] The Communist Party of India at its second Party Congress in February-March 1948 had raised the slogan: "The Telengana way is our way". It had declared all out support to the armed struggle of Telengana, called for developing similar struggles in several other parts of the country and given a call to develop working class movements in support of the Telengana struggle—all ultimately leading to armed insurrection.

There also took place important struggles such as the Vayalar-Punnapra struggle in Kerala state. There were the "armed peasant actions" in certain areas of West Bengal and Tripura and Worli peasant revolt in Bombay. There had taken place in different parts of the country a number of militant struggles—struggles where some sort of armed classes had taken place between the peasantry and the police although none of them had been sustained or developed into partisan struggle like in Telengana.

The working class, which had come out in support of the revolt in a Royal Indian Navy and for release of the Indian National Army prisoners during 1945-47 period "could not be brought into effective action" in support of the Telengana peasant armed struggle. There were "no solidarity strikes" in support of the Telengana struggle, either before the intervention of the Indian Union armies in September 1948 or during the three long years of the Telengana armed resistance upto October 1951. The call for a general strike of the railway workers on their own specific demands had also not materialised except in some centres. Sundaraiyya observed : *"The Telengana armed struggle alone had to carry the brunt of the offensive let loose by the armed forces of the Indian Government with the subjectively conceived aim of overthrowing the Nehru Government".*[35] *(Italics in the original).*

Subjective idealism, lack of preparation and development of material forces, lack of consultation and coordination and agreement between the higher and lower levels of the organisations, factionalism and bureaucratic attitude and functioning of the highest leadership of the party—all contributed to the weakness and decline of the Telengana movement in the face of the enemy attack. Self-exile from the mass movements in the earlier period brought confusion, dissent and despair among different sections of the working class against the backdrop of communal politics in the country. Rejection of the entire theses of the Andhra state unit and at the same time support to the armed struggle organised by it on basis of its own theses was somewhat a patch work. Was it not idealism and self-contradiction in the line and policy of the organisation? Its origin can be rightly traced to the old idea that the things are separate, different and unrelated. And that is the product of subjectivism and metaphysics at large. The Party secretary even wrote a series of article in 1948-49 criticising Mao-Tse-tung.

Thus, subjective idealism in different forms and metaphysical outlook dominating the party not only did actually hamper progress of the movement but also led to its disintegration and spoil, particularly at that crucial period of the organisation. Individualism, groupism, factionalism, liberalism and sectarianism caused havoc in the party organisation and all its associations and led to their vascillation, decline, division and degeneration. Objective idealism and interest of the working class became the first casualty in this process. This being particular manifestation of subjectivism countered materialist philosophy, deceived the people and largely strengthened the reactionary forces in the Indian politics.

It is generally estimated that 400 Communists and peasant militants were killed by police, military and landlord terror during 1946-51, excluding thousands of Koya people who died of disease in concentration camps. Some investigations put the figure nearer 6000. P. Sundaraiyya, one of the members of the Andhra State Committee Secretariat, noted that "The party and the revolutionary movement, faced with the cruel police attacks of the Congress government on the one hand and the wrong and sectarian policies pursued by the All India leadership on the other, had been extremely weakened and disunited".

It was against such a background that an editorial appeared in *For a Lasting Peace, for a People's Democracy* sharply criticising the political line pursued by the top leadership of the Communist Party of India. Following this and the consequent inner-party struggle, a drastic reshuffle of the Central Committee took place. A new Polit Bureau with C. Rajeshwar Rao as General Secretary was elected by the reconstituted Central Committee of the party.

The new political line worked out by the Central Committee and the Polit Bureau was the rejection of the programmatic understanding given in the second Party Congress and subsequently elaborated in what was called the "tactical line", rejection of the thesis of the single-state revolution, that is intertwining of the democratic and socialist stages of the Indian revolution; the rejection of the idea that the entire bourgeoisie including the rich peasantry had been transformed into enemies of the people's democratic revolution; and upholding the concept of the Chinese path for the Indian revolution and advocating the development of extensive agrarian struggles on the pattern of Telengana wherever condition permitted this.

There was a stiff opposition to this new political line, from an "extreme right opportunist angle". The party headquarters in Bombay was made the centre of this new opposition and S. Dange, Ajoy Kumar Ghosh and S.V. Ghate assumed leadership of this inner-party opposition. While this new opposition was allowed to function legally, a part of the central leadership as well as the leaders of the Telengana armed resistance had to function underground. In short, "the situation within the party", Sundaraiyya wrote, "*had deteriorated very much and the party was split into different trends and factions*".[36] (Italics in the original)

Soon after it was elected, the new Polit Bureau took stock of the "grave ideological-political situation"[37] of the party and came to the conclusion that restoration of the political-ideological and organisational unity inside the Communist Unity of India was possible only if it could secure the guidance and assistance of the leadership of the Communist Party of the Soviet Union (CPSU), a leadership which commanded the highest authority in the world communist movement. The new Polit Bureau immediately approached the leadership of the CPSU and Stalin, who agreed to render all fraternal and ideological assistance to solve the problems that had confronted the CPI.

In May 1951 Central Committee meeting was convened to apprise the Committee of the discussions held by the Indian Communists' delegation and to take necessary political-organisational discussions. Rajeswar Rao and the Polit Bureau which was elected a year earlier had submitted their resignation on the grounds that their continuation was not congenial to the reunification of the party in order to carry out the newly chalked out party line. The Polit Bureau was reconstituted and Ajoy Kumar Ghosh was elected General Secretary of the Central Committee. He threatened that unless the Telengana struggle was withdrawn immediately, he would be forced to issue a statement disowning it and a counter-threat was issued by Maddukuri Chandrasekhara Rao, the Secretary of the Andhra Committee that in that case the leaders of the Telengana movement would be forced to disown him and his leadership, kept him in check.[38] Thereafter, Ajoy Kumar Ghosh, General Secretary of the All-India party, without consulting the underground state leadership, constituted an "Election Committee" and authorised it to function as the *de facto* state committee.[39] The underground committee of Andhra sent a circular asking party members to ignore this committee except for election purposes.

Two draft documents of the party, as noted earlier, were approved in the meeting with the Soviet Communist Party Leadership in 1951. But the tactical line was not published for reasons of leadership conflict. The draft programme was adopted by the party in 1951.

The programme[40] of 1951 stated that the British imperialist rulers of India "established" the government of the leadership of the National Congress in August 1947. It was the same imperialist state and that the Congress Government was installed in power by the consent of the British imperialists as it was a government pledged to the protection and preservations of British capital. It noted that the industrialisation of country "is held at the mercy of the British and the Americans and who certainly are not interested in making

India an industrial country". The government represented the interest of landlords and princes, financial sharks and speculators and "the government hang on to the will of the British Commonwealth and British imperialists". To prevent the growing unity of the people against this rule of landlords and princes and reactionary big bourgeoisie collaborating with British imperialists, "the present government is utilising other means apart from police repression". The government, "unwilling really to break its ties with imperialism, it has shamelessly proclaimed the republic to be a part of the empire" and a member of the British Commonwealth. The division of the country and communal religious strife were used to drown the demands of the various nationalities of India for their free development, for reconstruction of the former mixed British provinces and the princely states in autonomous linguistic provinces in a united India.

Although universal adult franchise exists in the constitution of India and it can and will be used by the people "it is a deception of the people to say that election alone under this constitution can end the landlord-capitalist rule in the country and the imperialist hold over its life". The constitution "guarantees no rights to the people which are enforceable in any way or which are not subject to violation by the emergency autocratic decrees of the bureaucracy which is irremovable and inviolate". It "is not and cannot be called a truly democratic constitution but is a constitution of landlord-capitalist state, *tied to foreign imperialist interests* mainly British" and faced with these facts, the Communist Party's duty is to outline the tasks in the practical programme. (Italics added)

In the programme, it declared, *inter alia*, "the right of all nationalities of self-determination. The Republic of India will unite the peoples of the various nationalities of India not by force but by their voluntary consent to the creation of a common state" and that "the tribal areas or areas where the population is specific in composition and is distinguished by specific social conditions or constitutes national minority will have complete regional autonomy and regional governments, and full assistance to their development". It outlined the "Replacement of the police by militia. Elimination of the mercinary army and other punitive forces and the establishment of a national army, navy and airforce for the defence of India, closely linked with the people".

The programme provided for the "protection of industry against the competition of foreign goods in the country by promulgating appropriate laws". It prescribed for "withdrawal of India from the British Commonwealth of Nations and the British Empire" and "confiscation and nationalisation of all factories, banks, plantations, shipping and mining owned by the British in India, whether in their own name or under the signboard of Indian companies".

Finally, the programme held in conclusion that "*India is the last biggest dependent semi-colonial country in Asia still left for the enslavers to rule and exploit*".[41] (Italics added)

Organisational problems and differences however still persisted in the party. The two lines of thought confronted each other.

The programme of 1951 was amended by the Madurai Party Congress held in December 1953 and was put in abeyance by the Palghat Party Congress in 1956—characteristically the beginning year of destalinisation in the USSR—on the ground that, it needed more important changes. The party at this time discarded many vital formulations of Marxism-Leninism in its programme of 1951, adopted a more compromising attitude to the Indian ruling classes and thus actually began to follow the path of revisionism charted by Khruschev and Co., the new leaders of the Soviet Union. The party took them a conciliatory approach and gradually covered up the antagonistic contradiction between the state and people, specifically, the working class and peasants of India. Subjectivism and idealisation of the existing social order, was put in force, and that was reflected with the continuous conflict and struggle in the leadership of party over the years.

The government formed by the Communist Party of India in Kerala in 1957 had to align with the Central Government under Congress Rule and the big industrial houses like the Birla. The Fifth Congress of the Communist Party of India was held at Amritsar in 1959. There two documents were adopted which were held in non-party circles as containing a new perspective for the party and the left movement in the country. One was the addition of a new preamble to the party constitution which declared that the party "would strive to attain its objective through peaceful means"[42]. Secondly, the party constitution as amended at the Congress created an organisation structure which made it appear as if the party was being turned into a machine for running elections and carrying on other "legal and constitutional" activities, and Namboodripad writes that "together with the rapid expansion of party membership these changes in the organisational structure made the party look *like* any other party in the country, engaged in the same type of legal-constitutional activity."[43] and these changes were capable of being used to transform the party into a social democratic organisation. The politics of peaceful transition in India was envisaged in the Communist Party constitution.

The flood gates of subjective idealism, opportunism and of social democracy were thus opened up in the fifties and the party could not check and recover itself from that poisonous marsh and opportunism. The right deviation of the party became quite strong and pronounced under the leadership of the Dange-Ghosh clique and its smouldering with other party fractions set the unhealthy trend of bitter groupism and factionalism inside the party in the name of ideological fight! This apparently centred round the allegation on the issue of Dange's letter to the British Government during the period of freedom movement in the 1920s. The group which took up this issue in the name of fighting out revisionism, formed the CPI(M) in 1964 but gave no less support to the bourgeois constitutionalism, class collaboration and opportunism than that of the other as their activities and developments in politics confirm through the decades. Its party programme like that of the undivided CPI incorporates the fantacy of peaceful transition, parliamentary cretinism, class collaboration and labour aristrocracy which have largely gripped the party organisations of both the CPI and CPM.

The CPI(M) loudly declared itself to be committed to the struggle for "reforging the unity of the world communist movement" on the basis of struggle against "revisionism" and "sectarianism". In the Indian politics in 1967-69, the CPI with its strategic slogan of National Democracy pursued the tactics of collaboration with bourgeois parties, while the CPI(M) with its lip service to the strategy of people's democracy, adopted the "proletarian tactics" of using the differences among the bourgeois parties, actually stood for the reaction and the existing regime. Like the CPI, it declared "peaceful transition" of the Indian society, in its programme of 1964. This is their practical "struggle" against revisionism and opportunism!

The CPI(M) did not actually launch struggle of the working class and peasantry with a long-term approach for expansion of the party and working class hegemony. It merely followed the footprints of the CPI with much hullabaloo to support the Congress Party led by Indira Gandhi and Co. against the other faction of the Congress, unconditionally and without moving any charter of demand for the working class and peasantry, in 1969, on the ground of "countering" the right reaction. It actually helped and collaborated with this clique of the Congress. When the Communist Party of China launched campaign for cultural revolution to strengthen and consolidate the dictatorship of the proletariat, the CPI(M) along with the CPI denounced it in the same vein. Who did reap the benefit? Surely, the class of capitalists and landlords and their well-wishers and apologists—and finally the international finance capital *i.e.,* imperialism. These two instances are enough to expose their class compromise and class peace and "fight" against revisionism which the CPI(M) leaders "thought" as the main danger. To cover up the imbecility, Jyoti Basu the "leader" was sent to the UK in 1972 to propagate that "democracy" was trampled upon in India. What a great enthusiasm was for propaganda in the country of the old imperialist masters! Before that, he himself a "Marxist" minister ordered police action against the Naxalbari peasant movement in 1967 which killed scores of peasants and their families. It was really the service of a real "leftist"friend to the state of the comprador landlord and capitalist classes of the Indian Republic!

The vacillation of the CPI(M) leadership was exposed in 1972 when, the party's programmatic understanding and tactics had struck the rock, and Namboodiripad writes, "Failure to resolve the differences through these exchanges made it difficult for the leadership to function collectively, paralysing its work. This was reflected in the fact that the Ninth Congress of the Party held at Madurai (1972) could not be presented with an agreed political-organisational report. After the Congress and then for another four years, the stalemate continued in the leadership and was resolved only in 1976. But by then the General Secretary Sundaraiyya tendered his resignation which was accepted by the Central Committee".[44] Namboodiripad himself wrote[45] that on many issues "different stands" were adopted by different comrades and the oppositionists of the Sundaraiyya line were not in agreement (each taking his own independent line), but somewhat "a broad agreement" was reached on the line to be pursued. And this line was nothing but parliamentarianism in opportunist social democratic tradition in the name of "united action against authoritarianism". Such is the nature of collective leadership of the CPI(M) and its fight against the bourgeoisie and enemies of the working class and peasantry in the country.

This degeneration of the CPI(M) started in the late 1960s. Namboodiripad, philosopher of reformist surmons "The Tenali and Nur Mahal meetings of the Central Committees revealed the emergence of a definite ultra-left trend within the party, both on the international and national questions. An important fact helping its emergence was the Chinese Party's shift to the left as seen in the inauguration of the so-called Cultural Revolution".[46] Statement of a true Gandhian, not even of a liberal bourgeois leader! This is "Marxism" of the party like CPI(M)! And thus its general secretary, Namboodiripad yearned to seek "truth" in the process of class struggle in the society and exhibited his "profound knowledge" in Marxist philosophy! Did he seriously ever encourage and support class struggle against the exploiting classes? What becomes the true colour of the "leader" who slights the massive class struggle in a socialist country organised by the Communist Party led by the great revolutionary leader like Mao-Tse-Tung? In the late 1940s, Ranadive did the same thing by castigating the leadership of the Chinese Communist Party which was then set to capture power in China by revolution. Such statements of the Indian communist leaders only prove their ignorance, class collaboration, inaction and incapability, and unworthiness to the revolutionary cause of masses of the people. Their smattering only gave theoretical support to the right reaction and imperialist forces. It is strange and indeed pernicious that with such dishonesty, hypocritical stand, class collaboration and rank opportunism, the CPI(M) parade for unity in the international communist movement! It works as a close and trusted friend of the national and international bourgeoisie. Jyoti Basu, the leader was not ashamed to speak during his foreign visit in 1983 that socialist leaders like Stalin and Mao-Tse-Tung were not necessary in India, as Parliamentary Democracy had functioned well in the country and only some principles, rules and regulations were required to be changed! This is "Marxism" of Jyoti Basu, the "leader" of the opportunists. Actually, he is the most "aristrocrat left leader, actually a very faithful" person serving for the *status quo*, right reaction and imperialism. No wonder, he was the "leader" of the CPI, who criticised the food movement of 1959 in which as many as 82 peasants fell to the police firing of the reactionary Congress Government. This is enough to expose the treachery of social democrat leaders who are dead against the interest of the working class and peasantry. It is they, who substitute Marxism-Leninism with bourgeois liberalism, social democracy and most vulgar materialism with their malignant opportunism in the contemporary period of history.

In this regard, the main reasons for resignation of P. Sundarayya from the post of General Secretary of the CPI(M) in August 1975 (during the internal emergency) can be mentioned to understand actual conditions showing vascillation and contradiction inside the party's Polit Bureau. The document[47] notes that the resolution of the majority of the CP1(M) Polit Bureau approved the joint struggle with the pro-imperialist Jana Sangh at the centre of which functions the para-military and fascist storm trooper Rastriya Swayamsevak Sangh. Sundaraiyya thought that this resolution was detrimental to the party and that it would be isolated from the anti-imperialist and socialist forces in the democratic masses of the people in the country and abroad. He observed that, for its materialisation, the party's tactical line could not be implemented in the trade union, peasant and other mass organisations by the Polit Bureau.

It also failed to implement the same in the open and secret sections of the party organisation. Sundaraiyya drew attention to the fact that the matter of concretisation of the tactical line in practical aspects had been kept in the cold storage. He held that the matters like formulating of demands, supporting of the demands, getting support of the democratic sections and other classes, formation of the party branches, the method of working of the trade unions, the main class organisation, particularly bypassing the party centre at the all India level, and above the state committees, were not conducive to the party organisation. He observed that cadre deployment to the peasant front was poor which led to the lack of unity among the agricultural labourer, poor peasant and middle peasant, and lack of initiative of the responsible party units to implement the agrarian programme with importance. He pointed out the negligence to form secret contingents of the party organisation according to the resolution of the Mazaffarpur document. He viewed that the Polit Bureau, above all, ceased to play the effective role as the collective leadership. It is known from Sundaraiyya's resignation letter that the difference of opinion in the Polit Bureau had persisted since the beginning of 1969 which forced K. Basavapunnaiya at first and P. Rammurthy sometime later to resign from the Polit Bureau but, on the request of the other Polit Bureau members, resignations were withdrawn. But according to Sundaraiyya, the difference became sharp right before the Party Congress in 1972. It worsened at the time of the discussion of the Agrarian question (urgent duty of the party organisation), inspite of its adoption by the Party's Central Committee in Mazaffarpur in March, 1973. Even, while implementing the unitedly agreed agrarian and organisational resolutions, difference in opinion became more sharp in the leadership.

At the time of the declaration of internal emergency by the Indira Gandhi Government on 26th June 1975, Sundaraiyya confides[48], that the CPI(M) was quite unprepared and it became so much scattered, isolated and politically disunited that the Polit Bureau practically turned to be ineffective and non-functioning.

After the declaration of internal emergency the resolution of the Central Committee entitled "Declaration of Emergency and Later Situation", that was given final shape by the Polit Bureau and published on 2.9.1975, said that there had come the greatest opportunity to form United Front from below. This approach, writes Sundaraiyya, meant that all parties (including Jana Sangh), groups and persons would organise joint struggle and joint struggle committee in which the CPI(M) would be associated and "all efforts must be made for this", and side by side, "movement of this nature should be built up from below." Sundaraiyya held that this was nothing but formation of political United Front with the Jana Sangh. He exposed that organising joint struggle and formation of the joint struggle committee with the Jana Sangha and other rightist opposition parties had been "a continuing idea" of the CPI(M) party and its leadership. P. Rammurthy, Jyoti Basu and B.T. Ranadive and most Polit Bureau members came in favour of joining in the all India movement led by Jayprakash Narayan in 1974 against the Central Government. B.T. Ranadive presented a thesis in the meeting of the CPI(M) Central Committee in April 1975 contending that it was wrong not to join the demonstration outside the parliament on 6 March 1975, which was led by Jayaprakash Narayan. Central Committee circular to this effect was issued to the state committees, district committees and state plenums. At this time, E.M.S. Namboodiripad, Polit Bureau member, issued a statement confirming that the party was prepared for the joint struggle with Jayaprakash movement and electoral front with the Congress (organisation) party in some states. And just a few days before the declaration of emergency, Namboodiripad advocated for a front with the rightist opposition parties like Jana Sangh against Indira Gandhi Government, in an article entitled "On Bourgeersie and Bourgeois Democracy" in the *Deshaviman*, a party daily in Malayalam.

In his resignation letter Sundaraiyya referred to note 32/70, wherein Polit Bureau member B.T. Ranadive himself concluded that the Polit Bureau was being gradually eroding and it was no longer united. In a rejoinder to the same note, Sundaraiyya retorted that Ranadive himself was deviating from the resolution of the CPI(M) in 1967. Sundaraiyya reminded that though Ranadive spoke of the hegemony of the working class and its interest, he actually had capitulated before economism and spontaneity, instead of teaching the working class to conquer them.

In the seventies the CPI(M) worked to forge unity with the rightist parties, groups and fractions for fighting against the Congress Government at the centre. Now in the late 1990s, Namboodiripad and other CPI(M) leaders like Jyoti Basu and Surjit strive to have alliance with the Congress against the B.J.P.-led Central government for the sake of "secularism". It is most important to remember that the Congress led by the lady president swears and very recently passed the resolution that "Hinduism is the best guarantee of secularism" in India, which ultimately serves this interest of the capitalist and landlord classes. CPI(M) openly supported this party's efforts for government formation by defeating BJP-led government at the centre in April 1999. This is "Marxism" of CPI(M) and its fight against "revisionism" and "*Hindutva*"!

The influence and domination of religion and its philosophy on the Indian politics and its parties has continued all through the present century. One of its major institutions is the Rastriya Swayamsevak Sangh which is also known as the Sangh Parivar that has been forcefully propagating Hindu cultural nationalism since its inception in 1925. This organisation is firmly based on the doctrine of Rama and *Hindutva* and it has influence on culture and franchise of the majority community to a great extent. Jana Sangh, a rightist party was closer to it but Congress Party lately also tried to utilise its support for winning the elections by championing Hinduism at large. The Congress Party's Government at the centre was responsible for the holocaust that occurred in November 1984 in which the Sikh community was targeted for loot, arson and murder. It was the culmination of the atrocious policy pursued by the ruling Congress Party. The ruling Congress Party used the Hindu card at the same time. The latter tactic was sought to be met by the political forces of Hindutva by organising *Ekatmata Yajynas* in 1983. After the unfortunate assassination of Indira Gandhi, her son and successor, Rajiv Gandhi followed the policy of appeasing the hardliners among Hindus as well as Muslims. His initiatives led to the unlocking of the Babri Masjid and the worshipping of Lord Rama's image surreptitiously installed in the mosque in 1949. Later, the U.P. state government led by the Bhartiya Janata Party encouraged Vishwa Hindu Parishad (VHP) to stockpile sacred bricks at the disputed *Ram Janmabhoomi—Babri Masjid* site where the VHP wants to lay the foundation of the Ram temple. It was known that the concerned plot of land was disputed and the court had issued injunction against any act relating to permanent construction at that site.

The Bharatiya Janata Party (BJP), assisted by Vishwa Hindu Parishad and other organisations of its ideological fraternity "competed with Rajiv Gandhi's (Congress) party as virulently as it could. It pushed its hate agenda with determination and reaped huge electoral gains by cultivating the insecurities in the psyche of the Hindu community which the ruling Congress Party had helped in creating by playing the Hindu card for eight years. Communal clashes followed, in which the police and the bureaucracy failed to remain impartial, in large number of cases".[49] Communalism continued to grow unabetted in the largest democracy of the world!

All this culminated in the demolition of the Babri Mosque on 6th December, 1992 by the Hindu fanatics mobilised by the organisations like RSS and BJP. In the aftermath of the destruction, the Muslim community became the "target of the Hindu communalists, for having dared protest". The most barbaric acts were perpetrated as had happened in 1984 but on a very large scale.

Elections in the country have become more and more expensive, especially since 1980. New means for collecting huge funds are being devised, which strengthens the collusion between politicians, moneybags and bureaucrats. The administration has become lax; and, gradually anti-social elements have started to join the ranks of politicians. This process had started earlier with the Congress under the new "leader" in the early 1980s but others have not lagged behind. Industrialists used criminal elements to break strikes in the industries and launch rival trade unions. Their nexus with politicians helped the criminals to join politics. Throughout the 1980s and 1990s there have remained clandestine ground level understanding[50] between the Congress and their organisations to defeat Left Democratic Front candidates in states like Kerala.

Religious communalism, exploitation of labour and power in the parliamentary democracy thus have been enmeshed and integrated to protect and continue the rule of the comprador landlord and capitalist classes and domination of the international finance capital *i.e.*, imperialist powers, on the Indian soil. Subjective idealism warrants existence and sustenance of the oppressive regime and reaction by creating myth and illusion around the existing reality of the exploitation, pauperisation and suppression of labour resulting in the debasement of humanity. It thwarts human development, welfare and progress in the society and supports reaction in general.

Revolt against the ideology and practice of the CPI and CPI(M) was centred with the formation of the All India Co-ordination Committee of the Communist Revolutionaries in 1969, and later CPI(ML) in 1971. The formation of the party marked a radical departure from the organisation and ideology of the CPI and CPI(M) committed to class collaboration, shameless compromise in the tottering parliamentary democracy of India and hence reformism and revisionism. In the field of practice, however, the new party could not sustain and develop necessary strong organisation owing to its own subjectivism, weakness and above all, mounting attacks of India's centralised, imperialist state machinery and revisionist organisations. Nevertheless, it made a definite positive impact upon the left movement in a country like India in the more contemporary period. It stressed the necessity for organising armed struggle. But, it could not build up the organisation and adapt technique of combining the workers and peasants in proper unions for their protracted political movement in the Indian situation. As a result, the movement disintegrated and the party split into a number of groups which have been in practice until the present. The Communist Party of China fraternally advised and practically helped to set right its policy and practice in 1971, but that was of no avail to check its weakness and decline.

But, the whole process has brought about a phenomenal development in unleashing class struggle and unravelling the contradiction of the Indian society over the years. It has exposed the reactionary philosophy of the Indian ruling classes and their social democrat allies and opportunists in politics showing the relative advance of the materialist philosophy in politics. But it is still a very small force compared to the reactionary philosophy of subjective idealism and will have to proceed through many odds, obstacles and barriers in future.

The hold of monism or *Adwaitavad* as idealist philosophy is still very strong in the Indian society. In fact, it has been reinforced by Vivekananda, his Adwaita Math and many other institutions and authors over the years. But they all suffer from the lack of objectivity and that leads to compromise and collaboration at large. The inception of Congress governance in 1937 for 18 months, "was attended by compromise and opportunism", writes one contemporary author (Suhit Sen, First Ministries, *The Statesman*, Calcutta 4.7.99: Magazine Section, p. 4). This was "practical *Adwaitavad"* in Indian political struggle for power by the Congress led by Gandhi. The parliamentary left and its government have now become the modern Vedantist as they practise reformism, and compromise, oppose class struggle, support imperialist exploitation and take all such measures to maintain *status quo* in the semi-feudal and semi-colonial Indian society. They more idealise the existing social order in India.

Prof. R.K. Dasgupta writes that "Satyameva Jayate is our government's motto although truth has been a rare commodity in our public life since independence". (R.K. Dasgupta, The Perfect Language, *The Statesman*, Calcutta, 25-26 June, 1999) and speaks of the muddle in the real life of the society. There is indeed a great difference and divergence between the actual and the ideal, and hence, undenyingly existence of contradiction in social life. He seems to recognise it. The eminent scholar thereafter writes, "What is to be done now? I think it is still not too late to realise that the root of our culture is in the spiritual and moral tradition which is embodied in Sanskrit. And if we must now try to find our place in the modern world, the world of Bacon, Newton, Hume and Mill, the world of Marx and Freud, we must go back to the *Vedanta*. Sri Ramkrishna and Vivekananda, Rabindranath and Sri Aurobindo, have brought to us the message of the ancient India." (R.K. Dasgupta, The Perfect Language, *The Statesman,* Calcutta, 25-26 June, 1999). Spiritual and moral tradition is only a part of culture but not the root of the matter. Because they originate from the material condition of the life of the society based on the mode of production. In sum, economic foundation dominates in the whole historical process. Sanskrit does not mainly embody the culture of India as language itself is a great social phenomenon and an important product of the culture of the economic society. Culture in the main is demonstrated and embodied in caves, stone weapons, instruments of production, cave sketches, potteries, artifacts, archeological relics and inscriptions of the past which have been discovered so far. The roots of Indian culture are not in the spiritual and moral tradition which Sanskrit is supposed to hold fast, but in the real life process of ancient India's tribal communities. Sanskrit deals only a little on social developments and mainly concentrates on imagination, mystification and spiritualism, mostly devoid of the actual life of the society. Going back to the *Adwaita Vedanta* philosophy, heavily loaded with theism, cannot at all help one to understand the world of materialism of Bacon, Newton and Marx. With its subjectivism *Adwaitavad* cannot explain the world phenomenon but it abounds man's ignorance with mysticism and spiritualism that was strongly advocated by the earlier Vedantists like Vivekananda. Vivekananda gave primacy for spirit in relation to matter and failed to explain the process how the spirit enters and enjoins to become dominant in the matter. Concept of the domination of spirit over matter is quite old, utterly speculative and false. The *Adwaita Vedanta* philosophy was justly opposed and declared to be useless by Rammohan Roy, Vidyasagar, Debendranath Tagore and Akshay Kumar Dutta who were the pioneers of philosophic movement and renaissance of India in the nineteenth century. It is sad that scholars like R.K. Dasgupta see contradiction in the society but oppose the anti-Vedantic rational philosophical trend of Rammohan and Vidyasagar and idealistically, take shelter in the dark cave of *Adwaita Vedanta* philosophy for the sake of "peace". Their stand actually helps the comprador Indian ruling classes, exploiters their political parties and government.

Marxism or militant materialism is quite opposed to such a passive philosophical stand. It studies and unravels the contradiction, and can proceed by blasting the age-old fortification of the religious philosophy. Today there is no serious scientific dispute about the fact of evolution of nature as shown by the scientists. Evolution of nature is supported by anatomy, fossils, carbon dating, genetic evidence, the ages of rocks, etc. There is a continuous debate and controversy on the general theoretical exposition of evolution : how and why and when life began and species evolved. Such is the process of the progress and development of scientific knowledge and philosophical materialism in the world. The process is being daily enriched.

Bhupendranath Dutta much earlier observed that "the orthodox Brahminical priestcraft is engulfing Ramakrishnaism" and "it has not moulded the society according to its own ideal". It is following "the old beaten Brahminical rut." (Swami Vivekananda—*Patriot-prophet*, Calcutta, 1954, p. 185) The Mission's schools and colleges provide education mainly to the children of the well-off middle class that can afford its high cost, and propagate spiritualism at large. Those have mainly become the breeding ground for making future executives to serve the colonial state machinery of India that oppress the country's people. Mission like this indirectly has given moral and spiritual feed-back and support to the organisation and development of the right-wing institutions like the Rashtriya Swayam Sevak Sangha (RSS), Vishwa Hindu Parishad, Bajrang Dal over the years. For instance, at present, there are 35000 branches, 25000 centres and ten lakhs active worker-worshippers in the RSS who are active in Hindu Community services in the name of cultural nationalism. Their philosophy is certainly based on *Vedanta* in the cult of Ramachandra as the ideal king and incarnation of God. Organisations like Ramakrishna Mission do not criticise or oppose them. In fact, all of them are inter-linked and work in unison under the old beaten Brahminical rut and caste system in the name of *Vedanta*! The Indian state extends generous financial help for such missions' organisation and service.

All these institutions are generally aligned with the ruling classes and decadent forces of the society. They never oppose severe exploitation of labour and plunder of India by the imperialist finance capital. They idealise the existing oppressive social order of Indian society. *Vedanta* with its age-old idealist philosophy mystifies man's thought and the existing social order with spiritualism and salvation of soul and thus serves reaction at large. Science with spiritualism, integrated humanism and similar ideas of the ruling classes are the worst forms of subjective idealism based on the *Vedanta* philosophy.

The developments are indeed quite opposite to what Swami Vivekananda had visualised about the mission. He expressed the following view to the representative of *The Hindu*, Madras, in February 1897 : "The Chicago parliament was a tremendous success for India and Indian thought. It helped on the tide of *Vedanta*, which is flooding the world", and "There is every prospect. Before many years elapse, a vast majority of the English people will be Vedantins. There is a greater prospect of this in England than there is in America." (*Works*, Vol. 5, pp. 139-142). This speaks of his firm conviction in the *Vedanta* philosophy. Vivekananda spelt out the objective of the Ramakrishna Mission at its second meeting held on 5 May, 1897 and his words suggest that the mission was not conceived as a Hindu sect. He said that the "duty of the Mission is to conduct in the right spirit the activities of the movement inaugurated by Sri Ramakrishna for the establishment of fellowship among the followers of different religions knowing them all to be so many forms only of one undying eternal religion." Prof R.K. Dasgupta cites this statement for communication to the public. But the Mission's activity has not so far made any impact for the establishment of fellowship among the followers of different religions in India and abroad. Prof. Dasgupta writes that Vivekananda did discover in Ramakrishna's life and teachings "some unique features of spirituality which we now call neo-Vedanta. What I have called the Ramakrishna movement is essentially a *Vedantic* movement creating a neo-Vedanta" (*The Statesman*, Calcutta, 10.8.1999, p. 8) Thus neo-Vedanta is based on spirituality, and this is common to all the medieval and right-wing forces like RSS, Vishwa Hindu Parishad and Bajrang Dal which are opposed to the cause of the labour in general and in particular against the minority communities of India.

In his last important statement on Vedantism reported in the *Oakland Tribune* on 26 February 1900 Vivekananda said, "Vedantism is the only religion that can be taught without lies, without stretching the texts, without compromise". Vivekananda, through all his addresses, writings and letters, notes R.K. Dasgupta, "gave a new dimension and a new depth" to *Vedanta* which we now call neo-Vedanta" (*The Statesman*, Calcutta, 15.8.1999). This confirms *Vedanta's* distinction as a religion based on theism and spirituality—an old philosophy—that sanctions caste system and obscures the vile economic reality, inequality and class antagonism in the society. What the people will do with such a religious philosophy that sanctions caste system and daily tortures and smothers them all round? Indian people are severely repressed in unison by the colonial state and religion with old medieval practices.

In fact, much earlier, Romain Rolland observed, "Vivekananda's neo-Vedantism...spread like a burning alcohol in the veins of his intoxicated nation" (*Prophets of the New India*, p. 501). This had obviously countered secularism and no doubt created an adverse reaction in fomenting communalism in the Indian society and politics over the long period of time. No sensible person can deny this fact in the history of political development of India.

It is with the fideism and oneness of the *Vedanta* that the Congress Party leading the comprador Indian bourgeoisie of the majority community philosophically discovered "communalism" in the struggle of the Mopla peasants against the oppressive Hindu landlords and money lenders in 1921-22, in the uprising of Meo tribal peasants against the Hindu feudal prince of Alwar state in 1929-30, and in the imposition of tax on the Indian big business by the Indian Government in 1946-47. *Vedanta* very much came in to protect the class interest of the capitalists and landlords. M.K. Gandhi opposed the struggle of the naval ratings in 1946 against the British rule in India as "irreligious". Such is the relation of the religion and *Vedanta* philosophy with the actuality and world reaction. Parliamentary Left now holds and implements the same philosophy by curbing the opposition to the imperialist capital and its exploitation, by opposing class struggle and by practising class collaboration in India. They have become one with the Vedantists indealise the existing state of things in the material world.

It thus becomes clear that the pioneers of Indian Renaissance in the nineteenth century were very correct to criticise the *Vedanta* philosophy, and rightly called it a false and erroneous system, from the rational viewpoints of secularism, unity and progress of the Indian society. Idealist philosophy gradually suppressed and negated this trend of rationalist approach towards philosophical materialism. The latter with the aid of modern dialectical materialism must reverse the former in the interest of class struggle and steer clear the path of proletarian people's organisation and progress of the society. It is the urgent necessity. It will be the negation of negation in accordance with the dialectical materialism.

It can be stressed that, while exposig the basic contradiction in the international sphere, Mao-Tse-Tung addressed, "People of the world, unite and defeat the US aggressors and all their running dogs". (*People's Daily*, Peking, May 21, 1970).

NOTES

1. "Citation" in R. C. Agarwal, *Constitutional Development of India and National Movement,* S. Chand & Co., New Delhi, 1986, p. 55.
2. *Ibid,* p. 56.
3. *Ibid,* pp. 55-56.
4. Benoy Kumar Sarkar, *Naya Banglar Gora Pattan,* (Bengali), Volume I, Chakraborty, Chatterji & Co., Calcutta, 1932, p. 350.
5. *Ibid.,* p. 356 and p. 360.
6. *Ibid.,* pp. 364-366.
7. V. I. Lenin, National and Colonial Questions (Three Articles), Foreign Languages Press, Peking, 1975, pp. 30-37.
8. Sir Cecil Kaye, *Communism in India (1919-1924),* National Book Agency, Calcutta, 1971, p. 300.
9. Bhupendranath Datta, *Bharater Dwitiya Swadhinatar Sangram* (Bengali), Nababharat Publishers, Calcutta, 1983, p. 34 and p. 149.
10. Bhupendranath Datta, *Aprakashita Rajnaitik Itihas,* (Bengali), Nababharat Publishers, Calcutta, 1983, Section 2, p. 30.
11. *Ibid.,* Section-2, p. 31.
12. "Citations" in Y. Krasin, *The Dialectics of Revolutionary Process,* Navosti Press Agency Publishing House, Moscow, 1972, pp. 44-45. *Cf.* Bulletin of the Congress of the Comintern (in Russ.), No. 1, 27 July, 1920.
13. See Revolutionary Movement in the Colonies and Semi-colonies: Thesis approved by the Sixth Congress of the Communist International 1928, Moscow, People's Publishing House Ltd., Bombay, 1948 (Indian Edition).
14. Communist International, *International Press Correspondence,* Moscow, 18, December, 1930.
15. See Thesis of the Sixth Congress of the Communist International *(op. cit.).*
16. *Ibid.*

17. The Communist International, *International Press Correspondence*, Moscow, Vol. II, No. 2, 15 January, 1931, p. 44 and No. 8-9, 15 May, 1932, pp. 303-314.
18. The Communist International, *International Press Correspondence*, Moscow, No. 51, 1933, pp. 1153-1158.
19. M. Sharif, *Presidential Address*, Indian Philosophical Congress, Conference Volume, Aligarh, 1936.
20. *The Communist International*, September 1935, Moscow, pp. 1337-1349.
21. P. C. Joshi, The Nehru Legacy (Reprint), *Mainstream*, New Delhi, November, 1998, p. 24.
22. *Ibid.*, p. 23. To clarify the matter it is important to note that : *The Communist International*, (New York) in an editorial of October 1939, entitled "The Indian People Ask..." wrote, "The English imperialists have demanded that Germany withdraw from Poland and respect in full equality of the Polish people. That is an excellent demand but it will remain a contemptible hypocricy as long as England does not withdraw its troops from India and respect the full equality of the Indian people. Where the English imperialists piously raise their eyes and reply that the Indian people certainly could not be left to the mercy of their corrupt maharajahs, one must remind them that the majority of the Indian people are under direct English rule and that the corrupt Polish pans are not a whit better than the Indian Maharajhs and that it is *the concern* of the Polish and Indian peoples to rid themselves of their native tyrants....

    "...now not a gang of bankrupts but a great and noble people are turning to the oh-so-democratic, oh-so-honourable, oh-so-freedom-loving British bourgeoisie and asking what the English government's avowal of freedom, democracy and self-determination really means for the Indian people. Will the English imperialists refuse to the oppressed Indian people what they so magnanimously accord the oppressors of the Polish people, of the Ukranian and white Russian minorities?

    Of course, they will refuse it. But what they pass off the freedom, democracy and self-determination are only counterfeit banknotes, the use of which is mercilessly punished in their own empire. The freedom they mean bears the countenance of a Polish oppressor of peasants but not the countenance of the three hundred million Indian people."

    In an article entitled "How the British Imperialists Rule in India" by W. Leitner, published in *The Communist International* (New York) of April 1940 it was stated :

    "More than ever before, the people of India are today determined to throw of the foreign yoke. In the fight against British imperialism, they are unfolding not only the forces of national liberation, but the forces of their social and cultural progress too.

"In the last world war hundreds of thousands of young Indians, led by their belief in the promises of British politicians, allowed themselves to be sacrificed in an alien cause on the battlefields of Europe. The outbreak of the present war has been met by the people of India and first and foremost by its workers and peasants, with a more determined fight for independence. And this fact weighs more in judging the lofty war aims proclaimed by the British imperialists and their henchmen, the citrines, than all the thousands of their propaganda speeches."

This confirms the favourable and positive attitude of the Communist International toward the Indian freedom movement. To facilitate the freedom movement and national liberation struggles in different colonial countries, Communist International was declared "dissolved" by Stalin in 1943. (*cf. Keesings Contemporary Archives*)

Ranen Sen, one of the leaders of the Indian Communist movement writes that, in India, the arrested Communist leaders were transferred to different jails in the early period of 1942. Ranen Sen and some other leaders were transferred to Midnapore jail. Sen recollects that rumour spread that the party was likely to change the political line. Earlier, it was decided that the war was amongst the imperialist forces; but with the attack of the Soviet Union by the Fascist Germany "the world situation had changed." At this time, Deuli document of the Communist Party of India was prepared, which said that war was "changed into a people's war" and so it was necessary to "ensure victory of the Soviet Union." It was people's war not only to the people of Europe but also to the Indian people. It was necessary to ensure victory of the Soviet Union and so the Communist Party should support the war, inspite of the hard reality that the British imperialism was conducting the war from India.

This was the main content of the Deuli document. The document was actually prepared Sen confirms, by B.T. Ranadive while interned in the Deuli jail. S.A. Dange later confided to Sen that he himself did not oppose the document. There was intense debate on the document both inside and outside the party. At least P.C. Joshi and G. Adhikari, on whose leadership the main party centre was functioning secretly, also accepted the same line in general. Joshi wrote another article making the line more concrete and acceptable. (See Ranen Sen, *Bharater Communist Partir Itibritta* : Bengali, Nabapatra Prakashan, Calcutta, 1996, pp. 79-80).

23. E. M. S. Namboodiripad, *Reminiscences of an Indian Communist,* National Book Centre, New Delhi, 1987, p. 98.

24. *Ibid.,* p. 125.

25. *Ibid.,* p. 127 and p. 128.

26. *Ibid.,* p. 132.

27. *Ibid.,* p. 132.

28. *Ibid.*, p. 133.
29. See Cominform, *For a Lasting Peace and for a People's Democracy,* Documents of the History of CPI, Vol. VIII, New Delhi, p. 612.
30. See Namboodiripad, *op. cit.*, pp. 133-34.
31. *Ibid.*, p. 134.
32. See P. Sundaraiyya, *Talengana People's Armed Struggle,* National Book Centre, New Delhi, 1985, pp. 88-89.
33. *Ibid.*, p. 89.
34. *Ibid.*, p. 89.
35. *Ibid.*, p. 90.
36. *Ibid.*, pp. 92-93.
37. *Ibid.*, p. 93.
38. *Ibid.*, p. 112.
39. *Ibid.*, p. 112.
40. See *Three Communist Documents,* Published by the Committee for Inner-Party Struggle against Revisionism, Calcutta, 1963.
41. E. M. S. Namboodiripad, *op. cit.*, pp. 146-150.
42. *Ibid.*, p. 177.
43. *Ibid.*, p. 177-78.
44. *Ibid.*, p. 223.
45. *Ibid.*, p. 223.
46. *Ibid.*, p. 299. There was acknowledgement of dissent in the document of the CPI (M) Central Committee in 1968. It said, "Since our Tenali Convention of July 1964, when our programme draft was broadly endorsed for full three years upto August 1967, our Central Committee's official stand on the ideological questions, more or less, stood in suspense with the result that the entire struggle against revisionism, as far as the ideological issues under debate in the world Communist movement are concerned, was carried on solely relying on the contribution made by the Chinese Communist Party and reproducing them in our papers and pamphlets in different languages…" (Citation in Ranen Sen, *Bharater Communist Partir Itibritta*: Bengali, 1996, p. 169).
47. P. Sundaraiyya, *Why did I Resign from the Polit Bureau* (Bengali), Calcutta, 1976.
48. *Ibid.*
49. Surendra Mohan, Endemic Violence, *The Statesman,* Calcutta, 27 March, 1999; Yasin Malik, Communalism in Kashmir, *Frontier,* Calcutta, October 10-30, 1999, pp. 8-11.
50. *Ibid.*, and K. Madhaban Kutty, *The Southern Discomfort,* Har-Anand, New Delhi, 1999.

6

MILITANT MATERIALISM

Spectrum of Marxism

How is the world at the end of twentieth century under "globalisation", the present battle cry of imperialism against the people of this planet at the end of the twentieth century? This is at present the most important social issue of the human organisation. From the viewpoint of objective reality, its answer unfolds many issues and exposes the acute antagonistic contradiction under the capitalist system of the world dominated by the monopoly and finance capital in the beginning of the twenty-first century.

More than a quarter of humanity—1600 million people—are worse today than they were 15 years ago, according to the 1996 Human Development Report of the United Nations. According to James Guestav Speth, administrator of the UNDP, "We must face the fact that we live in a world where between 1960 and 1993 total global income increased by six-fold to $23000 billion and where average world per capita income tripled, but where three-fifths of humanity still live in a prison of poverty". *(The Statesman,* Calcutta, 21 July, 1996, p. 16 and the "editorial" dated 5.7.1996, p.8) The poverty line is obviously measured by the bare minimum subsistence of labourer. With this characteristic and indicator in the backdrop, it was observed that the gap in economic development has been widening, the report said. The world has become more economically polarised both between countries and within countries. The official added that if the present trends continued, economic disparities between industrial and developing nations will move from "the inequitable to inhuman". According to the official, "The net worth of the 358 richest people is equal to the combined (annual) income of the poorest 45 per cent of the world's population—2300 million". It is the consequence of the existing mode of production under monopoly capitalism in the world economy.

The developing countries with 80 per cent of the world's population, account for only 20 per cent of the world output. The gap in per capita annual income between the industrial and developing country group tripled between 1960 and 1993 from $5700 to $15400.

In countries like Brazil and Guatemala, the richest 20 per cent earn more than 30 times the poorest and even in the USA, the U.K., Switzerland and Australia, the difference is about ten-fold. As in the USA, the wealthiest one per cent of the population increased its share of total assets between 1975 and 1990 from 20 per cent to 36 per cent. The concentration of assets has become quite rapid, phenomenal and amazing over the years in the rule of finance capital.

The UNDP report adds that in more than 100 out of the 174 countries, the per capita income is lower than it was 15 years ago. In 19 countries, per capita income at present is less than it was in 1960 or before. Monopoly capitalism has violently divided mankind more than ever before in the globe.

In terms of Human Development (measured with the life expectancy at birth, educational attainment and real income) the top positions belonged to the developed industrial countries, while the developing countries slided down to the bottom. At the end of the list of 174 countries are Angola, Burundi, Mozambique, Ethiopea, Sierra Leone and Nigar. India lags behind Myanmar and Pakistan. Income growth alone cannot be the indicator of the quality of people's life for obvious reasons. In Pakistan, despite high economic growth, 61 per cent of its population lacked the health, education and nourishment.

Employment data for the past decade from 69 countries show that only 27 of the 46 countries with positive economic growth had little increase in employment. As many as 19 countries experienced jobless growth, including India and Pakistan.

Some 500 largest industrial multinational corporations now control 25 per cent of the world's economic output, employing only one-twentieth of one per cent of the world population. Industrial countries utilising much greater share of global savings had $1,50,000 worth of capital invested per worker as against only $13000 per worker in the developing countries in 1994.

Let us state and consider the following characteristics and results of the world economic development over the years : the richest 358 people have as much money as 45 per cent of the world's population; $ 18 trillion of the global gross domestic product is in the industrialised countries, $ 5 trillion in the rest; 15 per cent of the world's population has 85 per cent of the world income and 85 per cent of the world's population received only 15 per cent; of its income; the richest 20 per cent have 85 per cent of global income while the rest 80 per cent have only 15 per cent; and the poorest 20 per cent have only 1.4 per cent of it. In more than 70 countries per capita incomes had fallen during 1980s. And the saddest fact is that the two regions that have contributed to this devastating scenario are South Asia and Sub-Saharan Africa. Thanks to the monopoly capitalism and its parliamentary democracy, there are now 447 billionaires in the world estimated by Forbes Magazine, and, of them 149 (33 per cent) are in the USA, a powerful base of monopoly capitalism.

"Markets are ruthless", says Michel Camdessus, Managing Director of the International Monetary Fund, and he declares that it "will vigorously challenge those who do not adapt." The world's "common good", he surmons, "will be greatly helped by unions using their strength and place and government in dialogue to ensure that those who are unemployed through structural change are helped to retrain, to find new jobs and to carry their entitlements from job to job." (*IMF Survey*, International Monetary Fund, Washington, 15 July 1996, p. 239). In fact many unions have been performing this negotiation for decades and their result is the existing social order of highly concentrated global private property and wealth, glaring inequality and violent division of the population—the stage towards the "common good" of the philosopher, chief of the international finance capital of the present time! Clearly, his concern is only for the interest and domination of international capital and against the workers of the world.

The characteristics of the world economy indeed largely support and confirm the postulates and contentions of Marx-Engels on capitalist production *viz*., labour exploitation and mass pauperisation, centralisation and concentration of capital as private property, distribution as the product of the mode of production, uneven development of capitalism, relative surplus population, class domination and class contradiction in the society. It is naïve to think that the existing anarchic world order can be transformed by peaceful means. To maintain "peace", the international bourgeoisie is already far more armed to the teeth than ever. They maintain "peace" for preserving the present wage slave system in their own interest for global exploitation.

The developed industrial countries have parliamentary democracy and its government functioning under the rule of the law made by parliament for centuries. It is this system of government, the developed industrial countries' bourgeoisie idealise and have thrusted upon many countries of Asia, Africa and Latin America in the past colonial period and striking hard to foist upon them and the former socialist countries now-a-days. It is plain to see what a high degree of the concentration of income and wealth, labour exploitation, world-wide social antagonism and violent situation have been created within the parliamentary democracy. Under the thumb of monopoly capitalism – a great reaction – it has served, created and manifested great inequality and extreme social disparity over the years. It requires not much education to recognise what a violent rule the bourgeois parliament – an institution and product of capital and its market – has created and enforced in the world. But it is rife with strife and contradiction. The concentration and centralisation of wealth with the minority section of the population has proceeded uninterruptedly and unprecedentedly and it is this minority section which has established firm control in the parliamentary system and the state with the ownership of the means of production and domination of capital. It becomes evident that the parliamentary democracy has long before transformed itself as the forum for the dictatorship of the bourgeoisie to spread its influence and tentacles to support and consolidate the dictatorship of the international bourgeoisie. The result of capitalist development during the past two and a half centuries clearly prove this hard reality in the world.

Bourgeois parliamentary system including its election process during its long tenure has conditioned and assured the centralisation and concentration of capital and wealth in the hands of the minority section of the population, and the emergence and growth of monopoly capitalism in the world economy through exploitation of the mass of the people. A system that has invariably worked for the privilege of amassing of the riches and social power by the minority section of the people and internationalisation of capital actually means and ensures the domination and, hence, dictatorship of the ruling international bourgeoisie as well.

The process of capitalist production, exploitation of wage labour, the arbitrary character of distribution of its product enforced by the repressive state machinery and buttressed by the law and judiciary work in such a great co-ordination and unity that they together invariably condition, protect and enforce dictatorship of the minority, privileged bourgeoisie over time. No law in the capitalistic society can even slightly check this force and restrict the domination of the bourgeoisie in any manner. All the state laws under capitalism have conformed to it, ensured right to private property and its concentration that warrant the rule of capital *i.e.*, dictatorship of the bourgeoisie, in the name and form of parliamentary democracy. They have amazing unity and character that serve the process of capitalist production, acquisition through centralisation and concentration of capital *i.e.*, sway of monopoly capitalism all over the world with its own idea of globalisation.

Developed industrial countries with the old parliamentary system of government serving the interest of the bourgeoisie are now largely shedding their official social security schemes for the people and throwing out the workers at the mercy of the "ruthless market". The same course of action is being blindly adopted and implemented in other countries for the cause of reforms. Why, then, there is too much interest and clamour for the parliament, the forum of the bourgeoisie for its own dictatorship, and enthusiasm for participation in its election process on the part of the "Marxist" leaders at the present time? Why do they propagate parliamentarism, bourgeois constitutionalism and reformism among the mass of the people daily fleeced, exploited and oppressed under the dictatorship of the capitalist and landlord classes? Because the "Marxist" leaders, actually, social democrats, are disposed to the existing reactionary order of the society and sworn to serve the dictatorship of the bourgeoisie in whatever way and manner they can. The idea of some "Marxist leaders" to give some relief to the people of India in the existing social system of the country is simply naïve, reformist and opportunist with a desire to systematically cheat the people in the tottering parliamentary system. Ocean and mountain has never stopped the operation of the old colonial state machinery, its laws and statutes to sanctify continuous sucking of the blood of the Indian workers and peasants. The Government of the "Marxists" in West Bengal during more than two decades of their regime could do little to ameliorate the condition of the people with "some relief". On the countrary, many "Marxist" leaders have improved their economic position, acquired handsome private property and social status and they have become millionaires. Parliamentary "Marxists" and their government, in India, irrespective of the period of their tenure, are totally indisposed and incapable to remove even corpse of a running dog of imperialism from the city of Calcutta or remove a single brick from the solid structure of colonialism and imperialism at the Raisina Hill, New Delhi.

No law in India, for example, has ever worked to really improve the condition of life of the labourer. All laws of the Parliament and State Assemblies have invariably reformed and consolidated the joint rule of the comprador bourgeois-imperialist capital in the country, and they have been of no avail to the mass of the workers and peasants and ever-swelling number of unemployed and surplus workers in the country.

Bourgeois parliaments function to legalise sucking blood of the working people and certainly enforce the vile dictatorship of the capitalists and apparently in a sober manner. Outwardly, in the bourgeois democracy, there are democratic rights but they are so much clothed in the laws that most of the people comprising the workers and peasants, who are economically, socially and politically oppressed and downtrodden, cannot even really think of availing the "progressive" laws.

Changes in the government and parliamentary acts have failed to stop the uninterrupted process of labour exploitation, accumulation and concentration of private property and consequently, the dictatorship of the comprador bourgeois-imperialist capital on the Indian soil. No such reforms and changes would even slightly prick the rule of monopoly capitalism and affect the reactionary social order in any measure. "Globalisation" is the present slogan for further extending and deepening the rule of the international capital. It is being implemented by the dictatorship of the capitalists and landlords in many countries within the veil of parliamentary democracy and at the behest of the international finance capital.

Contradictions are being manifest in different parts of the countries like India and world exposing and signifying revolutionary crisis. Workers and peasants are becoming more restive against the offence of the axis of the native comprador and imperialist capitals, closure and lockout are throwing thousands of workers out of employment. The parliamentary "Marxists" are never tired of speaking and preaching of industrial peace and making every effort to embrace native comprador and international capitals with open arms in the name of industrial development. They now act just as "left" accomplices of imperialism. This their way and method of providing "relief" to the people and for this purpose they help to form "United Front" government at the centre with the support of a big party of the Indian comprador bourgeoisie.

All this exposes the dictatorship of the comprador bourgeoisie and landlord classes in collaboration with the imperialist capital – the reality of the bourgeois parliamentary system – established by the British colonial power in its own long-term interest in India. It is however on the wane and becoming more redundant over time.

Hence, participation in the bourgeois parliamentary election by the forces of the working class in the countries like India, Pakistan and Bangladesh would seem inconsistent, short-sighted, demoralising and counter-productive to further the cause of the workers, peasants and toiling masses. Participation in such elections would have only a very marginal effect to hasten class struggle, as the centre of gravity of contradiction is certainly developing fast outside the corrupt parliamentary arena and its system. To stress the work of a very marginal impact on the working class movement and leave the main field of working class movement in the hands of reaction means a service to the reactionary rule and neglect to the work of rousing the people for revolution. That would be unprincipled, confusing and disastrous. The working class organisation must have a firm stand against the illusion of the bourgeois parliamentary elections in the present period for resolving social contradiction.

The working class organisation, according to its principles and firm stand, in India must thoroughly expose the hollowness of parliamentary elections, bourgeois parliamentary politics and the parliamentary "Marxist" parties and groups. It must basically support extra-parliamentary struggles and other forms of democratic opposition and resistance against the existing reactionary social order by the exploited masses of the people.

The exploiting classes have generally succeeded to restore capitalism in Russia and China. In Russia 70 per cent of the gross domestic product is presently accounted for by the private sector and there are nearly 5 million share-holders in the private corporate sector. Chinese economy in 1995 registered 47 per cent of the industrial output contributed by the state-owned factories, 33 per cent by the township and village organisations and 20 per cent by the private sector. Some 10,000 to 20,000 Russian households have $5 million or more apiece in overseas bank accounts. Wages of the labourers have been shrinking as a proportion of household income in Russia from two-thirds (66 per cent) in 1992 to 40 per cent in 1995. In 1996, the richest 10 per cent of Russian were, according to official figures, earning 13.5 times as much as the poorest 10 per cent. "The discrepancies yawn not only between bosses and workers, but also between industries and between regions". This is the hard reality. The laws of capitalism prevail in the ruthless market. (*The Economist,* London, 1 June and 22 June 1996, p. 51 and 47, and *Ibid.,* London, 6 July 1996, p. 63).

The present governments of China and Russia are basically soft to the world monopoly capitalism and, therefore, generally opposed to a radical change. The working class organisation generally has to oppose their governments and ideology for obvious reasons.

Ascent and descent of forces, emergence and domination of different classes, restoration of the old order in the society, and revolution are all well within the operation and stronghold of dialectical materialism and they appear with their amazing nature and characteristics in the different periods of world history. The condition of labour is related with the phenomena.

Of the working age population in the high income capitalist countries, 3 per cent was absorbed in agriculture, 19 per cent in industry, 42 per cent in services and 6 per cent was unemployed in their total working age population. In the middle income countries, agriculture employed 18 per cent, industry 16 per cent, services 26 per cent and 4 per cent remained unemployed. In the low income countries, agriculture absorbed 44 per cent, industry 11 per cent, service 16 per cent while 2 per cent remained unemployed. Well over half of the world's working age population, some 2 billion people lived in the low income economies where annual income per capita was $695 in 1993. Another 40 million were elderly workers and a reported 50 to 60 million there worked as child labourers. Of the total working age population of 547 million in the high income economies, 30 per cent (164 million) was not in labour force; out of 1030 million in the middle income economies, 36 per cent (372 million) was outside the labour force and of the 1963 million in the low income economies of the less developed countries of Asia, Africa and Latin America 27 per cent (527 million) was not in the labour force. Overall, out of the 3.5 billion in the world's total working age population in 1995, as many as 1 billion (30.5 per cent) remained outside its labour force (*World Development Report*, 1995).

There are nearly 800 million (men, women and children) in the world's poor countries who go to bed hungry every day despite a substantial increase in food production in the last two decades, and endemic poverty being the major contributing factor. One-third of India's population is half fed due to poverty, and their number has been rising. India has one-third of the world's hungry, according to an international Hunger Project Organisation. The problem of global hunger and malnutrition has become quite ominous. In 1976, the Food and Agriculture Organisation (FAO) placed the number of malnourished people in the developing countries at 450 million. It now predicted that by the year 2000 the number of seriously undernourished would rise to 600-650 million. (*cf.* Y.P. Gupta, Hungry Planet, *The Statesman,* Calcutta, 3 June, 1999).

Will the Nobel Laureate Prof. Amartya Sen's welfare economics be of any practical help to redress the chaotic global economy? Certainly, it would be of no avail because the rule of monopoly capitalism has been the most oppressive stumbling block to the welfare and progress of mankind through the twentieth century.

First World War started in 1914 and ironically, in that orgy of carnage, Britain, France, Belgium, Tsarist Russia and later the USA "claimed" to be defending Serbian rights against the Austro-Hungarian and Ottoman Turk oppression. They actually wanted to carve out the Austro-Hungarian and Ottoman empires among themselves. It was done in the name of "ending all wars" and "making the world safe for democracy."

In 1942, Germany's Nazi Armies marched into Yugoslavia. Hitler's Luftwaffe rained bombs on Belgrade and other population centres. Nazis said they wanted to "liberate" the Croats and other Yugoslav nations from Serbian domination, just like they had "rescued" German minority in Poland and Sudetenland and "freed" Slovakia from the Czech rule. It was all designed for domination of Nazi Germany.

On the same premise, like the Nazis, the USA in 1999 had launched massive air attacks on Yugoslavia and inflicted heavy losses upon Yugoslav people on the plea of protecting Albenians in Kosovo province of Yugoslavia, "suffering" from its state oppression. Actually Kosovo was already granted autonomy to a great measure by the Central government. The North Atlantic Treaty Organisation had long before turned into an instrument for the U.S. domination in Europe and exploitation of its people.

The US-led machination had already forcibly separated and taken away Bosnia, Macedonia, and Croatia from the state of Yugoslavia. The Nato forces have already occupied these regions and reduced those into its colonies. U.S., German, French, and Italian troops already have occupied Bosnia, Skopje-Macedonia and Croatia and are on the ground of Albania. Poland, Hungary and Czech

Republic have now been pulled into NATO military alliance. Kosovo is being converted into another US-NATO protectorate. The USA has recently established military outpost in Bangladesh in collaboration with its government. It has threatened to intervene in the Kashmir affair. There is clear indication that the USA was no longer content to remain a silent bystander and reserved the option to intervene if India and Pakistan were not able to find a bilateral solution to the military conflict in Kargil sector of Kashmir. The US Ambassador to India Richard F. Celeste in a press conference on 4 June 1999, refused to rule out intervention adding that it was not being considered at this stage. The attitude is very clear.

Protection of ethnic minorities and human rights is only a pretext to suppress nationalities and violate human rights, used by the imperialists and their allies in different countries of the world. The government of Turkey, a member of the NATO for instance, has murdered more than 30,000 Kurdish men, women and children. Hundreds of Kurdish villages have been wiped off the map, and at least 2 lakhs people have been driven from their homes. The US militarists have 14 military bases in Turkey and thousands of troops there. US military actively assisted Turkey's (a NATO member) genocide of the Kurdish people. In 1995, thousands of Serbs were "ethnically cleansed" from their homes in Croatia by its dictator Franco Tudjman, a protégé of the U.S. and western European capitalist countries, who claimed that Nazi Holocaust never happened there. He forced removal of Serbs. "Operation Storm" was planned by US Army Generals advising the Croatians after their separation from Yugoslavia. Since the World War-II, the United States alone spent nearly $30 trillion to destroy Soviet Union and its allies. (Bill Williams, Operation Yugoslavia, *Frontier,* Calcutta, May, 23-29, 1999).

The European Union has grown out of the alignment of European monopoly capitalism and it is frantically operating for annexing the old colonial countries to its best economic and political interests through large trade and investment. Japanese monopoly capital is largely expanding its influence in the South-East Asia. Inter-imperialist rivalry is growing a pace with all its intensity.

All this actually reveals bellicosity and anarchic philosophy of the imperialist powers – coercion, bribery, struggle and domination— for exploitation of labour and realisation of more profit (surplus value) out of the mode of production of monopoly capitalism under "globalisation" at the end of the twentieth century. Materially, it is the domination of monopoly and finance capital at a higher level in the world economy. It is at present characterised with the most aggressive design and belligerent activities of the arch fascist U.S. Government formed, nurtured and controlled by the U.S. finance capital constantly thwarting peace, democracy, independence and sovereignty of countries in the world.

In the last one hundred and fifty years, great changes have taken place in the countries of Asia, Africa and Latin America. Changes came as a result of the struggles of the institutions of modern ideas against the regimes representing past and its social formation. The struggle for reform and enlightenment started in the earlier colonial period which educated, influenced and encouraged the people to assert in their rights for building up nations with their respective specificities and fight for national liberation against the oppressive rule and domination of colonialism and imperialism.

For instance, in the Arab World, al-Mawe group led by Mufti Mohammed Abduh, and in the Mghreb Shaykh Ben Badis, Tahir al-Haddad and Abdel Aziz Taalbi were influential reformists. Like the restorationist, the reformist trend emerged as a response to the perceived decline of Muslim power and encounter with the colonising western powers. From the second half of the nineteenth century gained hegemony in the Muslim world, but stagnated in the more recent decades owing to the attack of the opposite forces in the society.

Reforms suffered an initial set back in the Ottoman empire where successive attempts at reform failed, mainly because they were feebly attempted. The Turks' revolutionary turn was premised on the failure of Ottoman reforms in the earlier periods. Mustapha Kamal's activity was the first revolutionary response in the Muslim world. He abolished the Caliphet and established "an uncompromisingly secular republic, suppressed many religious institutions, proscribed the veil, prohibited polygamy, and enacted secular laws regulating property rights and women's rights on the basis of equality. No other Muslim country has so far equalled Ataturk's radical break from tradition and from the association of Islam with state power. Yet, in the eighties and nineties Turkey did not escape the resurgence of Islamism" (Eqbal Ahmad, Sacrificed in God's Name, *The Asian Age,* Calcutta, 6 February 1999, p. 13).

In Iran, the *coup d'etat* led first by Reza Shah Pahlevi and another engineered by the American Central Intelligence Agency in 1953 put an end to what might have been the most successful experiment in democratic reformism in the Muslim world. Under partial reformist regimes in a number of states —Tunisia, Algeria, Egypt, Syria, Iraq, Indonesia and Malaysia among others – instituted secular constitutions without effecting a radical break from the tradition of associating religion and power.

"Many of these secular authoritarian regimes are now being challenged by Islamist movements", Eqbal Ahmad concluded. It would be quite reasonable to compare this present development in the Muslims countries with the standpoint of Turkey, in the 1940s especially in connection with its position to the Indian situation at that time. M. Atay, leader of the Turkish Press Delegation then visiting India, declared that "Turkey does not believe in Pan-Islamism or Pan-Islamic Federation of any kind, nor even Pan-Turkism. Religion was personal and individual affair in Turkey and it was not allowed to influence the administration of the country. (*The Statesman,* 30 January, 1943).

Not a day goes past in Iraq without some combined political and cultural functions and demonstration against the US-British aggression. "If the American and British soldiers are so brave, let them come and face us directly, and not with their missiles", the choir sang. "Missiles fall on Iraq, but we will rebuild our country", the choir intoned. Their film show demonstrates how US soldiers committed atrocities during the Vietnam war and it aims to suggest that Iraq would be the USA's next Vietnam as it occupies Iraq.

Nearly 15 per cent of Pakistan's Muslims are Shias. The country has 2.7 million Christian population. Christian may also find themselves targeted under the Islamic law. "Christian rights will be trampled because we cannot interpret our laws under the same system", says Lahore's Bishop Alexander Malik. "We took part in the struggle for independence and now they want the concept of middle ages Muslim state imposed on this country, he observed."

In 1997 elections some 35 per cent of the registered voters in Pakistan actually exercised their franchise. That means some 65 per cent did not participate in it. Of the 35 per cent votes cast, the ruling Pakistan Muslim League Party got only 20 per cent, and the rest was obtained by the opposition parties. Official literacy figures show that only four out of every 10 people in Pakistan can read and write and the current government expenditure on education is less than 2.3 per cent of the country's gross domestic product.

It is thus evident that, like in all other countries, contradiction between the old traditional and reformist trends in the Muslim countries is current and that is growing over the years. They are subject to the same law of struggle for survival. The senile imperialist forces always try to align itself with the old, more conservative and decadent class forces for their exploitation, control and domination of the people in the Muslim countries, just as in other states.

Indian people, more especially the Muslims, cannot remain blind of or oblivious, to the changes and developments that have taken place in the Muslim countries over the past one hundred years. They can see at ease from the existing contradiction, the progressive movements and restorations that have already occurred in those countries through the present time. Changes actually take place in the society as a result of the struggle between the forces — past and present, order and reform, and decadent and progressive forces and ideas. It is the penetration and struggle of the opposite forces and institutions that constitutes the reality of the society and determines its course of development over the years.

Eqbal Ahmad, a contemporary author of Pakistan, has justly emphasised and drawn our attention to the fact that "Modernity is a historical process. It refers to the development of societies from one mode of production to another, in our age from an agrarian/pastoral mode to the capitalist/industrial mode of production. The shift from one mode of production brings revolutionary changes in the society. It compels a new logic of social and economic life, threatens inherited styles of life and forces transformations in the land, labour and capital." "And how peacefully and democratically a society makes this journey depends on its historical circumstances, the engagement of its intelligentsia, the outlook of its leaders and governments and the ideological choices they make." (Eqbal Ahmad, *op. cit.*).

The dominant feature in politics has been the existential style of deploying religion whenever it suits the political convenience of those in power in collaboration with imperialism. The resurgence of right wing religious movements in the eighties and nineties has become world-wide in order to aid and sanctify reaction in most of the countries in the world.

All sections of the democratic masses of the people have to learn from this materialist conception of history and must close their ranks for the progressive movement of society in favour of their interest, condition of labour and for independence and sovereignty of nations.

The grim socio-economic reality of the world is inevitably related and bound up with the political developments in the form of military organisations and their operations in different countries by the imperialist forces. The massacre of the Vietnamese from 1955 to 1975 as part of the titanic struggle against communism by the French and U.S. forces is a well-known fact. Imperialists have always extended support to innumerable feudal and military dictatorships in Latin America, Asia and elsewhere. The embargo imposed on Cuba, the military coup against the popularly elected progressive government of Allende in Chile, the invasion of the Caribbean nation of Grenada in October 1983, the seizure of Panama in December 1989 and conspiracy against the leftist Sandinista regime in Nicaragua speak of the naked imperialist intervention in the affairs of foreign countries in the more recent times.

The continuing attack on Iraq and Afghanistan by the U.S.A. demonstrates its imperialist design and atrocity through 2004. The UN sanctions after the Gulf war, a decision was virtually thrusted on the international body by the USA. As a result of the US-led military attack and consequent sanctions, UN after the gulf war in 1991, some 5,67,000 Iraqis have died due to disease, malnutrition and poor medical care. This is what developed capitalist countries call a bizarre "clash of civilisations"!

Israel, the chief U.S. ally in the Middle East that pursues a belligerent policy against the peoples of the Arab states, has not ratified the nuclear non-proliferation treaty and the 1972 biological and toxic commission's report although it has 200 nuclear warheads. In the process of the machination for the "human rights and self-determination" of nationalities led by the U.S.A. and other western imperialist powers, innocent citizens–Palestinians, Bosnian Muslims, Afghans, Chechynians and Kosovo Muslims–have became pawns on the chessboard of imperialist diplomacy and expansion of its area under their fascist military organisation like NATO and its command. The leaders of the imperialist countries like the U.S.A. and U.K. speak in the language of nineteenth century colonialists and their attitude towards smaller nations is often very hostile and belligerent. Living under the shadow of colonialism, their motive has been to break up larger nations and states such as Soviet Union and Yugoslavia and redraw geographical boundaries to promote their global economic and political interests. They always strive to redivide the world according to their own economic and political design. The third world countries under the conditions find it increasingly difficult to maintain their economic and political interests, and national sovereignty. Like in the first decade of twentieth century, many of them have now been reduced to *semi-colonial* countries—a category—development of which Lenin very rightly pointed out at that time. Whether one calls these countries semi-colony or "neo-colony" is not of much importance. For colonialism has been inherent and continuous in the development of world capitalism into monopoly capitalism to oppress and subjugate the countries and peoples of the world.

The most important and crucial phenomenon is that those countries have always been severely exploited by the imperialist capital, remained under their bully, yoke of imperialism and domination of international finance capital. Recently the imperialist forces have colonised Bosnia, Croatia, Macidonia and launched a fierce fascist attack on Serbia in the name of defending the right of Kosovo and for its "liberation" from the state of Yugoslavia.

Some 58,000 Americans died in the Vietnam war, compared to 3.8 million North and South Vietnamese soldiers and civilians killed from mid-1960s to 1973. In his 1995 memoirs, Mr. Robert

MacNamara, former US ex-defence secretary admitted that the policies in the Vietnam war were "terribly wrong" and he had reached this conclusion by 1967. Yet war was escalated in Vietnam by the U.S. imperialism. In his new book published in 1999, MacNamara writes, "wars between great and lesser powers...are certain to occur", and he asks, "But can we not reduce their severity by learning from history?" He thus acknowledges contradiction between the great and lesser powers, inter-imperialist rivalry and confrontation, and hence contradiction between the oppressor imperialist nations and oppressed nations in the world. The idea of reducing the severity of war in the atmosphere of intense rivalry among the imperialist forces for market-exploitation and overseas domination is only a misnomer, figure of speech, and a fantasy in the real world.

The imperialist forces always have ill-design against the weak countries and are racist in their core. After a secret, two-month tour of eleven African countries in 1947 British Field Marshal Viscount Montogomery, submitted a racist master plan for Africa. Public records just released in 1999, show that he submitted an imperial plan to turn the African continent into a white supremacist bulwark against their freedom and communism He concluded that the African is "a complete savage and is quite unable of developing the country himself." His theory of colonisation against the African independence movements was revealed in a recommendation to the British Government that said "we should have no nonsense with the United Nations Organisation about Tanganyika; it should be absorbed into the British bosom." He advocated continued white suzerainty over Africa, deemed Africans as "savages" and staunchly followed his predecessors and contemporaries in serving the empire. Professor Anthony Giddens, Director of the London School of Economics, delivered John Reith (first Director-General of British Broadcasting Corporation) memorial lecture in Delhi in March 1999. The main thrust of his thesis was that the globalisation that had taken hold of the world in the present time was a phenomenon without precedent. He said, it was "different from any earlier form of internationalism". Dr. Manmohan Singh, former Finance Minister of India, put forward a question to him whether it is "*a new avatar of colonialism*". Professor Giddens rejected this idea as "wrong", though he observed and conceded that globalisation "pierced many barriers, rammed into inertia and challenged the authority of groups controlling the state, religious and temporal institutions and even the family". Actually, globalisation is further extension, penetration and manifestation of imperialism—the highest stage of capitalism– in the world economy to firmly annex and subordinate the weaker countries. It takes place at a higher level in a matured phase of international monopoly capitalism and certainly engenders and supports colonialism. This is the only right conclusion that can be derived from the premises of Marx's Modern Theory of Colonisation expounded in the *Capital* (Volume One : Chapter 33).

Economic, political, military and diplomatic coercion, exploitation, and consequently, acute dependence of the weak countries are the main strands of imperialism. Racism, exploitation, subversion, graft, domination and subjugation of nations and states have become the criteria of "civilisation" under the monopoly capitalism in the world. Violence, massacre, *coup d'etat*, destruction and war are the products of the domination of atrocious international finance capital "modern incarnation" of Vishnu. Iraq has become its latest prey.

Capitalist market economy and militarism are inter-related and have been more integrated in the recent times. One conditions and recoils the other at large and forms the principal objective factor of colonisation in the present world. The U.S. administration proposed a real increase in the military budget in 1999 and the largest since the cold-war build-up of the mid-1980s, reports the *New York Times*, quoting administration and defence officials. It sought to increase of more than \$4 billion in the military budget for the fiscal year 2000 and about \$ 100 billion over the next six years.

Socialist leader Fidel Castro of Cuba, in his speech marking the 40th anniversary of the Cuban Revolution in January, 1999 exposed the nature of global free-market economy. He ripped into neo-liberal theoreticians, accusing them of being "more theologians than academics" for having turned their faith in the free-market system into a "religion". Castro labelled those who believe that human freedom and open markets go hand-in-hand as "hypocrites". He emphasised that the United Nations function under the "dictatorship of the Security Council and the dictatorship within the Security Council", referring to the most dominant role of the USA in the more recent period.

In India, contradiction is simmering even in the organisation like Swadeshi Jagran Manch, an offshoot of the Rastriya Swayamsevak Sangh. It made a frontal attack against the BJP-led government at the centre for "bartering away" the country's interests to the world's economic giants. Its resolution said : "The Vajpayee government has surrendered before the global economic monsters" in bringing such "retrograde legislations (Insurance and Patents Bills)", while "The World Bank and the International Monetary Fund are trying to reduce *the whole world into a U.S. colony*". Dattopant Thengdi, RSS ideologue said in the meeting of the Swadeshi Jagran Manch, "What hurts me more is that the Vajpayee government has bowed down to international pressure and conspiracy against India's economic interests". He observed that the third world war had already begun with the World Trade Organisation coming into existence" and added, "The only difference this time is it is being fought *economically* and not militarily". (*The Statesman*, Calcutta, 3 January 1999, p. 10 and 2 June 2004, p. 4)

Developments and facts thus expose the character and philosophy of the imperialist countries. At the same time, the above passage point out the very comprador character of the Indian big bourgeoisie and landlord classes their parties and governments at large. The so-called economic reforms, save the earlier regimes' enthusiastic hosting of the imperialist capital in Indian soil, were initiated by the Congress Government in 1991, and the more recent bills of concession to the imperialist countries were passed in the Lok Sabha with much disposition and pleasure by the Congress and Bharatia Janata Party together. Politically both act as faithful agents of imperialist capital in India. The CPI(M) flaunted to fight against revisionism but follow the old line of class collaboration.

Where does the philosophy of *Adwaitavad*, neo-vedanta and integrated humanity propagated by the parties of the Indian comprador bourgeoisie stand and lead to? Nowhere does it stand up but obediently crawls to the poisonous marsh of capitulation, that inevitably leads to the colonial dependence and slavery of the country and its people at the dictates of the ever more aggressive international finance capital.

The USA has long been engaged in militarisation on a very large scale and in a far more dreadful proportion. General Putt, as early as in the late 1950s, in evidence before the House Committee on Armed Services, explained that the United States Air Force aims at establishing a missile base on the moon, and considered that a warhead will be fired from the moon to the earth without any enormous expenditure of energy, since the moon has no atmosphere and little gravity. He declared that the moon "might provide a retaliation base of considerable advantage over earthbound nations". His testimony was reinforced by Richard E. Horner, Assistant Secretary of the Air Force for Research and Development, who saw in the establishment of lunar bases an opportunity of breaking through the nuclear stalemate. The moral which General Putt drew was that the United States must also occupy Mars and Venus. (I.F. Stone's Weekly of October 20, 1958)

"In reading of the plans of militarists, I try very hard to divest myself for the time being of the emotions of horror and disgust. But when I read of plans to defile the heavens by the petty squabbles of the animated lumps that disgrace a certain planet, I cannot but feel that the men who make these plans are guilty of a kind of impiety." wrote Bertrand Russell (*Commonsense and Nuclear Warfare*, 1959, pp. 18-20). He concluded that "powerful countries hitherto have had two kinds of purposes in their policy : on the one hand, they have sought the prosperity of their own countries; on the other hand, they have sought domination, political, economic or ideological, over other countries. The second aim has usually been pursued by means of war. But what is new in the present situation is that the pursuit of foreign domination by means of war is much less possible than it used to be." (*Ibid*. p. 40).

Bertrand Russell observed, "There are, one may say, three spheres of contest involved in the gradual approach of man towards wisdom. There are the contests with nature, the contests between men, and the contests within a man's own self. Each of these has its own history and its own importance...... It is not now barbarians who constitute the danger. On the contrary, it is those who are in the forefront of civilization."

These observations of Russell expose the ideology and philosophy of the powerful imperialist countries in the late twentieth century. In the same vein, they also disclose the contradiction between the imperialism and nations and actual operation of dialectical materialism in the development of the world history at large. All this can be hardly overemphasized or refuted.

We have now come to the end of our analysis and discussion which has been undertaken in the preceding chapters. To the recapitulate, Rammohan, Vidyasagar and Akshyay Kumar had declared and firmly spoke of the *uselessness and falsity* of the *Vedanta* philosophy in the practical life of man and lit up the lamp of reform and rational thought in India in the modern time. Debendranath disagreed with Sankara and his *Adwaitavad*. All this had a great significance in the society's development and progress. They did not write a comprehensive treatise on it for their preoccupation with social activity, but their literature and practical work support this *anti-Vadanta radical idea*. Undoubtedly, it was a prelude to the study of materialist philosophy in India and repudiation of subjective idealism of the old theology. It can be seen as the initial ground for start and progress of materialist philosophy.

A broad secular foundation was built up by the talent and social practice of the Indian people over a long period of history. An effort has been made to show it in the process of analysis in this work. But, whatever common, secular and rational thought evolved out of the practical life of the Indian society over the years has been coerced and suppressed in the struggles by the heavy armour of idealist philosophy reinforced with the fast religious doctrines and imperialism and its related politics of the transplanted parliamentariansm of the twentieth century in the country. Subjective idealism reigns through continuous irrationality of thought and anarchism in the Indian society.

The suppressed rationalist thought in India can rise up and move forward with the aid and strong support of militant materialism. Militant materialism finds its proper use, due appeal and acclaim in a distinct rational approach and vehicle of reason built up by the Indian liberal reformers of the nineteenth century. Objectively speaking, *Vedanta* philosophy would never help to make a secular India and with social equality, real material and social progress. Militant materialism is the only very weapon that can blast the old fortress of subjective idealism of reaction, free the Indian society and lead the country on the path of radical change and revolution in the interest of the masses of the Indian people.

It follows that, with the extension and development of class struggle and sustained campaign for it along with the addresses of the respective political and academic institutions, the theory of dialectical materialism as the revolutionary philosophy began to gradually spread and make some inroad in the Indian society in the crucial period of its independence movement conditioned and surcharged by religion and communalism–characteristic manifestation of the metaphysics, subjective idealism and sectarianism in the twentieth century. The philosophy of dialectical materialism naturally came in direct confrontation more and more with the subjective idealism which was largely fostered by the religious and spiritual interpretation and that worked for the class interest of the Indian princes, landlords, big industrialists and merchants who were firmly aligned with the British colonial and imperialist power ruling in India. Gandhi's non-violence, a spiritual concept, compromised with the British imperialism at different periods of time and recoiled the strong force of idealism in Indian society and politics over the decades.

Naturally, materialist philosophy in politics has not yet gained enough strength and momentum to struggle and undermine stronghold of the force of subjective idealism, the philosophy of the Indian ruling class and Pan-Hinduism reflected mainly in Gandhism. Gandhism is still the ideology of the state of a large semi-feudal and semi-colonial country like India and the Indian state takes all possible measures to propagate it daily among the people to serve its class interest at large in collaboration with imperialist capital.

In the social life, co-operation, human affection and loyalties work and grow with the process of the mode of production through the centuries. There is no doubt about it, but that is conditional, relative, temporary and transitory. Struggle between the opposite forces, precisely, class struggle, is the dominant and absolute in history. Gandhism, as the product of subjective idealism speaks of non-violence for class compromise and so it is inimical to the dialectical materialist philosophy. It covers up contradiction in actual developments of the society. It idealises Indian society's backward social formation characterised with a population of numerous castes, faiths and ethnic groups and languages suffering from inhuman exploitation of the comprador bourgeoisie and imperialism. Everyday, it is propagated through the media to mistify harsh reality of the society and blur the consciousness of the masses of the people in order to keep them under the feudal, capitalist and imperialist bondage and slavery.

Such is the idea and anarchic character of subjective idealism—the ideology of India's exploiter classes and their master, imperialism. People have little to do with it as this ideal does not serve the people's cause. The working class philosophy is the dialectical materialism i.e. militant materialism–the truly secular ideology–to defend their real interest as workers and toilers in the existing social order and conquer political power for emancipation of labour from the domination of the exploiting classes in the society. The Indian people, irrespective of caste, creed, religion, ethnic distinction has to follow this philosophy free from religious import and sectarianism in their practical life for a new democratic revolution and socialism. The existing regime only works for their oppression, exploitation and ruin. Equal economic and political rights and opportunity–and these are the main planks of the social democracy and united struggle of the people for achieving it –must not be related, confused or corrupted with the religion and spiritualism. In India, however, the opposite still works at large. All major parliamentary parties have shrewdly utilised religion and caste for their political gain in the corrupt and fast degenerating parliamentary system, and hence, opportunism with subjective idealism in the existing social order has risen at the new height in Indian society over the years. Nationalism of the vulgar Indian comprador bourgeoisie and its major parliamentary parties now means shameless services to and capitulation before the dominant international finance capital, reducing India more as an abject semi-colonial country. The parliamentary left has followed the same path by abandoning the basic tenets of materialist philosophy and scientific socialism over the decades. This state of anarchy constantly draws its nourishment from subjective idealism and vulgar materialism. Dialectical materialism makes its most radical departure from all the colourable thoughts of subjective idealism with its myths and spiritualism which befool the mass of the general people. Subjective idealism holds and worships the great vestiges of remote past to which mankind shall never return nor can make advance with it. It covers up all the vile exploitation of man by man and class antagonism in the society, stands for the existing order of things, keeps the people under great illusion and ignorance, and creates necessary atmosphere for continuous exploitation of countries and nations by the senile international finance capital. It preaches the ideas of sooth saying and man's salvation after death ! Scientific experiments and discoveries and facts of practical life in the bouregois society have continually exposed the falsity and crisis of the speculative philosophy and subjective idealism and thereby warranted the firm position of dialectical materialism.

It is seductive to fancy that the society would return to the days of the past. It is absurd to think that the persons of different "faiths" cannot and have not together composed a society and built up state and civilisation. Contact and cooperation, mutual relation, reciprocity and struggle against the common enemy have largely played a much greater role in making social life of man over the years.

In India, such a continuous process have been in operation through the ages. It is this historical process that has made a common life and composite culture based on its economic structure over the years. Many a time Indian people have fought together against their common adversary in the contemporary period. They unitedly fought against the oppressive colonial British rule in 1857 and created a brilliant history of national revolutionary struggle. The same was in full vitality which Marx observed in 1880s.

It continued further through 1916-1921 when the national united front with the Congress and Muslim League shook the foundation of British rule in India with revolutionary mass movement—a great historical fact well recorded and lauded by the Communist International, more especially in its Sixth Congress in 1928. This showed the trend of secularism, national feeling and progress of the society. Working people's ideology is concerned and rooted in their just struggle against the oppression and exploitation of the predatory and reactionary forces and its action is quite free from, and independent of individual's religion and faith. So it is their morality. Religious revivalism organised and motivated by the backward forces and exploiting classes and fomented with the petty politics and parliamantary reforms based on communal electorates made by British imperialism had created a sharp communal division and riot among the people, led to country's partition and brought havoc in the working class organisation and movement in India. It is the result of the philosophy and design of the ruling classes and their imperialist masters, which is heinously directed against the people and humanity.

Every action the India's colonial state machinery takes in the name of truth and non-violence is invariably designed to "civilise" the masses of the Indian people with pauperism, destitution, begging bowl, prostitution and corruption. Leaders and Ministers chant Ram Dhun, the song of *Hindutva* and "non-violence" for sanctifying corruption and all their anti-social activities. "Democracy" based on private property and market is taking its heavy toll of the human life in the crisis of capitalism and acute social anarchy at the end of the twentieth century. The "left" social democrats and their ministers enjoying all the privileges of the colonial and bourgeois state and being at large, corrupt, dare garland the pictures of the founders of scientific socialism and its revolutionary leaders ! Actually, it is all set to crush labour and humanity in the name of development and civilisation in the era of moribund imperialism. Whoever soberly states this objective condition in the decadent bourgeois order of the society appeases reaction, kisses the boot of imperialism and plays the role of agent of the enemy in the camp of the labour. Subjective idealism is of no help to the cause of the masses of the workers, peasants and toilers of the world. Only unravelling the contradiction through systematic organisation of class struggle favourably conditions the interest of the working class and leads the way towards victory of revolution and emancipation of labour.

The anarchic condition in the world economy has more aggravated over the years. Its contradiction is manifesting in the past cold-war period. As *The Economist* (London, 28 February

2004, p.27)observes in a special report," The nuclear age is set for a long and perilous half-life. The palpable relief, as the cold-war ended that the threat of Armageddon — a nuclear fight to the finish between the Soviet empire and the West— had been lifted, has proved to dispiritingly short-lived.If anything, the 21st century seems even more dangerous, because less predictable place". The working people have their right to defend themselves against war and build up a new society and a new civilisation for the mankind.

Hence, Dialectical materialism is the only universal philosophy, invincible weapon in the aid of the proletariat and revolutionary struggle of the people. Just one hundred and fifty years ago Marx-Engels,[1] founders of scientific socialism, observed : "The criticism of religion disillusions man to make him think and act and shape his reality like a man who has been disillusioned and has come to reason, so that he will revolve round himself and therefore round his true sun. Religion is only the illusory sun which revolves round man as long as he does not revolve round himself" and "It was still more reasonable that the liberal of the recent past combated the liberals of the present". Further, "The relation of industry, of the world of wealth generally, to the political world is one of the. major problems of modern times" and "the criticism of religion ends with the teaching that man is the highest essence for man, hence with the categoric imperative to overthrow all relations in which man is a debased, enslaved, abandoned, despicable essence......".

As Engels elucidated the premises of materialist philosophy in simple words, "Just as Darwin discovered the law of development of organic nature, so Marx discovered the law of development of human history : the simple fact, hitherto concealed by an overgrowth of ideology, that mankind must first of all eat, drink, have shelter and clothing, before it can pursue politics, science, art, religion, etc., that therefore production of the immediate material means of subsistence and consequently the degree of economic development attained by a given people of, during a given epoch form the foundation upon which the state institution, the legal conceptions, art and even the ideas of religion, of the people concerned have been evolved, and in the light of which they must, therefore, be explained, instead of *vice-versa*, as had hitherto been the case."

"But that is not all. Marx also discovered the special law of motion governing the present-day capitalist mode of production and the bourgeois society that this mode of production has created. The discovery of surplus value suddenly threw light on the problem, in trying to solve which all previous investigations, of both bourgeois economists and socialist critics, had been groping in the dark".[2]

Long ago Socrates visualised man's moral code absolutely independent and free from religion. After the October Socialist Revolution of 1917 in Russia, following Marx-Engels and recognising the continuity of class struggle in the society Lenin[3] wrote in 1920, "We reject all morality based on extra-human and extra-class concepts. We say that it is a deception, a fraud, a befogging of the minds of the workers and peasants in the interests of the landlords and capitalists. We say that our morality is entirely subordinated to the interests of the class struggle of the proletariat. Our morality is derived from the interests of the class struggle of the proletariat".

"The class struggle is continuing and it is our task to subordinate all interests to this struggle. And we subordinate our communist morality to this task. We say : Morality is what serves to destroy the old exploiting society and to unite all the toilers around the proletariat, which is building a new society of communists."

"Morality serves the purpose of helping human society to rise to a higher level and to get rid of the exploitation of labour".

Lenin, further observed that "The unity (coincidence, identity, equal action) of opposites is conditional, temporary, transitory, relative. The struggle of mutually exclusive opposites is absolute, just as development and motion are absolute", and that "Development is the 'struggle' of opposites".[4]

All this highlights and reinforces the basis of materialist philosophy i.e., dialectical materialism. Practical life of the society has proved its reality, humane nature and universality.

Only this philosophy can raise and save India and her people from the abject feudal and imperialist bondage, oppression and exploitation. This is the morale of time to the working class.

At attempt has been made in this work to show its relation, connection and operation in the Indian situation and politics of the past century. An analysis has been provided with the course of developments and their inter-lacing in the struggle between the subjective idealism and objective idealism and its transition to materialism. Its central thing is the class relation and class struggle in the society. The relative weakness and lack of progress of the materialist philosophy in politics against the onslaught of the idealist philosophy, in India, is never due to its deficiency in reserve and arsenal, but weakness of the leadership of the Communist Party of India, in practical operation, who often fell in the mire of subjectism and failed to act consistently and persistently in the interest of the workers and peasants. Policy advice and formulations of the Communist International with organisational steps and measures were never properly adhered to and systematically practised. That is why the situation had seriously deteriorated; the revolutionary social democratic movement could not make much headway and the Communist Party continued to remain fractured and fragmented, leaving the ground for subjective idealism propagated by the clergy and intellectual prostitutes to serve the ruling capitalist and landlord classes in collaboration with imperialism. But in the face of this opposition, a certain force is slowly growing with its experience in practice of class struggle and support of the people. "*With the thoroughness of the historical action, the size of the mass whose action it is will therefore increase.*" (Marx-Engels, *The Holy Family*). This is the 155th year of the publication of the Communist Manifesto, the finest master piece of materialist philosophy. Let its call reverberate in all parts of India and the world.

"The Communists disdain to conceal their views and aims. They openly declare that their ends can be attained only by the forcible overthrow of all existing social conditions. Let the ruling classes tremble at a Communistic revolution. The proletarians have nothing to lose but their chains. They have a world to win"[5] Workers, peasants, artisans and all toilers of India and other countries of the world must appreciate, get organised and act in accordance with this noble message to the mankind for the national liberation and emancipation of labour from the oppressive domination of the international finance capital in the globe.

NOTES

1. Marx-Engels, *On Religion,* Progressive Publishers, Moscow, 1956 p. 40, p. 42, p. 46 and p. 50.
2. Frederick Engels, Speech at the Graveside of Karl Marx, Marx-Engels, *Selected Works,* Vol. III, Progressive Publishers, Moscow, 1977, pp. 162-63.
3. V. I. Lenin, *The Tasks of the Youth League,* Foreign Languages Press, Peking, 1975, pp. 11-15.
4. V. I. Lenin, *On the Question of Dialectics,* Progressive Publishers, Moscow, 1980, p. 11.
5. Karl Marx and Fredrick Engels, *Manifesto of the Communist Party,* Progress Publishers, Moscow, 1967, p. 96.

APPENDICES

APPENDIX-I

INDIA
Development of Philosophical Thought

Rammohan Roy's view on the *Vedanta* was a very characteristic and revealing nature from the standpoint of reason, enlightenment and social progress. It made a definite break in India's social thought.

Seventeen illuminating lectures of Ramchandra Vidyabagish, first Acharya of the Brahmo Samaj, suggest that its philosophy recognised five organs for the working of the body and five sense organs for its knowledge, existence of matter and of its impermanence and dissolution, and mechanism of the nature. But according to Ramchandra, their co-ordination, working and control is done by the grace of the divine power of great consciousness of the universe.

Ishan Chandra Roy of the Sadharan Brahmo Samaj observed in the preface to Rammohan's *Vedantasar* that only *Upanishad* was the real *Vedanta* and that the *Gita* supported the truth of the advices of the *Upanishad.* He stated that Rammohan's *Vedantasar* was of a different kind as he did not write it, according to the *sutras*. He took up its necessary doctrines and made their brief explanation in his writing. Subject mater was the principal theme in this pamphlet. Rammohan reiterated Vedavyas's assertion that the nature of Brahmo could not be known by any means. By sense organs, energy and noble work, the ingredient material of Brahmo could not be known. (*Vedantasar*, p.1)

It is true that Rammohan used the *Vedanta* for helping propagation of his own thought but he never fully accepted the entire version current in the name of *Vedanta* among the public. For this reason, the common people, without recognising Rammohan's *Vedanta* as the real thought, took it as a caricature of the Vedanta. Principally, Rammohan advanced Brahmo thought based on the *Vedanta (Upanishad)*. But while it was impossible to worship on the line of extreme *Adwaitavad, Mayavad* preaching the world as false and illusory, and monastery declaring the knowledge of Brahmo for the household man as impossible and making, man indifferent to the good and bad in the society, Rammohan never hesitated or failed to protest such ideas. He did not say that the *Vedanta* was false, but he also did not preach that the *Vedanta* was infallible and gospel truth. Along with *Vedanta* and *Tantra*, ideas of many faiths, scriptures and religious personalities influenced upon Rammohan. (Gautam Niogy, Pandit Ramchandra Vidyabagisher Jibani: Bengali; in *Brahmo Samajer Byakhyan;* Bengali Sadharan Brahmo Samaj, 1977, Calcutta, pp. 167-70).

Luis Vivian Derozio wrote in *The East India Magazine,* "What his (Rammohan's) opinions are, neither his friends nor foes can determine. It is easier to say what they are not than what they are... Rammohan, it is well known, appeals to the Vedas, the Koran and the Bible, holding them all probability in equal estimation". ("Citation" in A. F. Salahuddin Ahmed, *Social Ideas and Social Change in Bengal:* 1818-1835; Leiden, 1965, p. 43). Debendranath Tagore acknowledged that Rammohan rejected idolatry and established Brahmo Samaj for preaching the worship of parabrahmo (concept of the kind, formless one and only single God) sanctioned by the *Vedanta*, among the people of India. He said that though Brahmoism was being propagated in many ways, but these were all branches and leaves of the seed sown by Rammohan. (Debendranath Tagore, *Brahmosamajer Panchabingshati Batsarer Parikshita Brittanta :* Bengali; Sadaharan Brahmosamaj, Calcutta, 1953, p. 8, p. 23, pp. 26-27 and p. 38).

Akshay Kumar Datta did not accept the view that Rammohan had believed in the infallibility of the *Vedanta*. Data wrote that "Although he (Rammohan) had collected the principles from the scriptures, especially from the *Vedanta* to establish his own viewpoint, there is no matter of doubt that he was not actually a Vaidantik but initiator of the faith on Brahmoism" (Speech at the

25th Annual Conference of the Brahmo Samaj, *Tatwabodhini Patrika,* 1854 Part 4, No. 139 ; see *Brahmo Samajer Byakhyan*, p. 187).

Debendranath strongly opposed the motion for preaching the idea of incarnation and idolatry from the alter of Brahmo Samaj. Brahmin, Sudra, Christian and Muslim — all had equal right in the Brahmo Samaj established by Rammohan. In the Charter of Rights for the Brahmo Samaj, Rammohan clearly forbade in writing that no picture or statue would be preserved in the Samaj. Brahmos would always have to proceed according to this will. Absolutely for keeping the words of the will, the oath of the Brahmos was prepared that says one "shall not worship any making, with the knowledge of all-creator *parabrahmo*". Rammohan had the great objective that there would be no quarrel on religion and all would be worshippers of the one God. From the *Upanishad* itself the scripture of Brahmo religion was redacted and nourished.

The defects of the *Vedas* became gradually exposed and then it was decided to collate whatever truth the *Vedas* contained. With the want of common sense and self-confidence of some members there occurred a commotion in the Brahmo Samaj when the authority of the *Vedas* fell. Rammohan was the first to adopt the *Upanishad* for the cause of India. (Debendranath Tagore, *op. cit.,* pp. 13, 16, 24-25, 27 and 38)

Pandit Shibnath Shastri wrote in the *History of the Brahmo Samaj* (Sadharan Brahmo Samaj, Calcutta, 1974) that Debendranath Tagore at first believed in the infallibility of the *Vedanta* and that faith was strengthened during the debate with Dr. Alexander Duff and Christian Missionaries but immediately after that, a debate started between him and Akshay Kumar Datta and editorial board of the *Tattwabodhini Patrika,* and the infallibility of the *Vedas* was ultimately rejected. (*cf.* Ramchandra Vidyabagish, *Brahmo Samajer Byakhyan,* Sadharan Brahmo Samaj, pp. 188-89).

Rammohan in *Vedantasar* himself postulated a state of things even before the *Vedas* and observed that the creation, existence and destruction of the universe was subject to the action of one and the only single supreme being, Brahmo. Life, all sense organs, space, air, halo, water, earth and the *Vedas* – all emanated from the Brahmo

(*Vedantasar,* pp. 2-4) Rammohan rejected idolatry. According to Rammohan, a person could attain the knowledge of Brahmo without joining in a monastery, unlike the concept of Sankar's *Vedanta.* In general, it appears that Rammohan in his *Vedantasar* recognised the *thing* and its *change*, in a very rudimentary form. In his letter addressed to the Governor General Lord Amherst dated 11 December, 1823, Rammohan himself questioned on the *Vedanta* and raised the fundamental issue on the relation between the matter and soul in these words: "Neither can such improvement arise from such speculations as the following, which are the themes suggested by the *Vedanta.* In what manner is the soul absorbed into the deity? What relation does it bear to the divine essence? Nor will youths fitted to be better members of society by the Vedantic doctrines which teach them to believe that all visible things have no real existence, that as father, brother etc., have no actual entity, they consequently deserve no real affection and therefore the sooner we escape from them and leave the world the better." He opposed establishment of the Sanskrit school and pronounced uselessness of the *Vedanta* in practical life of man.

From these facts, it becomes evident that Rammohan had reservation on the *Adwaita Vedanta* and Akshay Kumar's observation on Rammohan's view about the *Vedanta,* was more realistic and at the same time crucial and conclusive especially in the light of the comment of Derozio on Rammohan's thought.

To explore in the matter, it is necessary to incorporate the modern interpretation of *Adwaitavad.* As Sarvapally Radhakrishnan observed:

"Sankara does not assert an identity between God and the world but only denies the independence of the world....If we raise question as to how the finite rises from out of the bosom of the infinite, Sankara says that it is an incomprehensive mystery, *maya.* We know there is the absolute reality, we know that there is the empirical world, we know that the empirical world rests on the absolute; but the how of it is beyond our knowledge ....The greatest thinkers are those who admit the mystery (of the relation of God to the World) and comfort themselves by the idea that the human mind is not omniscient. Sankara in the East and Bradley in the West adopt this wise attitude of agnosticism" (*Hindu View of Life,* pp. 66-68).

In this regard he also added, "No theory has ever asserted that life is a dream and all experienced events are illusions. One or two late followers of Sankara lend countenance to this hypothesis, but it cannot be regarded as representing the main tendency of Hindu thought". (*Ibid.,* p. 69).

Thus Radhakrishnan sought to defend the absolute reality, theism and Sankara's *Adwaitavad* through the leeway of mystery and agnosticism of the west. And with this stand, the distinction of Rammohan's social view on the *Adwaita Vedanta* with that of Radhakrishnan on the same subject becomes quite noticeable and clear.

Prabhat Kumar Mukhopadhyay wrote in 1984 that Debendranath Tagore refused the *Vedanta* religion of Rammohan which was sanctified by the *Adwaita Vedanta* of Sankara, and established Brahmoism based on the *Bhaktivad* by collecting the Sanskrit texts of the Hindu scriptures, making those suitable for worshipping Nirakar Unitary God with his own interpretation in place of the hard radical religion of Rammohan's idea. And what was "*Samaj*", a centre for worshipping Brahmo of all religious persons was turned into a "*Mandir*" (Prabhat Kumar Mukhopadhyay, in introduction to *Rammohan-Smaran,* Rammohan Roy Smritiraksha Samiti, 1989, Calcutta, p.11).

In his Persian pamphlet *Tufat-Ul-Muahidin*, Rammohan raised the voice of defence in favour of one God and Unitarianism. In its introduction he wrote, "I proceeded on my travels and passed through countries chiefty within but some beyond the bounds of Hindusthan, with a feeling of great aversion for the establishment of the British Power in India". In the technique of Voltaire and Volney, Rammohan divided mankind into four classes; cheat, cheated, cheat and cheated and those who were neither cheat nor cheated. Brojendranath Sil noted that, in this writing of Rammohan, the influence of Locke and Hume could be found and he analysed therein the reasons of prejudices and their influences and that in this analysis, psychology had a greater influence than history.

Brojendranath Sil pointed out that the *Adwaitavad* of Sankara influenced Rammohan most, but, practically, he became sceptic about the scriptures and all kinds of traditional religious opinions appeared to him bereft of essence, or a collection of false or impure thoughts or distortions of truth. He observed that Rammohan's theosophy accepted both dualism and qualified monism in regard to the self and the world. Rammohan declared that the nation's scriptures, the repository of its total knowledge or probity had to be integrated in the light of the rationality of man. (Brojendranath Sil, Rammohan Roy: Bengali; in *Rammohan Smaran*, Raja Rammohan Roy Smritiraksha Samiti, Calcutta, 1989, pp. 378-379).

According to Amiya Kumar Majumdar, although Rammohan followed Sankaracharya, he did not blindly accept Sankara. In the interpretation of the Vedanta, Rammohan laid maximum stress on the scholarship and application of intellect. Shri Majumdar observed that Rammohan thought that Brahmo was the creator, protector and destroyer of the world, and in forming such a premise he was influenced by cosmological argument of the western philosophy and of the reason of causal effect in the *Naya Darshana*. Guided by the logic, Rammohan did not view that the *Vedas* had emanated from the mouth of God. The *Vedas*, according to Rammohan, contained the collection of thoughts which had originated from the feelings of men through the ages (*Ibid.*, pp. 203-11).

E.V. Paiyevskaiya, Soviet writer, held that by opposing casteism, other rites and practices Rammohan had not only attacked the base of Sanatan Hinduism but also undermined the foundation of the feudal society in India. He showed that the idolatry of the Brahmins were contrary to the practice of their forefathers and principles of their ancient scriptures. Rammohan's Unitarianism was only the imagination of God by a person knowing Brahmo. To Rammohan one God is the symbol of the unity of India. Paiyevskaiya cites that, Rammohan in a letter to Mr. Arnot expressed his extreme hatred against the British Rule in India, but he reconciled himself with the British rule within a short period, for the sake of benefit to the posterity.

Paiyevskaiya also observed that the two streams of social movement in India in the subsequent period – liberal policy and nationalism – got inspiration from the philosophical thought of Rammohan. (*Ibid.*, pp. 217-232).

From William Adam's account it is known that Calcutta's first Lord Bishop Middleton had allured Rammohan with a much higher post provided he embraced Christianity. Rammohan felt greatest shock and deep sorrow of life on this occasion and retorted to the Bishop, "My Lord, you are under a mistake. I have not laid down one superstition to take up another" (*India Gazette,* Calcutta, 8 October, 1829)

Last, but not the least, Rammohan questioned the very idea of the spirit being absorbed into the deity or matter as early as in the early 1820s. In the late nineteenth century, Swami Dayananda who interpreted the *Vedanta* in his own way and opined that matter and spirit are collateral in the universe, while Swami Vivekananda held that matter and spirit are parallel.

Of the three views, which is near the centre of the cause and standpoint of the objective idealism and materialism? Of course, the first one.

APPENDIX-II

MILITANT MATERIALISM

In the words of Newton's Principia, "Since the ancients (according to Pappus) considered mechanics to be of the greatest importance in the investigation of nature and science and since the moderns... have undertaken to reduce the phenomena of nature to mathematical laws, it has seemed best in this treatise to concentrate on mathematics as it relates to natural philosophy. The ancients divided mechanics into two parts : the rational, which proceeds rigorously through demonstrations and the practical. Practical mechanics is the subject that comprises all the manual arts.... But since those who practise an art do not generally work with a high degree of exactness, the whole subject of mechanics is distinguished from geometry by the attribution of exactness to geometry and of anything less than exactness to mechanics. Yet the errors do not come from the art but from those who practice the art.... Anyone who works with less exactness is a more imperfect mechanic, and if anyone could work with the greatest exactness, he would be the most perfect mechanic of all..."

Sir Isaac Newton's Principia, or The Mathematical Principles of Natural Philosophy (first published in Latin in 1687) is credited with having single-handedly laid the foundations for modern scientific world view. His foremost biographer Richard Westfall calls it "epoch making" : "nothing had prepared the world of natural philosophy for the Principia". It gave the world Newton's three laws of motion, his method of "fluxions", or calculus and his universal law of gravitation.

In 1859 Charles Darwin wrote, "I will here give a brief sketch of the progress of opinion on the origin of species. Until recently the great majority of naturalists believed that species were immutable productions and had been separately created... Some few naturalists... have believed that species undergo modifications, and that the existing forms of life are the descendants by true generation of pre-existing forms. Passing over allusion to the subject in the classical writers, the first author who in modern times has treated it in a scientific spirit was Buffon. But as his opinion fluctuated greatly in different periods and as he does not enter on the causes or means of the transformation of species, I need not here enter on details. Lamarck was the first man whose conclusions on the subject excited much attention... He upholds the doctrine that species, including man, are descended from other species. He first did the eminent service of arousing attention to the probability of all change in the organic... world being the result of law, and not of miraculous interposition."

"Evolution has become more than a science", writes Steve Jones while doing the work of a rewriting in the late 1990s of Charles Darwin's *The Origin of Species*. He observe that "its ideas are used wittingly or otherwise, in economics, politics, history, art and more". "Natural selection", "survival of the fittest", our human descent from the great apes—these Darwinian discoveries with certain variations are current and common place in the modern world.

Mechanics of the Universe and Origin of Species have generally formed the domain and spearheaded scientific investigation and research on the modern lines since that time. It has progressed uninterrupted under the aegis of the school of science discovering numerous and varied wonderful, phenomena and laws of nature with the passage time.

In 1929, American Astronomer Edwin Hubble discovered that galaxies in the universe are receding from one another at speeds that increase with the distance between them. Hubble's observations implied that the universe is expanding; that galaxies were closer to each other in the past; and that the universe was infinitely dense at one point sufficiently back in time. That moment of infinite density is considered to be the birth of the cosmos in the scenario of the universe's evolution known as the Big Bang model, which is currently popular among the astronomers. For years, they have been trying to measure the rate of expansion of the universe to know exactly how old the universe is. Named after Hubble the expansion rate is a constant at any given point in the universe's history, and the search for its exact value has become a high profile quest in the realm of science in the present time.

To get a reliable value of the Hubble constant, astronomers need to know the distances to different galaxies accurately, task that is not easily accomplished. The most commonly used method hings on using a type of stars called Cepheid variables. Cepheids fluctuate in brightness over a period of time. If an astronomer can identify cepheids in another galaxy, it is possible to get an estimate of the galaxy's distance using the observed periods and luminosities.

Two decades ago, estimates of the value of the Hubble constant fluctuated between 50 and 100, leading to estimates of the universe's age that lay between 10 and 20 billion years.

Using eight years of measurements by the Hubble Space Telescope, a team of astronomers led by Wendy Freedman of the Carnegie Observatories has determined that the value of the Hubble constant is 70, plus or minus 7, kilometers per second per mega per sec. Because of the scale of the of the universe cosmologists favour these strange units. What this number means is that, for every 3.26 million light years that lies between them, two galaxies are flying away from one another at 70 klometres per second. When inserted into various models of the universe, this value of the Hubble constant gives an age estimate for the universe between 13.5 and 15 billion years, which is consistent with age measurements obtained independently for the old stars.

The value of the Hubble constant touted in response to Freedman's estimate is slightly lower, lying between 53 and 65 kilometres per second per mega per sec. It arises from the observations of galaxies by another Carnegie observatory's astronomer, Allan Sandage, who has been using a different method to calculate the constant's value. Sandage is the grand-father of the Hubble constant search, having observed thousands of galaxies over half a century. His value gives a greater age for the universe, making it between approximately 15 to 18 billion years old.

This is not the first time that Freedman and her colleagues have announced a value for the Hubble constant. In 1994, they announced a preliminary value of 80 kilometres per second per mega per sec which implied that the universe was 12 billion years old, raising a big hue and cry among astronomers : how could the universe be younger than its old stars? Separate measurements had put the ages of the universe's oldest stars over 12 billion years. Back then, Sandage opined – as he had for the last two decades – that the correct value of the Hubble constant would be around 55, which made the universe about 17 billion years old, a value that was in no conflict with the observations of old stars.

Thus, a group of cosmologists announced in May 1999 that it has finally determined the cosmic number—called Hubble's constant—that leads to the universe's age. The universe is between 13.5 and 15 billion years old, the group proclaimed. The Freedman and Sandage Values both allow for a universe that is 15 billion years old, vindicating the standard Big Bang model of the universe. Robert Krishner of the Harvard-Smithsonian Center for Astrophysics, who himself has estimated the value of the Hubble constant using a different method and found it to lie between Freedman and Sandage values, points out that cosmologists used to disagree by a hundred per cent a couple of decades ago. "Now we are just as passionate about 10 per cent," he said.

The two space observations orbiting Earth – Hubble Space Telescope and the Compton Gama Ray Observatory were complemented with the launching of Chandra X-ray observatory in July 1999. Unlike the Hubble Space Telescope's circular orbit that is relatively close to the Earth, the Chandra X-ray observatory was placed in a highly elliptical (oval shaped) orbit. At its closest approach to Earth, the observatory will be at an altitude of 6000 miles. As its farthest, 86400 miles, it travels almost one-third of the way to the moon. Due to this elliptical orbit, the observatory circles the Earth every 64 hours; carrying it further outside the belts of radiation that surround our planet.

Three major elements of the Chandra X-ray observatory are the spacecraft system, the telescope system and the science instruments.

The telescope system contains in its heart the High-Resolution Mirror Assembly with special cylindrical mirrors so that incoming X-rays graze off the highly polished mirror surfaces and are funnelled to the instrument section for detection and study. The mirrors of the X-ray observatory are the largest of their kind and the smoothest ever created. The largest of the eight mirrors is almost 4 feet in diameter and 3 feet long. Assembled, the mirror group weighs more than 1 ton.

The Earth's atmosphere can absorb X-rays and therefore space based observatories have become very necessary and vital to study the phenomena and objective reality of the universe.

NASA's newest space telescope, called the Chandra X-ray Observatory, released images that promise to unravel the mystery of the structure and evolution of the universe in a way astronomers had only dreamt of till now. One of the stunning images was of a gigantic steller explosion which, what scientists feel, is evidence of a neutron star or black hole at the centre of the blast.

One of Chandra's first targets was the 320-year-old Supernova remnant Cassiopeia—A product by the explosion of a massive star that collapsed in on itself. Material from the explosion collided into surrounding material at 16 million kilometres per hour causing violent shock waves, like massive sonic booms, and creating a gigantic 50-million degree bubble of X-ray emitting gas. Chandra's mission is to see these high energy, invisible X-rays that are emitted from the hottest and most violent parts of the universe that ordinary telescope cannot pick up.

Another image that Chandra has picked up is of Quasar PKS 0637-752. It is so distant that we see it as it was six billion years ago and it is a luminous quasar radiating the power of 10 trillion suns from a region smaller than our Solar System.

The source of this astonishing energy is said to be a super massive black hole. Chandra X-ray image shows a powerful X-ray jet stretching across several hundred light years, which is most likely the result of a beam of extremely high energy particles. Galaxy clusters are the largest and most massive objects in the universe. They are enormous collections of galaxies, bound together into a cluster by gravity. Their mass is in the form of an incredibility hot, X-ray emitting gas that fills the space between the galaxies. (But neither the mass of the galaxies, nor the mass of the hot X-ray gas is enough to provide the gravity that we know, holds the cluster together.)

The important question is about the powerhouse that drives the explosive activity in many distant galaxies. The centres of many distant galaxies are incredible sources of energy and radiation – especially in X-rays. According to scientists, massive black holes are at the centre of these active galaxies, gobbling up any material – even a whole star – that passes too close. Chandra will make detailed studies that can probe the faintest of these active galaxies, and study how their energy output changes with time and how these objects produce their intense energy emissions in the first place.

So, it is not serene and void above, no matter what our eyes, or science fiction movies tell us. Scientific probe "shows that the universe is a violent, vibrant in ever-changing place where temperatures reach millions of degrees, objects accelerate by gravity to the speed of light and magnetic fields, more than a trillion times stronger than the Earth's, cause stars to crack and shiver". Within the instrument section of the Chandra X-ray observatory is a high resolution camera and it is regularly "recording X-ray images, giving scientists an unequalled look at violent, high temperature occurrences like the death of stars or colliding galaxies". Earlier universe was thought to be quiet, peaceful and soothing. It is no longer correct, as scientific discoveries and objective reality have disproved and negated the former idalist view.

When the vast clouds of gas collapse, the result can often be the formation of stars. Most of the condensed cloud becomes star but some of the material forms a disc around it from which planets and comets arise. Such discs have been observed around young stars, but not around the older ones like our own sun.

Let us look into the core of our planet. Earth's core, a seething mass of molten iron, is bubbling at about 9930 degrees fahrenheit. British scientists have very recently declared. "It is important because the whole dynamics of the Earth depends on knowing the temperature inside it," Professor Mike Gillan of University College, London, told the Press, "The Earth changes over time. Things are slowly moving. You see the effects of this through volcanoes and earthquakes and in order to have a really basic understanding of this, you absolutely need to know the temperature deep down inside the Earth because that is driving everything," he added.

A quantum object— A sub-atomic particle such as an electron or neutron, for example—can behave either as a discrete particle or as a wave, depending on how one looks at it. In the well-known 'two-slit' experiment, a single particle is fired at barrier with two slits in it. On the other side of the barrier, one can detect a pattern of interacting ripples, as if a wavefront had washed up against both slits at once, passed through, and created an interference pattern of peaks and troughs on other side.

Getting a single particle to appear to behave like a wave, by passing through both slits at once, is what physicists call 'quantum superposition' of two alternative states. The act of seeking to observe precisely what is going on disturbs the system, bruising the ambiguities of the quantum world with the certainties of everyday physics.

The wave-like properties of electrons and neutrons are routinely exploited in scientific research, and recent work has demonstrated quantum superposition in larger objects, such as atoms, pairs of atoms and even small clusters of atoms.

A stunning advance is reported in the journal *Nature*, where Anton Zeilinger of the University of Vienna, Austria and his colleagues demonstrated a version of the two-slit experiment with buckminsterfullerene, a single soccer-ball-shaped molecule made of sixty linked carbon atoms (abbreviated as C60). They show that a beam of excited C60 molecules behaves as a wave, producing a diffraction pattern when shone at a grating. They also show that C70, a larger cousin of C60, obeys the quantum rules of wave-particle duality, making this the largest object ever demonstrated to show quantum properties.

Matter consists of quark arid leptin. Mind or brain is the highest product of matter. The degree of man's consciousness depends upon the complexity of his brain. The wonderful blueprint of the brain and nature's detailed craftsmanship with the complex network of neurons inside it is still beyond the reach of the best of human minds. It continues to elude man since it is in the vast and absolute domain of nature of which man himself is just a part and product.

The complexity of the human brain is second only to the complexity of the universe. Structurally a full grown brain is a highly efficient electro-magnetic system of a mass of nervous tissues consisting of more than 10 billion cells weighing up to 2 per cent of the body's weight, but consuming more than 25 per cent of the system's total energy consumption. That means it consumes on an average 12.5 per cent more energy than other vital organs of the body. The brain caps this excess energy mainly for structuring consciousness as the material world is reflected on the thinking brain. (Sources: Science Reviews – *The Statesman*, Calcutta, 6 September, 20 September, 4 October and 25 October 1999).

Long before, Frederick Engels, materialist philosopher and collaborator of Marx wrote that "We have once again returned to the mode of outlook of the great founders of Greek Philosophy, the view that the whole of nature, from the smallest element to the greatest, from grains of sand to suns, from protista to man, has its existence in eternal coming into being and passing away, in ceaseless flux, in unresting motion and change. Only with the essential difference that what in the case of the Greeks was a brilliant intuition, is in our case the result of strictly scientific research in accordance with experience, and hence also it emerges in a much more definite and clear form". He observed that "The whole of nature accessible to us forms a system, an interconnected totality of bodies, and by bodies we understand here all material existences extending from stars to atoms, indeed right to their particles, in so far as one grants the existence of the last named." (Frederick Engels, *Dialectics of Nature*, Progress Publishers, Moscow, 1976, pp. 30-31 and p. 70).

Extending this idea further Georgi Plekhanov wrote, "*...the foundation of our dialectics is the materialist conception of nature.* Our dialectics is based on materialism and would collapse were materialism to collapse. And *vice versa:* the *materialist theory of cognition* would be incomplete, one-sided – more than that, it would be *impossible* without dialectics.

"With Hegel, *dialectics* coincides with metaphysics; with us dialectics rests upon the *study of nature*...the absolute idea is only an *abstraction from motion* which gives rise to all *combinations and conditions of matter*....According to our *materialist* – teaching the contradictions within conceptions are the reflections, *translated in the language of thought,* of the contradictions within *phenomena* due to the contradictory nature of their common basis, that is to say, *motion*....the course of *ideas* is explained by the course of *things, the course of thought by the course of life* "(*Selected Philosophical Works*, Vol. III, Moscow, 1976, p. 79 : Italics in the original).

Plekhanov explained the relationship and distinction between nature and social phenomena as follows: "The rising of the sun is in no way connected with men's social relations, either as cause or as effect. As a natural phenomenon, it can, therefore, be contraposed to men's conscious aspirations, which, too, have no causal tie with it. But it is quite different when we have to deal with *social* phenomena, with history. We already know that history is made by men; therefore human aspirations cannot but be a factor of the movement of history. But men make history in one way and not in another, in consequence of a particular necessity which we have....Once this necessity is given, *then given too, as its effect, are those human aspirations which are inevitable factor of social development. Men's aspirations do not exclude necessity; but are themselves determined by it.* It is, therefore, a grave logical error to contrapose them to necessity."

"When a social revolution is brought about by a class striving for its liberation, that class acts in a way that is more or less expedient in achieving the aim desired; in any case its activities are the *cause* of that revolution. However, together with all the aspirations that have brought them about, these activities are themselves a *consequence* of a definite course of the economic development, and are, therefore, themselves determined by *necessity*" (*Ibid.,* p. 180).

As a result of this process, the hard reality has been that the world is now violently divided more than ever, between a minority rich capitalist class, master of the monopoly capitalism and a very vast majority of working people. Class antagonism has been immanent and struggles inevitably grow, develop and manifest in a particular course of development in the practical world. Material forces working through their class organisations and property relations actually counterpose and confront among themselves in the society with the existing dominant one remaining in power by force, or that is overthrown by *the other* which had already grown and become more powerful over time. Struggles continues on. In general, religion, with conversion being one of its tenets, does not combat but shields and protects the oppressors and exploiting classes and their collaborators all over the world. It has long ago fallen as the ideology in the service and counsel to the ruling oppressor classes and fascist forces for keeping the oppressed masses of the people in the check. No religious institution can actually become the saviour of man. There can be nothing more ridiculous and fetish than the theory of spirit, *atman avatar*, creationism and Gospel of Salvation to the mankind. It is with great insight, objectivity and clarity of vision. Iswar Chandra Vidyasagar pronounced the *Vedanta* false as early as in 1853.

The morality of religion has now been reduced to the alms given by the international bourgeoisie from its treasuries filled with the blood-soaked money from the ruthless exploitation of the international proletariat and people of the world. The morality of the oppressed working people, as history evidenced, is class struggle and fight against the world reaction. Emancipation of labour from the wage slave system under monopoly capitalism, is the real salvation —the result of continuous, long-term collective action of their own organisation. The alienated man must be his own master and make history.

APPENDIX-III

DECLINE OF THE INDIAN NATIONAL CONGRESS PHILOSOPHY (1925)

"We were straining every nerve to secure the co-operation of our Mohammedan fellow-countrymen in this great national work. We sometimes paid the fares of Mohammedan delegates and offered them other facilities...

All wings of the nationalist party were now united; and educated Islam joined hands with them on the Congress platform. Never did the prospects of the effective and united work seem more hopeful....Mrs. Annie Besant, who had hitherto identified herself with the work of the Theosophical society and the Hindu Educational movement joined the Congress held in Madras in 1914....

When the Congress met in Bombay in 1915, she (Mrs. Annie Besant) called a meeting to consider the question of the formation of a Home Rule League....The general feeling at that time was that such an organisation would serve to overlap and perhaps weaken the Congress....

I have no desire to re-awaken the memories of events which are now well nigh forgotten but I must say that the (Home Rule) League served to create the *first division* in the Congress camp after the reunion. I did not join it nor did many of the ex-presidents of the Congress. It is no exaggeration to say that it was the Government that set in motion the impulse that placed Mrs. Besant in the presidential chair of the Congress....The first visible sign of disunion among the members of the Nationalist party after the Lucknow Congress (1916) was, as I have observed, the formation of the Home Rule League and the second was the movement for the election of Mrs. Besant as a President of the Congress....

Communal representation being accepted (under the Act of the British Crown and Parliament and enforced by the Government of India), what we had to decide was the percentage of Hindu and Mohammedan members in the Legislative Councils; and here we had the Lucknow Convention of 1916 to guide us. Whether we should accept it as it was, or modify it in any way, was the subject of anxious consideration by the (Joint Reforms) Committee. We finally decided to proceed substantially upon the lines of the Lucknow Convention. The evidence that we received varied, as may be imagined, in a most remarkable manner. There were *extremists* on both sides —Hindus who would make little or no concession, Mohammedans who would go much further than the pact. We thought that the golden mean accepted at Lucknow was a fair solution, and consistent with the legitimate claims of both the communities. The question has been re-opened in Bengal by the Swarajists for party purposes. The proposals of the Swarajists have roused the indignation of the Hindu Community, while they have been acclaimed with enthusiasm by the Mohammedan leaders. They constitute the veritable apple of discord....

What a change now from those times —what a deterioration in the public life of the province (Bengal), when mendacity and malice are the weapons, offensive and defensive, employed by those who call themselves the apostles of self-Government and promise *Swaraj* to their countrymen! *Swaraj* means self-restraint in the great books of the Hindu religion where the word is first used. It means, as now employed by a certain class of people, license to use the meanest of mean tricks for the furtherance of their ends. If this is what we have in the green, what may we not expect in the dry?...

Where do we see the like of it (*Swadeshi*) in the Non-Co-operation Movement at least in Bengal?... Or where now do we find in literature or in journalism the inspiration of a patriotic impulse brushing aside all that is mean or contemptible or spiteful, leading national life upwards and onwards towards the fulfilment of a nobler destiny? *We see none of it*. It is all words from start to finish, or ill will and hatred, robbed in the garb of patriotism, or at least, it is separation, isolation from the larger interests of humanity. As a nation we are to live, prosper and flourish by detachment from the wider concerns of mankind. The sap that feeds humanity is to be cut off from us, and we are to flow down the stream of life, unfed, unsupported by the culture, the art and the civilisation of the rest of mankind, rejoining in our isolation, taking pride in our aloofness. To me the thought is intolerable. It must stunt our national growth, make us dwarfs where others are giants....

... The cult of Non-Co-operation, which dominated the political horizon, today stands suspended. Its constituent features, with one exception, have been dropped. All the boycotts, save that of foreign cloth, have been withdrawn. The fact is an open *proclamation of its failure* on the part of the leaders of the movement. A victorious general rushing to an assured triumph, with the monuments of his success strewn around him, would never think of abandoning, suspending or modifying his programme. It is a confession of failure, which no plea, however plausible and however closely it may be linked with a great name, can obscure. By all impartial spectators its doom was indeed foreseen and was felt to be inevitable. As far as the great leaders were concerned, Non-Co-operation had its roots in an intense and consuming love of country, coupled with hatred of the British Government, and all associated with it in the administration of the country. But as regards the non-co-operating masses, hatred of the British Government, its officials, and Englishmen in general, was the impulse. And when a sentiment is firmly rooted in the public mind it grows and expands. And from a hatred of the Government to that of political and religious opponents and of other castes and creeds, the transition was rapid and irresistible. Mr. Gandhi is my authority for it. He said that 'it was apparent that Non-Co-operation could not, in the present state of things, be presented by the nation as a national programme', for, said he, 'they were non-co-operating among themselves by carrying on a programme of hatred and violence amongst themselves'. It is this sentiment of hatred fostered amongst the masses, directed in the first instance against the British Government, that came, by a natural process of growth to be extended to all others who worshipped in a different temple, culminating in those communal and caste feuds that have darkened our recent history. I cannot help thinking that these leaders were playing with fire, and they have intensified a feeling already latent, that in this development has been attended with disastrous results. Of course, we all admire the supreme solicitude and earnest efforts of Mr. Gandhi to secure Hindu-Muslim unity. But, in judging of the communal strife, which we all deplore, let us not, for the sake of historic justice, forget the part the Non-Co-operation Movement had in fostering and promoting it....

Non-Co-operation may help us to stand on our own legs by making us wholly dependent upon our own resources and activities. But at the same time, it cuts off from the perennial and ever sustaining sap afforded by the culture and civilisation of the world, and the wide outlook which is a stimulus to progress. We cannot stand alone, isolated and detached from the rest of mankind, but must be in close association with them, giving to them what we have to give, receiving from them what we have to receive, swelling the common fund of human knowledge and experience. We thus broaden and elevate our own culture and civilisation by the touch of the world forces....

...We cannot remain wedded to the past. We cannot remain where we are. There is no standing still in this world of God's provide. Move on we must, with eyes reverentially fixed on the past, with a loving concern for the present and with deep solicitude for the future. We must, in this onward journey, assimilate from all sides in our character, our culture and our civilization, whatever is suited to our genius and is calculated to strengthen and invigorate it, and weave it, into the texture of our national life. Thus co-operation, and not non-co-operation, association and not isolation, must be a living and a growing factor in the evolution of our people. Any other policy would be suicidal and fraught with peril to our best interests. That is my message to my countrymen, delivered not in haste or in impatience, but as the mature result of my deliberations, and of my life-long labours in the service of the motherland.

[*cf.* Surendra Nath Banerjee, *A Nation in Making* (1925), Paschimbanga Bangla Akademi, Calcutta, 1998, p. 102, p. 119, p. 204, pp. 231-33, p. 290, pp. 303-04, and pp. 383-84 : Italics added]

.... In 1916, Annie Besant attended the Lucknow conference of the Indian National Congress with her followers and Home Rule banner. About the beginning of the year 1917, she started a new propaganda under the cry of "Home Rule".... Theosophical organisations controlled by Mrs. Besant took up the idea warmly and helped to establish branches of the Home Rule League all over the country....M. K. Gandhi who had returned to India from South Africa at the end of 1914, "was busy in his own sphere reclaiming the extremists" with Hindu religious ideology back into the folds of the Congress, and eventually succeeded in the work started much before by Annie Besant, Subba Rao and others.

The election of the president once over again, inaugurated party factions within the Congress. The Bengal Congressmen fell out amongst themselves and men like C. R. Das openly joined the extreme party to widen the gulf. Mrs. Besant, who was arrested and released later, was "acclaimed" President by the unanimous vote of all the Provincial Congress Committees. "This was the starting point", P.C. Ray pointed out, "of the creation of a new party in India which very soon developed as the moderate and, later, as the Liberal Party, and this was also the first Congress at which the elder statesmen of the country lost their control over deliberations." Gandhi was earlier acquainted with Mrs. Besant and kept himself abreast of the developments in the Home Rule League. Extremists were welcome to the Home Rule League and Congress "through the partially opened door." "We heard", says Indulal K. Yagnik, "that Mr. Gandhi helped in bringing about this settlement" in the political arena.....

Thus did Gandhi, a rising star, cast his first shadow on the political horizon of "Nationalist India".....

The conduct of the Home Rule agitation on the lines it was run, completely changed the aspect of the Indian politics. For the first time in the history of India politics had been given a *religious tinge*. Mrs. Besant's Home Rule League, however, finally succumbed to the influence of M. K. Gandhi. With the growing ideological, difference and crisis, Mrs. Annie Besant had resigned the presidentship of the All India Home Rule League and Gandhi was elected its new president in Bombay on 3.10.1920. There he proposed and got changed its creed and renamed as Swaraj Sabha, at the All India General Meeting of the members. Mohammad Ali Jinnah pointed out that the constitution of the Home Rule League could not be changed except by its council and that when three-fourths of the members voted for. It could not be changed on the recommendation of a sub-committee and with a bare majority in the general meeting. "To secure *Swaraj* for India in conformity with Article 1 of the constitution of the Indian National Congress", Jinnah there moved the amendment in the general meeting of the Home Rule League in October 1920. The amendment fell, constitution of the Home Rule League was altered with a bare majority in the meeting and a resolution was passed that persons unwilling to work according to the altered constitution could leave the organisation. Home Rule League with its changed name, "Swaraj Sabha" became a part of the Non-Co-operation Movement that led to political decay and turmoil.

[*cf.* Matlubul Hasan Saiyid, *Mohammad Ali Jinnah : A Political Study*, Lahore, 1945, pp. 121-122, 128, 133-34, 161, 192 and 261-63].

BIBLIOGRAPHY

Abbott, John, *The Keys to Power*, Methuen, London 1932.

Abdulla, Yusuf Ali, *A Cultural History of India during the British Period,* Taraporevala, Bombay, 1940.

Adenwala, M.D., *From Rammohan to Gandhi,* New York, 1956.

Agarwal, R.N., *National Movement and Constitutional Development of India,* Metropolitan Book, Delhi, 1956.

Ahluwalia, B.K., and Shashi Ahluwalia, *Muslims and India's Freedom Movement,* Heritage Publishers, New Delhi, 1985.

Appadorai, A., *Democracy in India,* Oxford University Press, Calcutta, 1942.

Appadorai, A., *Indian Political Thinking in the Twentieth Century from Naoroji to Nehru,* Oxford University Press, Madras, 1971.

Bishop, Donald H. (ed), *Indian Thought : An Introduction,* New York, 1975.

Bose, Nirmal Kumar, *Culture and Society in India,* Asia Publishing House, Bombay, 1967.

Buch, Amritlal Maganlal, *The Spirit of Ancient Hindu Culture,* Baroda, 1921.

Besant, Annie Wood, *The Future of Indian Politics,* Theosophical Publication House, London, 1922.

Borden, Carla, (ed), *Contemporary Indian Tradition,* Smithsouien Institution Press, Washington, 1989.

Chekki, A.D., *The Social System and Culture of Modern India,* Garland, New York, 1975.

Chopra, P.N., *Religions and Communities of India,* Vision Books, New Delhi, 1982.

Campbell-Johnson Allan, *Mission with Mountbatten,* Robert Hale, London, 1951.

Das, Bhagawan, *The Philosophy of Non-Co-operation and of Spiritual Swaraj,* Tagore & Co., Madras, 1922.

Dasgupta, Surendra Nath, *History of Indian Philosophy,* Vols. I-V. (1922-55) Cambridge University Press, reprint 1977.

Datta, Rajani Palme, *India Today,* Manisha Granthalaya, Calcutta, 1975.

Datta, Prabhat K., *Polities of Region and Religion in India,* Uppal Publications, New Delhi, 1991.

Dyakov, A.M., *The National Problem of India Today,* Nauka, Moscow, 1966.

Engels, Frederick, *Anti-Duhring,* Foreign Language Publishing House, Peking, 1975.

Engels, Frederick, *Dialectics of Nature,* Progress Publishers, Moscow, 1970.

Ezakiel, Issac A., *Swaraj or Surrender,* Bombay, 1921.

Gangulay, B.N., *Concept of Equality,* Indian Institute of Advanced Study, Simla, 1975.

Gangulay, Nagendranath, *India What Now?* George Allen Unwin, London, 1933.

Ghoshal, U.N., *A History of Hindu Political Theories,* Oxford University Press, Calcutta, 1923.

Ghoshal, U.N., *A History of Indian Political Ideas,* Oxford University Press, Calcutta, 1932.

Ganpat, Laxman, *Indian Democratic Reforms,* Bombay, 1881.

The Gazetteer of India, Vols. I-III, Government of India, New Delhi, 1975.

Indamdar, N.R., ed., *Political Thought and Leadership of Lokmanya Tilak*, Concept Publishing Company, New Delhi, 1983.

Indian National Congress, Collection of Resolutions (1920-23), *Allahabad Law Journal,* 1946.

Indian National Congress, Collection of Resolutions (1940-46) *Allahabad Law Journal,* 1946.

Indian National Congress, The Indian National Demand (Summary of the Nehru Report and Proceedings of the all Parties' convention), Calcutta, 1928.

Ishwaran, Karigaddar, *Tradition and Economy in Village India,* Allied Publishers, Bombay, 1967.

Jha, Akhileswar, *Modernisation and the Hindu Socio-Culture,* B.R., Publication Corporation, New Delhi, 1978.

Jain, S.P., *The Social Structure of Hindu-Muslim Community,* National Publishing House, Delhi, 1975.

Karve, Irawati and Damle, Y. B., *Group Relations in Village Community,* Pune, 1963.

Kattacckal, *Religion and Ethics in Adwaita,* New Delhi, 1982.

Lenin, V. I., *Collected Works,* Vol. 39, Progress Publishers, Moscow, 1968.

Lenin, V. I., *Materialism and Emperio Criticism,* Foreign Language Publishing House, Peking, 1975.

Lott, Eric, J., *Vedantic Approaches to God,* London, 1980.

Marx-Engels, *Selected Works,* Vols. 1-3, Progress Publishers, Moscow, 1975.

Mittal, Kewal Krishan, *Materialism in Indian Thought,* New Delhi, 1974.

McDermott, Robert A, and Narovane Viswanathan S., *The Spirit of Modern India, Writings in Philosophy, Religion and Culture,* Thomas & Crowell, New York, 1974.

Menem, Aubrey, *The New Mystics and the True Indian Tradition,* James and Hudson, London, 1974.

Morrison, John, *New Ideas in India during the Nineteenth Century,* Simpkin, Marshal & Co. London, 1978.

Mueller, Friederick Max, *Lectures on the Origin and Growth of Religions of India,* Indological Book House, Varanasi, 1964.

Mathew, C.V., *The Saffron Mission,* Delhi, 1999.

Moore, R.J., *Churchill, Cripps and India 1939-1945,* Oxford University Press, London, 1979.

Moore, R.J., *End Games of Empire,* Oxford University Press, London, 1988.

Moore, R.J., *The Crisis of Indian Unity,* Oxford University Press, London, 1974.

Mukherjee, Radhakamal, *The Culture and Art of India,* Munsilal Manoharlal, New Delhi, 1984.

Noble, Margaret, Elizabeth, *The Web of Indian Life,* Longmans Green & Co., London, 1918.

O'Malley, Lewis Sydney Steward, *Popular Hinduism: The Religion of the Masses,* Cambridge University Press, 1935.

Perrett, R.W., ed., *Indian Philosophy of Religion,* Dordrecht Kluwer Academic, New York, 1989.

Potter, Karl, *Pressuppositions of Indian Philosophies,* London, 1976.

Prasad, Rajendra, *India Divided,* Ananda–Hindusthan Prakashini, Calcutta, 1947.

Radhakrishnan, Sarvapalli, *Eastern Religion and the Western Thought,* Oxford University Press, Delhi, 1974.

Radhakrishnan, Sarvapalli, *The Heart of Hindusthan,* G.A. Natesen & Co., Madras, 1932.

Radhakrishnan, Sarvapalli, *The Reign of Religion in Contemporary Philosophy,* Madras, 1920.

Ramkrishna Mission Institute of Culture, *The Culture Heritage of India,* Vols. I-V, Calcutta, 2001.

Savarkar, V.D., *Hindutva,* Pune, 1923.

Smart, Ninian, *Doctrine and Argument in Indian Philosophy,* London, 1964.

Vidyabhusan, S.C., *A History of the Medieval School of Indian Logic,* Calcutta, 1909.

INDEX